Reflections on the Music of Ennio Morricone

Reflections on the Music of Ennio Morricone

Fame and Legacy

Franco Sciannameo

LEXINGTON BOOKS
Lanham • Boulder • New York • London

Published by Lexington Books
An imprint of The Rowman & Littlefield Publishing Group, Inc.
4501 Forbes Boulevard, Suite 200, Lanham, Maryland 20706
www.rowman.com

6 Tinworth Street, London SE11 5AL, United Kingdom

Copyright © 2020 by The Rowman & Littlefield Publishing Group, Inc.

All rights reserved. No part of this book may be reproduced in any form or by any electronic or mechanical means, including information storage and retrieval systems, without written permission from the publisher, except by a reviewer who may quote passages in a review.

British Library Cataloguing in Publication Information Available

Library of Congress Cataloging-in-Publication Data

Names: Sciannameo, Franco, author.
Title: Reflections on the music of Ennio Morricone : fame and legacy / Franco Sciannameo.
Description: Lanham : Lexington Books, 2020. | Includes bibliographical references and index. | Summary: "By analyzing Ennio Morricone's formative years as a music practitioner and his transition into composing for the screen, Franco Sciannameo studies the best of Morricone's popular compositions and concert works as he explores Morricone's legacy, its nature, and its eventual impact on posterity"— Provided by publisher.
Identifiers: LCCN 2019050581 (print) | LCCN 2019050582 (ebook) | ISBN 9781498569002 (cloth) | ISBN 9781498569026 (pbk) | ISBN 9781498569019 (epub)
Subjects: LCSH: Morricone, Ennio—Criticism and interpretation. | Motion picture music—History and criticism. | Music—20th century—History and criticism. | Composers—Italy.
Classification: LCC ML410.M79 S35 2020 (print) | LCC ML410.M79 (ebook) | DDC 781.5/42—dc23
LC record available at https://lccn.loc.gov/2019050581
LC ebook record available at https://lccn.loc.gov/2019050582

This book is dedicated to Alessandro Savasta
in memory of Sergio Miceli (1944–2016)

Contents

List of Figures ix

Foreword xi

Acknowledgments xiii

Introduction 1

1 In the Open City 9

2 Once Upon a Time Babylon 31

3 In the Lion's Den 47

4 Toward a New Consonance 77

5 Scoring Social Justice 95

6 Legacy 117

Appendix 1: *Piccolo Concerto* 1961 and 1962 Programs 143

Appendix 2: *Canto Morricone* 159

Bibliography 169

Index 173

About the Author 185

List of Figures

Figure 1.1	Concerto per orchestra, mm. 302–307. Ennio Morricone (Suvini Zerboni, 1990)	18
Figure 1.2	Concerto per orchestra, mm. 214–218. Ennio Morricone (Suvini Zerboni, 1990)	19
Figure 1.3	Concerto per orchestra, mm. 352–358. Ennio Morricone (Suvini Zerboni, 1990)	20
Figure 1.4	Concerto per orchestra, mm. 542–545. Ennio Morricone (Suvini Zerboni, 1990)	21
Figure 3.1	Harmonica's Theme	58
Figure 3.2	Frank's Allusive Theme	59
Figure 3.3	Jill's Theme	59
Figure 3.4	Main Titles: Segment 1	65
Figure 3.5	Main Titles: Segment 2—Part 1	66
Figure 3.6	Central Theme	66
Figure 3.7	Marcia degli accattoni (Beggars' March)	67
Figure 3.8	Deborah's Theme	70
Figure 3.9	Cockeye's Theme (Childhood Memories)	71
Figure 3.10	Poverty Theme	71
Figure 5.1	Johann Sebastian Bach. St. Matthew Passion BWV 244. First four measures from the orchestral introduction to Part 1	101
Figure 5.2	Girolamo Frescobaldi. Ricercar cromatico dopo il Credo from Fiori Musicali, Op. 12 (Venice, 1635)	103
Figure 5.3	Girolamo Frescobaldi. Ricercar cromatico dopo il Credo from Fiori Musicali, Op. 12 (Venice, 1635) Motif used by Ennio Morricone	103
Figure 5.4	Ali's Theme	104

Figure 5.5	Gabriel's Oboe, from *The Mission*	108
Figure 5.6	Conspectus Tuus, mm. 1–7 from *The Mission*	109
Figure 5.7	Finale, mm. 1–4 from *The Mission*	111
Figure 6.1	Secondo Concerto per flauto, violoncello e orchestra, mm. 458–462. Ennio Morricone (Suvini Zerboni, 1991)	129
Figure 6.2	Secondo Concerto per flauto, violoncello e orchestra, mm. 579–683. Ennio Morricone (Suvini Zerboni, 1991)	130
Figure 6.3	Roma (pensando al "Ricercar Cromatico" di Girolamo Frescobaldi) per soprano, voce recitante maschile e ensemble, mm. 20–22. Ennio Morricone (Suvini Zerboni, 2010)	137
Figure 6.4	Roma (pensando al "Ricercar Cromatico" di Girolamo Frescobaldi) per soprano, voce recitante maschile e ensemble, mm. 53–55. Ennio Morricone (Suvini Zerboni, 2010)	138
Figure 6.5	Roma (pensando al "Ricercar Cromatico" di Girolamo Frescobaldi) per soprano, voce recitante maschile e ensemble, mm. 147–152. Ennio Morricone (Suvini Zerboni, 2010)	139

Foreword

For cinephiles outside the Italian-speaking world the name of Ennio Morricone tends to be most closely associated with the genre of Spaghetti Westerns encapsulated by Sergio Leone's *A Fistful of Dollars* and *The Good, the Bad and the Ugly*, Roland Joffé's epic drama of proto-liberation theology *The Mission*, and Giuseppe Tornatore's lavish and nostalgic semi-biography *Cinema Paradiso*. However, Morricone's compositional output, both for cinema and the concert hall, was much broader than this and is deserving of better understanding by scholars and fans alike. In particular, his position as a radical composer working at the cutting edge of new music may prove revelatory to those unaware of this aspect of his oeuvre.

In this respect Morricone is not unique. The career of his almost exact contemporary, the Greek composer Nikos Mamangakis (1929–2013), who is best known for his scores for the German filmmaker Edgar Reitz's *Heimat* series, followed a very similar trajectory with a deep early engagement with high modernism (especially that of the Darmstadt school). Like Morricone, Mamangakis became interested in electronic music, in his case studying with Josef Anton Riedl, the director of the Siemens Studio in Munich. Through their interactions with avant-garde aesthetics, and the assimilation of new technologies, both composers developed a notable sensitivity to timbre which resulted in novel sonic combinations in their cinematic outputs. At the same time, both could very readily operate across the "divide" between art music and popular music, the latter being as much their vernacular as the former, in contrast, for instance, with Bernard Herrmann who often struggled to compose music in a popular style that evinced authenticity.

Of course, the scale of Morricone's filmography alone is simply immense and dwarfs that of almost every major film composer, including Max Steiner, one of the most prolific figures of Hollywood's "Golden Age." The Internet

Movie Database lists more than five hundred individual films and television shows since the inception of his career in 1960, when he was an uncredited contributor to the score for Franco Rossi's *Morte di un amico* (Death of a Friend).

Hitherto much of the most significant scholarship on Morricone has either been of relatively limited scope or in the Italian language (thus resulting in a more restricted readership), and the most important book-length study thus far is Sergio Miceli's 1994 monograph *Morricone, la musica, il cinema*. This wonderful and insightful new book by Franco Sciannameo, which examines Morricone's entire career and output in considerable detail, and with musicological rigor, is therefore a major landmark for anglophone readers.

As an Italian academic teaching in one of the USA's highest ranked universities, and as an equally eminent performer and musicologist, Professor Sciannameo is ideally placed, both culturally and academically, for this study. He has written widely on Italian film music, and his monograph *Nino Rota's The Godfather Trilogy: A Film Score Guide* is the standard reference on this seminal group of scores. His firsthand knowledge and understanding of the social and artistic milieu in which Morricone's output arose offers the reader rich insights into the motivations of the composer and his directors. Equally, the inclusion of his own English translation of the interview conducted with Sergio Leone by the film critic Francesco Mininni shortly before the Leone's death will be invaluable in the greater understanding of the nature of the collaboration between the director and composer.

Among the films he considers are ones which will be less familiar to many viewers. In particular, a group directed by Pier Paolo Pasolini, or for which he is credited as a writer, feature strongly, including the extraordinary *Teorema* (1968). The inclusion of a new translation of Pasolini's thoughts on the function of film music will be particularly welcome to scholars, though even for this most intellectual and articulate of filmmakers, "what music adds to the images, or better, the transformation that it works on the images, remains a mysterious fact difficult to explain."

This critical reflection on Ennio Morricone's fame and legacy stands as a worthy tribute to a man now in his tenth decade who is regarded by many as one of the greatest living exponents of the art of film composition. Grasping with both hands the problematics of explanation alluded to by Pasolini, Franco Sciannameo elucidates the totality of his achievement, both as a composer for visual media and of autonomous works written for the concert hall.

David Cooper
Emeritus Professor of Music
University of Leeds, UK

Acknowledgments

There are many individuals involved in the process of writing and publishing a book, which begins with the optimistic intention of bringing the task to fruition within months only to evolve into years as the subject matter becomes thicker and all details seem indispensable for an accurate expression of the author's intentions. So, who should be thanked as those who proved vital to the making of a book about a well-known composer like Ennio Morricone whose music over the course of the past sixty years has altered the way we look at, and listen to, films?

I begin by thanking Ennio Morricone himself for having reminisced with me about people and facts of musical life in Rome from the 1960s onward. Second, this book owes a fundamental debt of gratitude to the late Sergio Miceli (1944–2016), a friend and colleague who supported this project with his musicological rigor and ever-present polemic spirit.

Alessandro Savasta's counsel at Edizioni Suvini Zerboni, publishers of Morricone's concert music, has gone above and beyond. His quick timing in answering questions and providing material showed a keen desire to participate in the development of a critical work on a major composer whose works he represents.

I thank viola virtuoso Maurizio Barbetti, a staunch collaborator and interpreter of Morricone's music, for his willingness to discuss interpretive factors pertinent to the complexities of performing Morricone's music under the composer's supervision.

A special thank-you is due to film critic Francesco Mininni for authorizing me to quote his extensive interview with Sergio Leone in my English translation.

I thank my dear friend and esteemed colleague at the University of Leeds, David Cooper, for conversations and collaborations that took part on both sides of the Atlantic over many years. Film musicology was the main focus of our common interests but also academic pedagogy, leadership, the well-being of our students, and the human factors playing into decisive roles for the future of young musicians. David was the first reader of this book's drafted chapters. His support and insight were essential for me to continue writing—and his contribution of a foreword is indeed a much-welcomed gift. Thank you, David!

Reflections on the Music of Ennio Morricone: Fame and Legacy would have not had a beginning or an ending if not for the continuous support of Louise Cavanaugh Sciannameo, wife, literary critic, leader in higher education communications, and fierce editor of my conceptual vagaries. Morricone's music is, indeed, a constant in our lives' soundtrack, and this book is its listening guide.

Solving technical matters is necessary to turn a "manuscript" into a printed product. A team of individuals have dedicated time and special skills to make things right. I offer thanks to Kristin Heath, Music & Catalog Librarian at Carnegie Mellon University Libraries, for her knowledge and readiness to retrieve rare sources of information pertaining to my research, and Danny English for setting in uniform style the numerous musical examples disseminated throughout the pages of this book. I thank the editorial staff at Lexington Books for cradling my manuscript from "proposal" to marketable product. Finally, I thank the manuscript's anonymous readers for spending time with my work and providing me with generous and insightful commentaries.

Introduction

This book of reflections on the music of Ennio Morricone was born out of conversations I had with the late Sergio Miceli (1944–2016) about teaching film music in relation to his volume *Morricone, la musica, il cinema* (1994) and the collaborative work he wrote with Ennio Morricone, *Comporre per il cinema: Teoria e prassi della musica per film* (2001).

Miceli was, by his own definition, a non-aligned musicologist. A maverick and a scholar, he dedicated his research, enthusiasm, and combative spirit to enhance a field of inquiry not fully embraced by the Italian musicological establishment of his time: film music.

Miceli wrote extensively about the function of music in cinema with emphasis on the film scores of Nino Rota (1911–1979) and Ennio Morricone. With the latter he created a partnership dedicated to the teaching of the practice and theory of film music and the contextualization of its history. Miceli and Morricone offered advanced seminars at the Accademia Musicale Chigiana in Siena from 1991 to 1997 and occasionally at the Scuola Musicale di Fiesole and in Basel's Akademie der Musik. The results of their teaching and classroom interactions were collected in a volume entitled *Comporre per il cinema: Teoria e prassi della musica per film* (2001), preceded in 1994 by the publication of Miceli's *Morricone, la musica, il cinema*. These two texts constitute point of departure for further studies on Morricone's music and on the theoretical/historical views and legacy of Sergio Miceli—musicologist, poet, and painter. His substantial library is now open for consultation at the Fondazione Ugo e Olga Levi in Venice.

The goal of *Reflections on the Music of Ennio Morricone* is to present various phases of Morricone's career in light of newly obtained information and fresher contextualized perspectives. The sections included in Chapter 1—"In the Open City"—"The Holy Year," "A Family Man," "Goffredo Petrassi: My

Michelangelo," "*Concerto per orchestra*," "Darmstadt: A New Bayreuth," and "A Problem Solved" elaborate upon the composer's formative years as a music practitioner endowed by ironclad discipline and work ethic. From playing trumpet in Rome's clubs and recording studios to arranging commercial music for multifaceted occasions, Morricone kept himself busy. He made an honorable living as a musician and gained remarkable experience that shaped the development of his career.

In fact, the sections included in Chapter 2—"Once Upon a Time Babylon"—"*Piccolo Concerto*," "Arranging, Re-arranging, and Re-cycling," and "Voices from the Italian Riviera and the Bay of Naples," probe Morricone's unforeseen success as arranger-in-chief at the newly established RCA Italiana recording studios in Rome and at the revamped programming aspirations of the Italian radio and television broadcasting networks. Commercial achievements like selling millions of copies of Paul Anka's single *Ogni volta* (Every Time) and hundreds of sophisticated arrangements prepared for the 1961 and 1962 seasons of *Piccolo Concerto*—a television show featuring a quality orchestra of symphonic proportions—made Morricone the most sought-after arranger in Italy (see the programs of *Piccolo Concerto* in Appendix 1).

Consequently, the intrapreneurs behind the immensely popular Italian song contests organized in Sanremo and Naples feuded over Morricone's availability to spice any arrangement with sound bites and clever citations alluding to the classical repertoire—a clear Morriconian imprimatur that made his arranging inventiveness the crown jewels of several recording collections released in the 1960s and 1970s.

The reputation of the young man who dared to influence commercial music with the gravitas of conservatory training did not escape the attention of filmmakers and producers who lured him into the glitzy world of composing for the silver screen.

Chapter 3, "In the Lion's Den," is dedicated to the Sergio Leone–Ennio Morricone collaboration, a partnership that reached a reputation similar to those of Federico Fellini and Nino Rota, Alfred Hitchcock and Bernard Herrmann, and Steven Spielberg and John Williams.

"In the Lion's Den" chronicles the birth of the Italian Western as a genre and as a popular cultural phenomenon. The narrative of this chapter is based on Sergio Leone's last interview granted to film critic Francesco Mininni and published in 1989, the same year of the filmmaker's death. The freshness of perspectives expressed in those pages, available here in English for the first time, placed Morricone's collaboration at the level of an inspiring cocreator.

The unexpected success of the first three Italian Western films starring Clint Eastwood, *Per un pugno di dollari* (1964), *Per qualche dollaro in più* (1965), and *Il buono, il brutto, il cattivo* (1966) attracted the attention of Hollywood's moguls who engaged both director and composer to conceive a grand-scale trilogy based on the "once upon a time" concept of fabled lore. The project was realized over a number of years but not without taking a strong emotional toll on both Leone and Morricone, whose stressful relationships with Hollywood were never ideal. The new set of three films, *Once Upon a Time in the West* (1968), *Once Upon a Time . . . the Revolution* (1971), and *Once Upon a Time in America* (1984), unfolded unevenly over a period of sixteen years, a factor that derailed any sense of continuity expected of a trilogy. These three lengthy films ended up revolving around themselves like isolated planets linked only by their relentless critiques of American ways of life. Morricone composed splendid musical frescoes for the *Once Upon a Time* films which further solidified his reputation as one of the best film music composers of all times—a heavy responsibility for the conservatory-trained composer who continued to maintain, albeit for the benefit of a restricted audience, the flame that sustained him as the creator of experimental concert works.

Chapter 4—"Toward a New Consonance"—features "*Suoni per Dino*," "Sonic Dimensions and Shades of *Giallo*," "The Animal Trilogy," "Sampling 'Pink,'" "Pasolini's 'Color-blind' Palette," "A Cherished Note," and "A Little *Gebrauchsmusik*," and focuses on the enduring power of that creative flame. Morricone joined the Gruppo di Improvvisazione Nuova Consonanza, an ensemble specialized in improvising music of extreme radicalism. In addition, a landmark composition of this period, *Suoni per Dino* for viola and two tape recorders (1969), based on the interplay between elements derived from live performance and electronic devices, was immediately recognized as an adventuresome proposition that contributed to realign Morricone with the current trends of avant-garde music. Shortly after *Suoni per Dino*, the release of *Dimensioni sonore* (Sonic Dimensions), a series of ten RCA LP recordings whose realization was equally assigned to Morricone and Bruno Nicolai, validated the practical and creative benefits derived from the fusion of acoustical and electronic sounds. *Dimensioni sonore* and similar experimentations served to fuel the emerging film genres thriving on horror, crime, gothic, and sex. In general, the quality of these films was arguable but the appearance of genial works like Dario Argento's Animal Trilogy kept the expectation of the aficionados of these cult films high. They always panted for more.

Argento's Animal Trilogy included *L'uccello dalle piume di cristallo* (The Bird with the Crystal Plumage, 1970), *Il gatto a nove code* (The Cat O'Nine Tails, 1971), and *Quattro mosche di velluto grigio* (Four Flies on Grey Velvet, 1971), scored by Morricone in a novel procedure consisting of the deployment of modular systems arrangeable as needed like mosaic pieces, something he had been experimenting with at the RCA laboratories and with some of his concert works.

The section in Chapter 4 ambiguously entitled "Sampling 'Pink'" refers to Morricone's approach to cinematic musical comedy, a genre he mastered magnificently as shown by the soundtracks for the three-film series inspired by *La cage aux folles*, after the French farce by Jean Poiret starring Ugo Tognazzi and Michel Serrault. The comedy film *La cage aux folles* (Édouard Molinaro, 1978) and its sequels *La cage aux folles II* (1980) and *La cage aux folles III—"Elles" se marient* (1985) presented the composer with a wonderful chance to show his intelligent, sarcastic, and caustic musical sense of humor displayed in a virtuoso comedic tour de force that well complemented the films' brilliant cast as they constantly move about at the rhythm of a tip-toeing version of Youmans' *Tea for Two*, sunlit by the sultry Saint-Tropez environment.

By contrast, the encounter between Morricone and poet/writer/filmmaker Pier Paolo Pasolini projected the composer into the committed world of the Italian intellectual left. The Morricone–Pasolini relationship never blossomed into a full friendship; however, it brought interesting results as the two strong personalities drew inspiration from one other's works. Morricone treasured a short essay on the function of music in film that Pasolini wrote upon the composer's request for the release of *Dimensioni sonore*. Ultimately, still under Pasolini's literary spell, Morricone tried his hand at some intellectual cabaret songs in an effort to integrate serious and popular music, a constant he has cultivated throughout his career.

Chapter 5, "Scoring Social Justice," lies at the core of this book. It focuses on Morricone's commitment to various real-life events as well as historically fictitious ones. The chapter's beginning, subheaded "Justice, Class, Ethnicity, and Radicalism" reviews *Sacco e Vanzetti*, the 1971 film by Giuliano Montaldo based on the real story of two Italian anarchists arrested in the Boston area in 1920 under the suspicion of having committed armed robbery and murder. They were executed on the electric chair on August 23, 1927, after an extenuating international debate that turned a negative milestone in American jurisprudence. Montaldo's film added a dramatic component to the Sacco and Vanzetti tragedy. The character of the music in *Sacco e Vanzetti* oscillates between the somber and the vernacular as exemplified by *The Ballad of Sacco and Vanzetti* and *Here's to You* sung by activist singer Joan Baez who wrote their stirring lyrics. There is no question that the combined portrayal of homophobia, politics, sharp division of popular sentiments, superb acting, and the music of Morricone with Baez contributed to making *Sacco e Vanzetti* a cinematic masterpiece.

Chapter 5 also includes "Fighting for Algiers," "In the Names of Bach and Frescobaldi," and "A Rap for Ali and a Cha Cha for Rebecca"—all subheadings pertaining to the 1966 Gillo Pontecorvo's film *La battaglia di Algeri* about the 1954–1962 Algerian War for independence from the French. Pontecorvo's film is regarded as one of the best docudramas ever produced, and Ennio Morricone's music, inspired by Johann Sebastian Bach and Girolamo Frescobaldi, contributed a dense patina of sadness, jubilation, and exceptional numbing contemplation when atrocities were committed by both sides. Finally, a rap, based on Morricone's *Ali's Theme*, now popular in the streets of Algiers, celebrates Ali La Pointe, a martyr of the Algerian revolution and a protagonist of Pontecorvo's film. The rap is heard at the conclusion of the 2017 documentary by Malek Bensmail, *La bataille d'Alger, un film dans l'histoire*, a sort of meditation on Pontecorvo's film. The rap for Ali should remind us of the stark contrast in which the cha cha titled *Rebecca* is heard in the original film when a mass killing of French citizens is perpetuated by the Algerian rebels. The lyrics of the song heard from a jukebox: "Hasta mañana Rebecca / Espero que tú no vas a olvidar" are tragically ironic for the youth dancing around the record player. There was no *mañana* for them and certainly nothing to *olvidar* as their lives were to be taken in a matter of seconds.

The Mission (Joffé, 1986) is a cinematic powerhouse dealing with the frictions between colonial Spain, Portugal, and the Jesuit missions built in Brazil, Argentina, and Paraguay over the destiny of the Guarani tribes. Joffé's film is gripping as the protagonists—Robert De Niro, a slave trader turned Jesuit priest, and Jeremy Irons, Father Gabriel who plays the oboe—ultimately sacrifice their lives in an effort to save the Guarani from enslavement on the part of the colonial powers. A series of heart-wrenching episodes are wrought together by one of Morricone's best film scores, if not his very best. *The Mission*, 1987 Oscar nominee for best score, did not receive the coveted price, much to the disappointment of everyone involved in the making of the film. Morricone, crushed by disappointment, patiently waited for 2007 when the Oscar for a lifetime achievement was conferred upon him. The section in Chapter 5 entitled "Sunken Oboe," a take on Salvatore Quasimodo's poem *Oboe sommerso* (1932) and Father Gabriel's legendary oboe playing while "submersed" in the rain-soaked jungle, analyzes the score of *The Mission* on the basis of conversations I had with Morricone shortly before his 85th birthday.

Finally, this chapter concludes with a reflection on the tragic figures of Alexandros (Alekos) Panagoulis, the Greek political dissident; Pier Paolo Pasolini; and the fictitious Father Gabriel as the bearers of the composer's emotional makeup and poetic humanitarian sensibility.

In Chapter 6, I argue about Morricone's legacy, its nature, and its eventual impact on posterity. The composer has been rather adamant in regarding his catalogue of concert works as his legacy for the music history books. The rest, including hundreds of arrangements and the soundtracks to some five hundred films, I would consider more or less as ephemeral, subjected to revivals according to the unpredictable vagaries of the public's desire for nostalgia and retromania.

That said, this chapter begins when Morricone's public appearances as composer/conductor of his own music ended; the farewell concerts of June 2019. Before hundreds of thousands of adoring fans, Morricone's favorite film music was put, one more time, on full display. Now, it is left up to time to decide the future of that repertoire.

The first half of Chapter 6 pays homage to the Morricone everybody loves with a description of a number of sensational recordings, beginning with *We All Love Ennio Morricone*, a tribute to their favorite maestro by a group of artists from all over the world created on the occasion of the 2007 Oscar. This collection reaches its golden moment when Reneé Fleming sings *Come Sail Away* from the 1990 made-for-television film *Voyage of Terror: The Achille Lauro Affair*.

More gems are to be found in the four-CD collection called *Canto Morricone*, songs drawn mostly from celebrated film music themes. This elusive Morricone songbook (see its content in Appendix 2) is followed by *Yo-Yo Ma Plays Morricone*, an outstanding anthology of especially prepared arrangements for cello and orchestra of Morricone's favorite tunes. It is a unique instance in which a soloist of international reputation has taken on a program of Morricone's music originally written for motion pictures.

A music category dear to Morricone is represented by a selected number of works standing, stylistically and formally, between the commercial and the artistic. They consist of large cues from the soundtrack of films like *The Mission*, *State of Grace*, *Bugsy*, *Casualties of War*, and *The Hateful Eight*, among many others, which the composer presented often in concert as a departure from the usual medley of sweeping, familiar melodies. These pieces do not carry a specific tune but are built upon refined sonorities of post impressionistic, expressionistic, and avant-garde flavor. For the average Morricone fan, these works are excursions into less familiar territories which could function as an invitation to experience the music of the "other" Morricone.

The second half of this legacy chapter includes my descriptions of selected catalogue works including: *Gestazione* (1980), *Secondo Concerto* (1984–1985), *Terzo Concerto* (1991), *Quarto Concerto* (1993), *Ombra di lontana presenza* (1997), *Missa Papae Francisci* (2015), and *Roma* (2010).

As these titles are personal choices, I want to pause, reflect, and conclude with *Roma* (Thinking about Frescobaldi's "Ricercar Cromatico"), a little-known chamber work scored for soprano, male speaking voice, flute, oboe, clarinet, piano, violin, viola, and cello based on a poetic text written by Morricone's granddaughter Valentina. The work is Morricone's synthesized homage to his beloved city and to the Frescobaldi motif, present, like a signature, in many of his concert and commercial compositions from the beginning to late days of his career.

This intimate work alone, I would argue, could represent the essence of the Roman composer's ascent to fame more accurately than the glamorous Walk of Fame star etched in the sidewalk of Hollywood, a place far away from his beloved home in the heart of Rome.

Opinions differ on whether Ennio Morricone, who has made a fortune with his commercial and film music, deserves also a well-carved niche in the pantheon of contemporary Italian music along with his fellow composers who struggled to have their voices heard. The idea that Morricone be accorded special treatment because of his celebrity status may not bode well for some. However, such is not a good reason for neglecting the composer's concert music. On the contrary, it should be explored scientifically and enriched by outstanding performances presented in a totally "isolated" fashion from his commercial music. Morricone's concert music is part of the intimate diary of a man who never lost faith in his art. He was and, he indeed remains, confident that the day of appreciation for his legacy is at hand.

I do not know when, where, or if Ennio Morricone will make his archives available to scholars. It could happen under the auspices of a well-known institution or through a foundation created for the occasion, perhaps. What I know, however, is that this treasure trove of information will be of immense relevance, not only for the compilation of Morricone's definitive *catalogue raisonné* of more than one hundred titles of concert music, but for their systematic planning of performances and recordings as part of the tortuous trajectory followed by Italian music in the course of the past sixty years.

Franco Sciannameo
Pittsburgh, PA, August 2019

Chapter One

In the Open City

Ennio Morricone was born in Rome on November 10, 1928, to Mario Morricone, a freelance trumpet player, and Libera Ridolfi, a housewife turned shopkeeper. The family lived in Via S. Francesco a Ripa in the heart of Rome's working-class neighborhood of Trastevere. Then in 1932, they moved to larger quarters in Via Luciano Manara, also in Trastevere.[1] The Morricone family included five children: Ennio, Adriana, Aldo, Maria, and Franca. Aldo died at age three in 1938, the same year Ennio enrolled in the Conservatorio di Musica Santa Cecilia to study trumpet under the tutelage of Umberto Semproni and Reginaldo Caffarelli.

In 1943, Roberto Caggiano, a good musician who developed a career in Latin America in the 1950s, taught the three-year basic course in harmony at Santa Cecilia, a mandatory requirement for all instrumental and voice students. Morricone credited Caggiano for encouraging him to pursue composition studies; in fact, Caggiano helped him complete the prerequisite four-year harmony program by adding a semester to the basic harmony course he was already taking. That accomplishment paved the way for Morricone to enroll, in 1944, in the composition's middle-level curriculum consisting of courses in counterpoint, fugue, and composition, which he pursed under the guidance of Carlo Giorgio Garofalo (1886–1962), Alfredo De Ninno (1894–1965), and Antonio Ferdinandi (1901–1987).[2] These courses and a host of academic subjects were to be completed and certified through state examinations within a three-year period. Concurrently and clandestinely—Conservatory regulations forbade students to pursue professional activities before obtaining a proper diploma—Ennio Morricone played trumpet in nightclubs, subbing, at times, for his indisposed father and/or performing next to him in the renowned dance ensemble of bandleader Costantino Ferri.

The Open City, 1943–1945 Rome, so vividly portrayed by Roberto Rossellini in his neo-realist film *Roma città aperta* (Rome Open City) and by several prestigious writers active in the city during and after the war, became the theater of tragic/euphoric "rites of passage." The fall of Fascism, the German occupation, and the clamor of the Anglo-American troops parading through the city as liberators created a perplexing juxtaposition to the defeated or betrayed—depending on the point of view—German occupiers who missed no opportunity to inflict atrocities upon the population on their retreat to the north. The war and the horrors of the Rome Open City days and the everyday shortages and vicissitudes working people and a hopelessly destitute lower middle class had to suffer remained a painful memory in the ensuing peacetime filled with unhealed wounds and unsettled scores. During these transitional, traumatic times, Morricone and his father continued to play clubs, now under bandleader Alberto Flamini. While Costantino Ferri, known for his film scores and conducting activities during the Fascist era, had catered to the German military stationed in Rome with dance music and songs that suited their taste, Alberto Flamini and his band dished out as much jazzy, American dance music as they could muster for the benefit of the American and Canadian military officers and their mistresses patronizing the fashionable Hotels Mediterraneo and Massimo d'Azeglio.[3] That noted, jazz-influenced, "syncopated" music, as it was called, was somewhat tolerated in Fascist Italy. In fact, it even became fashionable in high societal circles accented by a hint of transgression. A trove of magazines devoted to popular songs and singers, fashion advertising, cinema, the discographic industry and the ever-growing popularity of the state radio EIAR (Ente Italiano Audizioni Radiofoniche) bear witness to the cultural contradictions that took place in those turbulent times.[4] Finally, the landing of the Allied troops on Italian soil in 1943 ushered in an overt process of Americanization that quickly turned into a staple of political propaganda in the long-lasting battle between the pro-America, Vatican-sponsored Democrazia Cristiana (DC)—the Christian Democrat ruling party after the April 18, 1948, elections—and the Moscow ideologically influenced Communist Party—Partito Comunista Italiano (PCI)—representing the opposition. Furthermore, the implementation of the Marshall Plan provoked a flood-like distribution of American films and sound recordings throughout the Italian territory.[5] Thereafter, EIAR, whose acronym was changed to Rai (Radio Audizioni Italiane) in 1947, assumed the role of the "voice of the Italian people" by broadcasting the type of entertainment music that the now "liberated" citizens of the new republic would have wanted and needed to enjoy notwithstanding that the ownership of radio receivers and ability to pay annual subscription to the network was still below European standards.[6]

In the postwar years, the stars aligned auspiciously for Ennio Morricone. On October 11, 1946, the Conservatorio di Musica Santa Cecilia granted him the degree in trumpet performance that he had worked hard for, and his composition studies heralded some noticeable vocal works. The following year, Morricone was engaged as trumpet player and arranger for some Shakespearean theatrical productions staged at Rome's Teatro Eliseo, an experience in the field of incidental music that became an essential tool in his professional kit. Then, more calls came, this time from the Teatro Sistina located nearby the Eliseo. The Teatro Sistina, under the visionary management and artistic stewardship of impresarios Piero Garinei and Sandro Giovannini, aka Garinei & Giovannini, was a sort of "Broadway on the Tiber" which, over the coming four decades morphed the old Italian "Teatro di rivista," an idiosyncratic mixture of operetta, cabaret, vaudeville, and musical theater, into fully exportable Broadway-style productions.[7] Morricone's activities as trumpet player and arranger in the pit of the Teatro Sistina ran parallel and clandestinely again to his composition studies at Santa Cecilia even during the final three years spent under Goffredo Petrassi. However, such a step forward in terms of professional status—from night clubs to musical theater—forged Morricone's strong work ethic that took nothing for granted but demanded hard work, persistence, and the ever-important cultivation of a network of fellow practitioners who, like him, made their living by making music with their hands, lips, and vocal cords. Ennio Morricone, born and raised in the Roman working-class neighborhood of Trastevere, embodied the image and temper of the Renaissance artisan at the ready, crafting on demand statuary (or immortal melodies) of classical beauty.

THE HOLY YEAR

The year 1950 marked the Holy Year, the universal Catholic observance also known as *Giubileo* (*Jubileum*), or *Anno Santo*, instituted by Pope Boniface VII in the year 1300. The yearlong celebration calls for millions of Catholics from around the globe to gather in Rome every twenty-five or fifty years for a ritualistic pilgrimage aimed at gaining the *indulgenza plenaria* (plenary indulgence), the forgiveness of sins bestowed upon the faithful by the Pope. The 1950 Holy Year proclaimed by Pope Pius XII, the charismatic Papa Eugenio Pacelli (1876–1958), was an event of extraordinary significance; attended by some three million pilgrims, it showed the supreme leader of the Catholic Church at work delivering the faithful from the horrors of a war that changed the course of civilization perhaps forever. Thus, the Catholic concept of wholesale forgiveness assumed fundamental significance in 1950.

To place more emphasis on the Anno Santo celebrations, which began with a solemn ceremony in St. Peter's Basilica on December 24, 1949, Giulio Razzi, director of programming for the Italian state radio and later television organization,[8] came up with the idea of having some popular devotional songs and Marian hymns collected, harmonized, and arranged for chorus and orchestra for eventual performance and broadcast by the Turin and Rome radio symphony orchestras and choruses. Razzi charged the project to noted ethnomusicologist Giorgio Nataletti as principal investigator and Diego Carpitella.[9] It appears that Nataletti, who was also a professor at Santa Cecilia, asked young Morricone to arrange the collected material for chorus and orchestra. Again, it seems that Morricone was paid well for the assignment, which consisted of two collections divided into devotional popular religious songs and hymns in honor of the Virgin Mary, very pertinent in 1950 since Pius XII proclaimed the Anno Santo the year of the Assumption of Mary into heaven. To this day, no records concerning performances or the whereabouts of the arrangements have come to light and Morricone's recollections on the subject appear to be scant.[10]

A FAMILY MAN

Most importantly, Marian celebrations aside, it was also in 1950 that Ennio Morricone met Maria Travia, a friend of his sister Adriana. Their courtship culminated in marriage on October 16, 1956. Meanwhile, at Santa Cecilia, Morricone completed the counterpoint and fugue program, a score of aggregate academic subjects, and successful admission to the advanced composition class of Goffredo Petrassi. Also, taking full advantage of the educational venues available at Santa Cecilia, Morricone completed a three-year program in choral music composition and conducting; however, for unclear reasons he did not pursue a final degree. It is safe to assume that it was Morricone's participation in this program that inspired Giorgio Nataletti to select him for harmonizing and orchestrating the Anno Santo collections mentioned above. Furthermore, on July 14, 1952—at the conclusion of the second year in the Petrassi composition studio—Morricone was awarded a secondary diploma in wind/brass ensemble instrumentation and added to his composition portfolio a group of piano works.

The composer's work ethic, faithful to the need and desire to make a living by writing music, prompted the 24-year-old Morricone to accept an invitation from Rai to compose incidental music for radio dramas—an assignment much welcomed by composers who later specialized in film music (one should look at the careers of luminaries in the field like Bernard Herrmann and Nino Rota who followed similar paths). Once inside the Rai network, Morricone was given the opportunity to test his skills as an arranger of commercial music. In 1953, he was offered, through the efforts of bass player and comrade-in-arms Giovanni Tommaso, the chance to arrange the music for nineteen broadcast sessions of a show entitled *Nati per la musica*. The successful show featured accordionist virtuoso/songwriter Gorny Kramer and pianist/singer/actor Lelio Luttazzi who were to dominate the Italian radio and television entertainment scene for decades to come. These much "Americanized" progressive musicians encouraged, or rather demanded, that Morricone arrange American style, a learning experience the composer embraced enthusiastically.[11]

Now in the penultimate year of Petrassi's composition class, Morricone contributed to the studio some imposing works, including *Distacco I* and *Distacco II* for voice and piano, *Verrà la morte* for voice and piano, *Oboe sommerso* for voice (baritone) and five instruments on text by Salvatore Quasimodo, and the *Sonata per ottoni, timpani e pianoforte*. This work was selected by Petrassi for public performance in the annual presentation of his students' works. Morricone's classmates Giovanni Zammerini played piano and Bruno Nicolai conducted. *Sonata per ottoni, timpani e pianoforte* is the first official opus number Ennio Morricone entered into his catalogue.

On July 6, 1954, Ennio Morricone graduated in composition under Goffredo Petrassi. Now officially out of the academic paternalism imposed by Santa Cecilia's regulations, Morricone was free to make a living by placing his professionalism at the service of the music industry on one side and his most daring compositional thoughts on the other.

In fact, Morricone was busy throughout 1955 ghost arranging and composing/supervising film music, radio dramas, and incidental music for other composers, activity he somehow continued to pursue notwithstanding the restrains imposed by eighteen months of compulsory military service that took place between the towns of Montereale, Siena, and Rome. Even during the military service, it appears that Morricone's compositional skills turned useful as he was "asked" by his superiors to transcribe a number of popular works for military band. At any rate, following the military discharge on October 16, 1956, Ennio Morricone and Maria Travia married in the Trastevere church of the Saints Cosma e Damiano. After a brief honeymoon in Taormina (Sicily), the newlyweds moved to an apartment in Via Mattia Montecchi in their beloved neighborhood of Trastevere. Meanwhile, Morricone continued his jobbing activities for Rai, arranging music for the orchestras of Guido Cergoli and Cinico Angelini in addition to the already mentioned bands of Kramer and Luttazzi. The collaboration with Angelini became particularly profitable as the very popular, conservative bandleader fostered the careers of budding young singers who won top prizes at the national song festival of

Sanremo and major recording contracts.[12] Thus, Morricone's arrangements, always innovative and highly sophisticated and yet sensitive to the popular taste of the time, came to be regarded as the essential ingredient for a singer's immediate success.

With the birth of Marco in 1957, Ennio and Maria Morricone contemplated the security of a steady job. Academic accolades and the composition of "serious" music guaranteed professional status but no income unless provided by a governmental institution through teaching/administrative functions. Freelancing, on the other hand, paid well, offered excitement and . . . much instability, a risk Morricone, the family man, could no longer afford. He decided to apply for the position of director of the Conservatorio di Sassari in Sardinia. Fate intervened, and Morricone's candidacy for the bureaucratic position on a large island, beautiful but out of the mainstream of the musical world, was rejected. The young family remained in their beloved Rome where Morricone was able to complete his first major orchestral work, *Concerto per orchestra*, which he dedicated to his teacher Goffredo Petrassi.

GOFFREDO PETRASSI: MY MICHELANGELO

Goffredo Petrassi (1904–2003), born in Zagarolo, a town in the Roman countryside near Palestrina—the hill town that gave Giovanni Pierluigi his surname—began his career as a boy soprano in the Vatican's Schola Cantorum (papal choir). There, he learned firsthand the sacred/secular contrapuntal orthodoxy that he passed onto his composition students at Santa Cecilia over many decades of teaching. Petrassi was a towering presence, an institution in itself, at the Conservatorio. Memorable for those who witnessed it was the ritual scene of the maestro surrounded by his disciples descending the large staircase of the school at the conclusion of evening classes. In Morricone's time, the likes of Firmino Sifonia, Aldo Clementi, Domenico Guaccero, Boris Porena, Mauro Bortolotti, and Bruno Nicolai poured out of the building onto bustling Via del Corso where they dispersed; only one or two students walked Petrassi to his house in Via Germanico. Real "lessons" were imparted during those walks, recalled Morricone. In fact, it was during a walk to Via Germanico following Morricone's graduation day on July 6, 1954, that Petrassi advised his pupil not to take any commitments for two years because something remarkable was going to happen to him in the course of that period. "To this day, I still do not understand what he meant by . . . two years!" pondered Morricone.[13]

Petrassi composed a *Concerto per orchestra* in 1933–1934, a time when Italian music, overwhelmed by the late spasms of operatic *verismo*, strived to find a new identity by adopting neo-classical formulae, halfway between Stravinsky and Hindemith, that the avuncular Alfredo Casella propagated among young progressive composers. Soon, stylistic labels like "neo-madrigal, "neo-Baroque, and "neo-classical" acquired favorable currency in the sociopolitical climate of the time, which rushed to equate rational musical structures to the new urban renewal *Razionalismo* sponsored by Mussolini and realized by architect Marcello Piacentini. That said, Petrassi's *Concerto per orchestra* remains a work of merit driven by steady motoric pulsations that became a quasi-metaphysical principle of Petrassi's music. *Concerto per orchestra* is an example of orchestral virtuosity and technical mastery, qualities that Petrassi valued above the expressive factor.

In 1940–1941, Petrassi composed *Coro di morti*, a *madrigale drammatico* based on a text by Giacomo Leopardi that quickly occupied an iconic place in the composer's oeuvre.[14] The work was viewed as foreshadowing the horrors of the Second World War and the ensuing civil war that tore Italy, a still relatively young nation, apart. At about the same time, Béla Bartók expressed in works like *Music for String Instruments, Percussion and Celesta* (1936) and *Concerto for Orchestra* (1943) his own anguish over the catastrophic fate of Hungary and the rest of Europe vis-à-vis the Nazis advances. *Concerto for Orchestra* was viewed by many as "the most powerful of Requiems, one that perhaps only an atheist could have written. It is a lament for men's inhumanity to man, but also a positive vision of a world in a kind of harmony in which chaos and order, the primeval enemies, are held in dynamic equilibrium."[15] Others saw it as Bartók's negation of the solid alternative to the Second Viennese School that he had established through radical compositions such as the two *Violin Sonatas*, the *Fourth String Quartet*, and the *Music for String Instruments, Percussion and Celesta*.

By 1955—one year after Morricone's graduation—Petrassi had composed five concerti for orchestra[16] in styles that reflected his gradual adoption of atonality, serialism, and avant-garde techniques, thus challenging audiences worldwide, critics, and his own students past and present. Petrassi's *Secondo Concerto* (1951), scored for woodwinds in pairs, 2 French horns, 2 trumpets, timpani, and strings, was written in a language more tonally polarized than that of the preceding cantata *Noche oscura* (1950–1951)[17] in which the composer approached 12-tone serialism for the first time, albeit in a very cautious manner.[18] Preeminent in this concerto though is the development of germinal counterpoint that expands gradually like a patch of oil in a manner strongly resembling the Bartók of *Music for String Instruments, Percussion and Celesta*.

In other parts, the composer resorted to neo-Baroque peculiarities like the "hook" of three notes—a J. S. Bach signature—which Petrassi used abundantly in his *Primo Concerto* and that fascinated Stravinsky (*Jeu de cartes* and *Dumbarton Oaks*) and Hindemith (*Kammermusiken*) among others. In substance, one could view Petrassi's *Secondo Concerto* as a sort of friendly match between Bartók and Stravinsky, not a surprise if one considers that Paul Sacher and his Basel Chamber Orchestra—an organization particularly vital to European composers of the Bartók and Stravinsky schools—commissioned Petrassi's *Secondo Concerto*.

A symphonic plan that showcased the principle of genetic developments growing out of fragmented patterns framed *Terzo Concerto* (1953), subtitled *Récréation concertante*. Thus, Petrassi's score looks like a sort of laboratory (he called it *Récréation*) for orchestral writing for writing's sake, which he mapped out with oases of static moments. During such moments, the fragmented patterns mentioned above suspended their genetic mutation process, issued a "call to order," proposed new thematic material, and restarted the generative process until they reached the next patch. *Terzo Concerto*, Petrassi's "credo to orchestral writing" had a strong influence on his pupils.

Quarto Concerto (1954), scored for string orchestra, presented Petrassi with a paramount challenge: avoid falling too deeply into Bartók's domain. A daunting task considering that *Music for String Instruments, Percussion and Celesta* (1936) and *Divertimento for Strings* (1939)—both Sacher commissions—were well established in the repertoire by 1954. Nevertheless, Petrassi continued to follow the Bartók technique of germinal counterpoint expansion he had previously exploited in the *Secondo Concerto* and sought new directions in string ensemble writing that not only alighted Bartók's lesson but reached as far back as Beethoven's late string quartets.

When the Koussevitzky Foundation commissioned to Petrassi the composition of *Quinto Concerto* (1955), the composer found himself again in competition against Béla Bartók if only for reasons of circumstantial association. In fact, both composers had written their concerti for the Boston Symphony Orchestra through commissions from the Koussevitzky Foundation, thus it was expected that Petrassi's work measure up to the gold standard set by the Bartók's masterpiece eleven years earlier.[19]

With *Quinto Concerto*, Petrassi returned to the orchestral richness of *Primo Concerto* albeit in a darker, more somber mood akin perhaps to Mozart's *Masonic Funeral Music* K. 477. Conceived in two parts: I. *Molto moderato—Presto*; II. *Andantino tranquillo, mosso con vivacità—Lento e grave*, *Quinto Concerto* is a kaleidoscope of brief statements each meant to showcase the instruments of the orchestra in solos, pairs, or groups. These statements are developed as thematic and timbrical variations on a musical motto he underscored with the words *lieta no, ma sicura* in his youthful *Coro di morti*. The quotation of this two-voice fragment may suggest that Petrassi wished to embed the "ghosts" of Serge and Natalie Koussevitzky, *Quinto Concerto*'s dedicatees, into the score through the symbolic quotation from a *madrigale drammatico* whose text dealt with man's condition after death: *lieta no* (not happy), *ma sicura* (but assured). Furthermore, toward the end of the piece Petrassi inserted a passage reminiscent of *Tristan und Isolde* as a reference to Serge and Natalie or perhaps for personal reasons.

Quinto Concerto removed Petrassi from Bartók's late choreographic narrative and brought him closer to Alban Berg's elegiac yet contained expressiveness of the *Violin Concerto*, another masterpiece bearing a strong mournful significance.

Petrassi's concerti for orchestra composed between 1932 and 1955 influenced Ennio Morricone greatly in the course of his formative process. So, it is natural that Petrassi's teaching is particularly evident in Morricone's own *Concerto per orchestra* composed in 1957 as we will observe in the pages ahead.

CONCERTO PER ORCHESTRA: A SUCCINCT DESCRIPTION

Ennio Morricone's *Concerto per orchestra* was performed for the first time on March 24, 1960, at the Teatro La Fenice in Venice. Rai, the Italian national radio and television network, broadcast that performance nationally on August 7, 1960.[20]

Here is a succinct description of a forgotten work whose score's rich craftsmanship, daring contrapuntal solutions, and timbrical subtleties comprise the efforts on the part of a young composer to establish himself as the legitimate heir to the great school of composition that Goffredo Petrassi had instituted at Santa Cecilia.

Although the architectural structure of this remarkable piece of music is planned as one continuous movement, it is divided in three distinct blocks built on sharply enunciated "horn calls," disposed in ascending and descending patterns that clearly assign trombone and trumpet concertante roles throughout the piece.

Block 1 covers the first five minutes and 25 seconds of music. It begins with a vigorous down beat marked *ff* (*Allegro con vigore*) sustained by the trombone but quickly joined by razor sharp "horn calls" (*fpp*) played by trumpet and French horn (doubled by bassoon) followed by tuba, cellos, and basses.

Upon reaching the agogic marking *e con spirito*, the sonic fabric begins to "liquefy" by means of canonical counterpoints played *legato* by the woodwinds—teased by the piccolo's tiptoeing version of the opening horn calls—while the strings' web of sixteenth notes, played *alla punta* and *sul ponticello*,

Figure 1.1. Concerto per orchestra, mm. 302–307. Ennio Morricone (Suvini Zerboni, 1990). Courtesy of Edizioni Suvini Zerboni.

provides the background to the whole section. The sonic liquefaction leads to a calm *intermezzo* introduced by the muted trombone playing *pianissimo* in echo with bass clarinet and bassoon. The violins then take over the melodic line in lyrical fashion until m. 51, when, accompanied by repeated eighth notes (clarinet and bassoon), the trombone leads the dialogue to a breaking point consisting of three 3/8 measures marked *Ritenuto e Fortissimo*.

There is no question that this section echoes similar passages in Petrassi's *Secondo* and *Terzo* Concerti.

Now, returning to the original 3/4-time signature, a section marked *Meno* shows delicate arabesques played by woodwinds, muted French horn, and trombone supported by triple piano strings playing minor third measured thrills *sulla tastiera*. Then, the episode crashes into a spirited *Tempo Primo*. Here too, there is Petrassi's hand in addition to some joyful (or sarcastic) bassoon rhythmical frolics encountered in Stravinsky's *Jeu de cartes*.

This section is followed by an extended, delicate, and lyrical development that concludes through a gradual crescendo punctuated by hints of the opening horn calls. Everything finally comes to a halt before resuming full force with a pickup beat to a false caesura leaving the trombone in charge of leading the whole orchestra in a violent episode marked *Molto rit. Sostenuto marcato* that resolves upon a *ritenuto* peroration. At this juncture, Block 1 begins its conclusion through a gradual dismantling of the whole construction.

An empty 8/4 measure separates Block 1 from Block 2, which is marked *Andante calmo*. It begins with a melodic line played *pianissimo* by cellos and double basses, quickly answered by French horn, trumpet, and trombone playing *Il più piano possible* (see Figure 1.2).

Then, a "velvety" moment prepares the clarinet's arabesque entrance, a reminder of the English horn solo in Petrassi's *Quinto Concerto*. Clarinet and violas converse until joined by piccolo, oboe, bassoon, and muted trumpet. This chamber music mode changes when the violins *con sordina* soar into an ethereal turn of phrase marked *Un poco più lento*, soon joined by the trumpet (*senza sordina*). Another great Petrassian moment? Yes, but Morricone interrupts his lyrical reverie with a triple piano reiteration of the opening horn calls.

This episode gives way to scalelike *poco movendo* interventions played by the bassoon followed by English horn, oboe, and ultimately the violins before unleashing a cataclysmic sound wave that climaxes through a *fortissimo* trumpet call answered by the timpani. Thus, the episode concludes in a rather mysterious way.

Next, trumpet and trombone, holding the note "A," lead the way to a gradual participation of the full orchestra in what would appear to be the anticipation of a tumultuous ending. Instead, the *crescendo* falls held by the

Figure 1.2. Concerto per orchestra, mm. 214–218. Ennio Morricone (Suvini Zerboni, 1990). Courtesy of Edizioni Suvini Zerboni.

fading sound of the French horn, then "terraced" strings playing harmonics and *pianissimo*, very soft timpani roll, and muted French horn are joined at m. 298 marked *Andante calmo* by oboe, English horn, and bassoon for the vanishing dissolve of Block 2 held until the start of Block 3.

Block 3 is a non-conventional fugue of large proportion lasting for one-half the length of the whole *Concerto*. It begins with a 12-tone subject played by the trombone. The countersubject is heard followed by its retrograde inversion embellished by an "ambiguous" game of triplets played by English horn and violas (see Figure 1.3).

Then, a two-measure statement, a vivid reminder of Petrassi's *Primo* and *Secondo* Concerti, leads to the *Poco ritenuto* that is an episode based on the countersubject. The following *A Tempo* could be considered a *Stretto*, although one announced rather prematurely by the trombone playing in a *quasi recitativo* style introducing the subject and countersubject in augmentation.

A series of episodes based on contrapuntal entries leads to a *Fortissimo* return of the subject in augmentation played by the violins together with the countersubject played by the woodwinds. This brief contrapuntal tour de

Figure 1.3. Concerto per orchestra, mm. 352–358. Ennio Morricone (Suvini Zerboni, 1990). Courtesy of Edizioni Suvini Zerboni

force disintegrates into *e rallentando molto* that functions as a lead-in to a beautiful *Adagio sereno*, an extended section in triple piano playing a lyrical transformation of the subject punctuated by bell-like interventions provided by the muted French horn and woodwinds almost in pointillistic fashion and

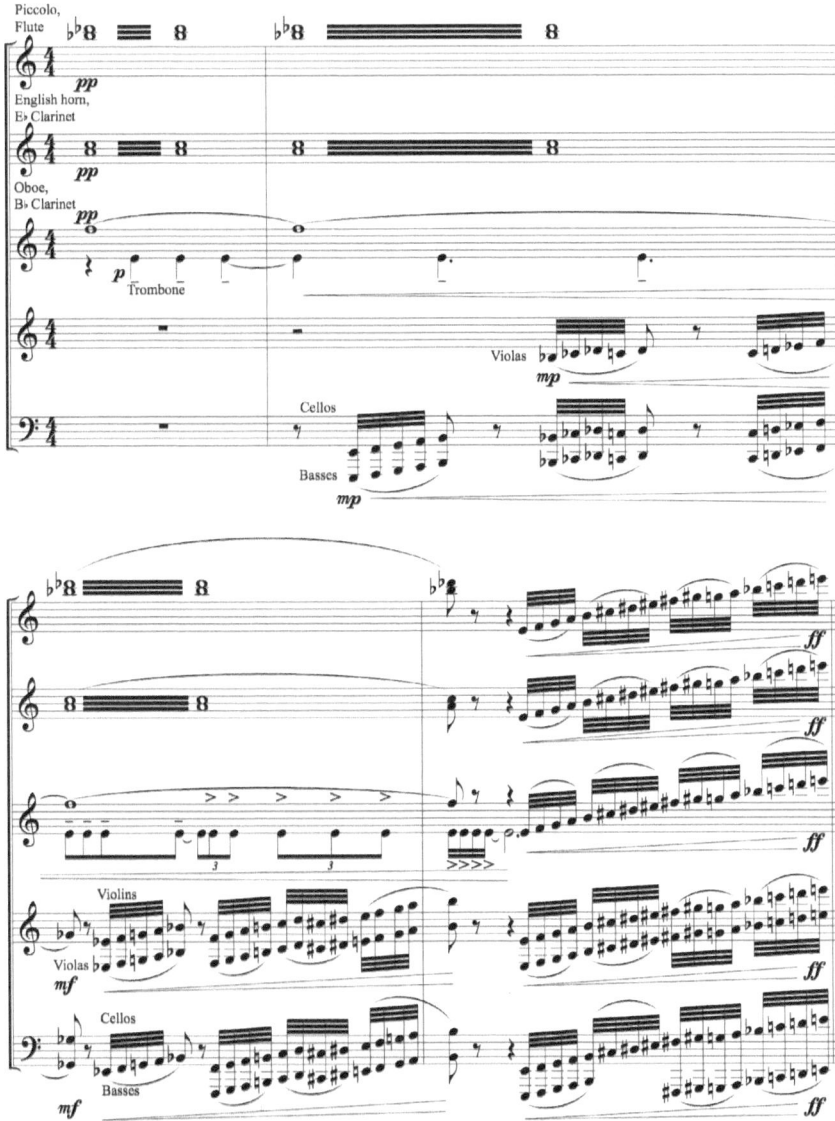

Figure 1.4. Concerto per orchestra, mm. 542–545. Ennio Morricone (Suvini Zerboni, 1990). Courtesy of Edizioni Suvini Zerboni

sustained by pulsating quarter-notes played first by cellos and double basses, then by timpani.

The soft pounding of the pulsating timpani—halfway between Petrassi's *Quinto Concerto* as well as Brahms' opening of the First Symphony and Puccini's *Madama Butterfly*—vanish in order to give way to a *Presto*, which can be considered as the first of a succession of four codas concluding with a fleeting, lancing *Fortissimo* that aims at an invisible target (see Figure 1.4).

DARMSTADT: A NEW BAYREUTH

Morricone's *Concerto per orchestra* was both homage to Petrassi and the beginning of a professional emancipation from him as shown by three works completed by the end of 1958: *3 Studi per flauto, clarinetto e fagotto* (1957), *Distanze per violino, violoncello e pianoforte* (April 1958), and *Musica per 11 violini* (late 1958).[21]

Distanze and *3 Studi* are two solid examples of chamber music that Morricone constructed with decisive, lyrical, Webern-inspired pointillism. They show the composer's concern about his predicament: that of a 30-year-old family man with no fixed income determined to make a living by composing music. Possible solutions to this conundrum pointed to three options: seeking an academic, government-sponsored appointment; securing an administrative/artistic role in the cadre of Rai-TV national network; or, alternatively, becoming a freelance professional gaining access to the alluring world of commercial music by relying upon the support of his professional network. After the first two options failed to materialize as noted earlier in this chapter, Morricone, the Trastevere working man with wife and child, held steady to his entrenchment in the serious music world and its proselytizing stance. This was a situation destined to become a duality, a "double aesthetic," as he labeled it later in life, that Morricone carried and has managed all these years.

In 1958, Darmstadt, the West German town near Frankfurt am Main in the Hesse State, was in the throngs of full reconstruction after being reduced to ashes during the war. For music and musicians, it represented a New Bayreuth of sorts whose Internationale Ferienkurse für Nueu Musik had become the destination that living composers worth their salt needed to attend to either subscribe to the Darmstadt-imparted dogma or resist it. Strong personalities like Pierre Boulez, Karlheinz Stockhausen, and Luigi Nono reigned supreme in Darmstadt. Others, including Bruno Maderna and Luciano Berio, acted like pallbearers at the wake of the fading rhetoric of Adorno, which in September 1958 was going to be disrupted by the participation of John Cage, whose arrival shook the whole fabric and philosophical views of many in the music avant-garde world of the Ferienkurse.[22]

The Italian participation in the Darmstadt Internationale Ferienkurse für Nueu Musik, September 2–13, 1958, edition was representative of the young forces reshaping new music in Italy during the postwar years. Ennio Morricone joined a group of colleagues on their pilgrimage to Germany although none of his music was going to be performed there, nor had he been offered a speaking role. He went to Darmstadt to listen, absorb, and debate about his thoughts and his future. Others were active participants: Luciano Berio lectured and introduced works he had realized at the Studio di Fonologia Musicale della Rai Milano, including *Perspectives* (1957), and Bruno Maderna presented *Continuo* (1958). Franco Evangelisti had a more preeminent role than his two compatriots; he presented his electronic piece *Incontri di fasce sonore* (1956–1957), realized at the Studio für elekronische Musik des Westdeuschen Rundfunks Köln, and *Proiezioni sonore*, while *Strutture per pianoforte solo* (1955–1956) was performed by David Tudor. Another piano authority, Aloys Kontarsky, performed Aldo Clementi's *Composizione n. 1* (1957). Maderna conducted *Canti 1 e 3* from *Tre canti* op. 1 (1957) by Antonio Titone performed in a version for soprano, clarinet, bass clarinet, piano, and viola. Walter Marchetti's *Spazi II für Kammerensemble* (1958) was performed by the Italian ensemble Incontri Musicali, also conducted by Maderna. Boris Porena's *Vier kanonische Lieder auf Texte von Paul Celan für Sopran und klarinette* (1958) was offered by soprano Zofia Stachurska and pianist Ferruccio Gonizzi. Niccolò Castiglioni and Franco Donatoni presented, respectively, *Inizio di movimento per pianoforte* (1958) and *Tre improvvisazioni per pianoforte* (1957). At the same time, Roman flute virtuoso Severino Gazzelloni dazzled the audience with Berio's *Sequenza I* (1958) and Maderna's *Musica su due dimensioni* for flute and electronics (new version 1958). Another Italian, concert pianist and music historian Massimo Bogiankino, stood by on the sidelines like Ennio Morricone.

A look at the Ferienkurse 1958 programs shows how the formidable array of music, composers, and performers operated under the clout of Arnold Schoenberg. The much-anticipated participation of John Cage, himself a pupil of Schoenberg in 1934–1935; the ironclad institutional presence of Luigi Nono, assisted by his wife Nuria Schoenberg, Arnold's daughter; violinist Rudolf Kolisch, Schoenberg's brother-in-law; and the performances of Schoenberg's own (1) *Suite für Kleine Klarinete, Klarinette, Baßklarinette, Geige, Bratsche, Violoncell und Klavier* op. 29 (1925–1926), (2) *Serenade für Klarinette, Baßklarinett, Mandoline, Gitarre, Geige, Bratsche, Violoncello und eine tiefe Männerstimme* op. 24 (1920–1923), and (3) *Drei Satiren für gemischten Chor* op. 28 (1925) were followed by the world première of the Darmstadt-commissioned *Cori di Didone* by Luigi Nono. One could say that the 1958 Ferienkurse was a true homage to Schoenberg, and, consequently, to the historical "Nueu Musik" he once represented. Nevertheless, John Cage's pathbreaking lectures on *Changes*, *Indeterminacy*, and *Communication*, enhanced by works performed by the composer and David Tudor, engulfed the Schoenbergian establishment with such a high level of perplexity that they provoked a fundamental rethinking about music altogether marked by outbursts of nervous skepticism.

It is not known how much and how directly Morricone absorbed John Cage's extremely nuanced command of the English language or the German translations of his lectures provided by the courses' organizers since Morricone was not familiar with either. Surely though, the wealth of musical examples accompanying Cage's lectures, the performances, and the many debates in any language taking place afterwards were sufficient to leave an indelible impression on all participants. Decades later, Morricone reflected about the use of music in cinema in clearly Cagean thinking. He said:

> Upon confronting John Cage's lectures and performances [in 1958] I slipped into a very heavy state of shock, then I reflected upon it. The whole meaning is that music once separated from the instrumental context, or the human factor, insects or any other living object acquires another meaning. I refer here to the final portion of the Manifesto, to the fact that music needs in cinema absolute silence.[23] When they say that I gave my best to Leone's films it is absolutely false. The merit is Leone's who leaves music isolated, cleansed of other sounds and elements of reality. Music needs space when representing a sound that comes from the elsewhere, indeterminate and does not generate from the screen either. The screen generates a flat image, which without music could remain as such. Music offers it a sense of vertical depth and horizontal dynamism all possible if surrounded by silence. This is necessary because the auditory system, therefore, the brain is not in condition to hear, comprehend multiple sounds of different contemporary provenance. We will never be able to understand four people talking simultaneously.[24]

In the same breath, Morricone had no qualms in pronouncing Luigi Nono a great composer:

> When I heard *Cori di Didone* for the first time [in Darmstadt] I had the impression that composition as manifestation of civilization had reached the peak of its being and probably the beginning of its decadence. When a civilization reaches its apogee, it can only roll back. I love him very much and I believe that in some ways he was among the few who have influenced me. *Cori di Didone* (1958) and *Canto sospeso* (1956) are two compositions of great density.[25]

A PROBLEM SOLVED

Distanze per violino, violoncello e pianoforte and *3 Studi per flauto, clarinetto e fagotto* were composed before Morricone's trip to Darmstadt. *Musica per 11 violini* was written after his return.

The title *3 Studi* indicates: studies, plans, maps, blueprints, schemata that objectify three instrumental voices as if they were styluses tracing trajectories with different color ink. In fact, there is a sense of spatial geometry pervading this score but no apparent beauty of expression. It is a score to be looked at rather than performed as the players' subjectivity would and could "breathe" unwanted life into the notes, thus forcing paths in unplanned directions.[26] By contrast, *Distanze*, a Webern-inspired composition that comes to life through the romantic sound of a piano trio (piano, violin, and cello), comprises a series of fragments grouped in a tripartite structure (ABC) preceded by twelve introductory measures for a total duration of some seven minutes.

The introductory measures present a series of seven notes that establish Morricone's unorthodox application of Viennese serialism while anticipating the strong contrapuntal construction of the whole work. Nevertheless, the lyrical élan that pervades *Distanze* shows the composer's emancipation from Petrassi's teaching and a nod to Roman Vlad (1919–2013), a very influential Roman composer/critic at the time who was very fond of Anton Webern's expressive power of pointillism.

Distanze offers performers and listeners plenty of "sighs" and alternating moments of extreme tension, which establish a narrative drenched in *Sturm und Drang* feelings.[27]

Ennio Morricone, a near-professional chess player, was fond of referring to *Musica per 11 violini* as a numerical game of twelve constructed with inflexible logic upon a series of twelve sounds whose permutations and compositional parameters result in having one violin remain silent all the time, eliminating one violin part from the score's nomenclature. That said, though, *Musica per 11 violini* is too complex a piece to be performed without a conductor, which means that player number twelve—waiving a bow or a baton—becomes the necessary element for completing the team.

Composed upon return from Darmstadt, *Musica per 11 violini* is scored for a principal violin, or better, a team leader that interacts with five violins placed on the right and five on the left, setting the stage for a series of episodes divided into three sections held together by two hinges, as if they were the panels of a tryptic-like scoreboard whose sonic palette stays within the instrumental boundaries established by Webern in his *Fünf Sätze für Streichquartett*, op. 5 (1909), to cite a "classical" example.

The first thing that emerges from this piece, aside from its gestuality when performed live, is the determination with which Morricone resolved the issue of timbre through subtle variants, despite the apparent monochromatic uniformity of eleven violins. However, it is the relationship between instrumental solutions and overall architecture that established the dramatic and agonistic ritualization of the score beginning with the physical positioning of the instruments organized according to functional principles: the team leader in the middle and five violins at the left and five violins at the right as mentioned before.

As with *Concerto per orchestra*, I offer a succinct description of this short work (6:45 minutes) according to the score published in 1973 by Éditions Salabert, Paris. It consists of seventy-five measures divided in three sections connected by two hinges that unfold as follows: Section A (mm. 1–29) shows in the first three measures the violins on the left, exposing the 12-tone series in pointillistic fashion to which the violins on the right respond with intertwined, impalpable trills mediated by the principal violin at the center. In this section, uniformity between left and right groups is reached on m. 13, where the migration of a sonic-micro event coalesces into a fuller sound: a *fff pizz. sul ponticello* played by violin six on the left engaged, from mm. 14 to 29, by all eleven players twice in systemic fashion covering the chromatic scale without serial regularity. In terms of game strategy, the sound gesture bounces as if it were a ball from player to player with no specific consequences—except when approaching hinge 1 (mm. 30–33). This portion consists of clustered notes and rests presented in terraced strata, from violin six on the right to violin six on the left, following a notational progression that goes from sixteenth to double-dotted half notes and, after a one-eight rest, from sixteenth notes of violin six on the left to double-dotted half notes of violin six on the right. Then, a total quarter rest puts the sound flow on hold before unleashing Section B (mm. 34–44), a truly passionate contrapuntal *ffff*.

Thereafter, a cathartic *pppp* suspension leads the discourse to hinge 2 (mm. 45–49), which establishes the note C as the climactic point of the composition and the beginning of Section C (mm. 50–69). This section showcases the principal violin engaging the other instruments one at a time in progressive order like fast-break action in a game of soccer. Then, at m. 70, all players crash into each other signaling that the game may be approaching its end at which point violin five "dribbles the ball" by performing a ricochet of sixteenth notes septuplets executed *col legno battuto descrescendo* to *pppp*.

A coda (mm. 70–75) alights ten violins holding a clustered pedal while the principal player soars into a lyrical cadenza.[28]

Musica per 11 violini is central to the antiphonal topoi Morricone inherited from his studies of Flemish polyphony; the sonic experimentations of the Venetians Adriano Willaert and the uncle–nephew duo Giovanni and Andrea

Gabrieli; the Roman polyphony of Palestrina; and the architectural constructiveness of Girolamo Frescobaldi. *Musica per 11 violini* can be viewed not only as a game that would have attracted Wittgenstein's attention and the masters of speculative counterpoint headed by Johann Sebastian Bach, but as a scanning of the composer's compositional strategies present and future as he positioned and repositioned on an imaginary sound/game board isolated and aggregate bodies of sound searching for natural sonic responsorial occurrences and/or melodic expansions which were to become the signature Morricone affixed to hundreds of arrangements of commercial songs and much music for the screen discussed in this book.[29]

NOTES

1. Trastevere, from the Latin *trans Tiberim*, an historic working-class neighborhood situated on the west bank of the river Tiber south of the Vatican, is presently known for its bohemian funkiness, countless artisans' shops, restaurants, pubs, and the colorful nightly gatherings of youth.

2. Carlo Giorgio Garofalo, known mostly for his sacred music, composed a number of large symphonic works, including *Sinfonia romantica* and *Concerto per violino e orchestra*, which was written for and premiered in Rome by Remy Principe. The same soloist, concertmaster of Rome's Augusteo Orchestra (the forerunner of the present Orchestra dell'Accademia Nazionale di Santa Cecilia) and revered Santa Cecilia professor, premiered in the 1930s Antonio Ferdinandi's *Concerto per violino in sol minore*, also written to suit Principe's talents. Ferdinandi, in addition to his pedagogical duties at Santa Cecilia, was a member of the double bass section of the Augusteo/Santa Cecilia Orchestras throughout his professional life. Alfredo De Ninno gained national reputation for his important historical and theoretical treatises currently in use.

3. For details on the musical activity in dance clubs in Rome in the immediate postwar period, see Andrea Malvano, *L'arte di arrangiar (si)* (Lucca: Libreria Musicale Italiana, 2015).

4. See Franco Monteleone, *Storia della radio e della televisione italiana* (Venezia: Marsilio, 1992).

5. The 1948 Marshall Plan, or European Recovery Act, consisted of a 12-billion-dollar endowment fund (120 billions in current money) dedicated by the United States Treasury to help rebuild those countries in western Europe devastated by World War II.

6. See Monteleone, *Storia della radio e della televisione italiana*.

7. Lello Garinei and Marco Giovannini, *Garinei e Giovannini presentano: Quarant'anni di teatro musicale all'Italiana* (Milano: Rizzoli, 1985).

8. Florentine-born Giulio Razzi, director of programming for EIAR, then Rai, was the son of Ida Razzi, sister of Giacomo Puccini's wife Elvira. Thus, Razzi enjoyed somewhat the benefits of nepotism.

9. Giorgio Nataletti (1907–1972) and Diego Carpitella (1924–1990) were two much-esteemed academics who devoted their efforts on behalf of the development of ethnomusicological studies in Italy.

10. On the occasion of the Anno Santo 2000, Morricone published *Cantico del Giubileo* (Ricordi, 2000), a work for chorus and orchestra echoing his popular choral fresco *On Earth as It Is in Heaven* from the film *The Mission* (1986).

11. It is important to credit bandleader Pippo Barzizza (1902–1994), a pioneer of jazz music in Italy, for having published *L'orchestrazione moderna nella musica leggera* (Milano: Edizioni Curci, 1952), a fundamental guide to Italian arrangers.

12. For a scholarly analysis of the Sanremo phenomenon, see Roberto Agostini, "Sanremo Effects: The Festival and the Italian Canzone (1950s–1960s)," in Franco Fabbri and Goffredo Plastino (Eds.), *Made in Italy: Studies in Popular Music* (New York: Routledge, 2014), 28–40.

13. See Sergio Miceli, *Morricone, la musica, il cinema* (Milano: Ricordi/Mucchi, 1994), 33, n13.

14. *Coro di morti, madrigale drammatico* is scored for male chorus (TB); 4 French horns, 4 trumpets, 3 trombones, tuba, timpani, percussion, 3 pianos, and 5 double basses. (Edizioni Suvini Zerboni, Milano.)

15. See David Cooper, *Bartók: Concerto for Orchestra* (Cambridge: Cambridge University Press, 1996; 2nd edition, 2004), 2.

16. By the time of his death, Goffredo Petrassi had composed eight concerti for orchestra. For exhaustive analyses of Petrassi's works see *Petrassi*, a cura di Enzo Restagno (Torino: EDT [Edizioni di Torino], 1992) and/or John S. Weissmann, *Goffredo Petrassi* [in English] (Milano: Edizioni Suvini Zerboni, 1980).

17. *Noche oscura, cantata for coro misto e orchestra* (SATB, 3 flutes, 2 oboes, English horn, 2 clarinets, bass clarinet, 2 bassoons. contrabassoon, 4 French horns, 4 trumpets, 2 trombones, bass trombone, tuba, timpani, 2 percussions, harp, strings). Text by San Juan de la Cruz.

18. However, Petrassi affirmed in several interviews that he had adopted 12-tone serialism for the first time in *Sesto Concerto* (1956–1957).

19. *Quinto Concerto*, dedicated to the memory of Serge and Natalie Koussevitzky, was written in celebration of the Boston Symphony Orchestra's 75th anniversary. Its premiere took place in Boston on December 2, 1955, Charles Münch conducting. Béla Bartók's *Concerto for Orchestra*, dedicated to the memory of Natalie Koussevitsky, was premiered by the Boston Symphony Orchestra conducted by Serge Koussevitzky on December 1, 1944.

20. Morricone's *Concerto per orchestra* is scored for piccolo, flute, oboe, English horn, E flat clarinet, B flat clarinet, bass clarinet, bassoon, French horn in F, trumpet in C, trombone, tuba, timpani, snare drum, and strings. It was published by Edizioni Suvini Zerboni, Milano, in 1990.

The performance of the Orchestra del Teatro La Fenice conducted by Erminia Romano was recorded before a live audience during the Stagione Sinfonica Primavera 1960 on March 24 at 9:00 p.m. The present listening guide is based on the 2002 recorded performance of the Orchestra dell'Accademia Nazionale di Santa Cecilia conducted by Andrea Morricone released in 2002 by Milan Records—198 791-2 in disc 4 of a compilation box set of four CDs entitled *Io, Ennio Morricone*.

For a fuller analysis of this work, see Franco Sciannameo, "Ennio Morricones *Concerto per Orchestra* (1957)," in Guido Heldt, Tarek Krohn, Peter Moormann, and Willem Strank (Eds.), *Ennio Morricone* (München: edition text + kritick, 2014), 119–40.

21. These three pieces were necessary stylistic departures from the neo-classical and neo-modal imprints that characterized Morricone's precedent works like *Sestetto per flauto, oboe, fagotto, violino, viola e violoncello* (1955), *Trio per clarinetto, corno e violoncello* (1955–1956), and *Invenzione, Canone e Ricercare per pianoforte* (1956). These works can be heard in the LP *Ennio Morricone, Musiche da Camera*, RCA, R1 70761 (2) 1985.

22. See Martin Iddon, *New Music at Darmstadt: Nono, Stockhausen, Cage, and Boulez* (Cambridge: Cambridge University Press, 2013) and Antonio Trudu, "La distruzione del tempio: John Cage a Darmstadt nel 1958 (e prima, e dopo)," in Sergio Miceli (Ed.), *Norme con ironie: Scritti per i settant'anni di Ennio Morricone* (Milano: Edizioni Suvini Zerboni, 1998), 313–46.

23. Morricone refers here to *Comporre per il cinema: Un manifesto*, a text he prepared for the conclusion of a cycle of seminars in film music held in Fiesole, Tuscany, in 1999 and 2000. This text is available in Italian in Ennio Morricone e Sergio Miceli, *Comporre per il cinema: Teoria e prassi della musica per film* (Venezia: Marsilio, 2001), 299–306, or in English in Ennio Morricone and Sergio Miceli, *Composing for the Cinema: The Theory and Praxis of Music in Film*, trans. Gillian B. Anderson (Lanham, MD: Scarecrow Press, 2013), 249–52.

24. *Ennio Morricone racconta . . .* (parte terza) in *Colonne sonore*, maggio 2005. Morricone's quotations are taken from a three-part interview published by Stefano Sorice in the periodical *Colonne sonore: Immagini tra le note* issued as Anno III-n.12–13 (2005), Anno III-n.14 (2005), and Anno III-n.15 (2005). English translations are by the author.

25. *Colonne sonore*, maggio 2005 (see note 24 above). English translations are by the author.

26. *3 Studi per flauto, clarinetto e fagotto* can be heard in *Ennio Morricone, Musiche da Camera*, RCA, R1 70761 (2) 1985—Marienne Eckstein, flute; Vincenzo Mariozzi, clarinet; Rino Vernizzi, bassoon; and Franco Tamponi, conducting.

27. *Distance* was published by Éditions Salabert in 1973 bearing a dedication to Picci and Gillo Pontecorvo. This work can be heard in *Ennio Morricone, Musiche da Camera*, RCA, R1 70761 (2) 1985—Fulvio Leofreddi, violin; Alfredo Stengel, cello; Arnaldo Graziosi, piano; and Franco Tamponi, conducting.

28. *Musica per 11 violini*, published by Éditions Salabert in 1973, was dedicated to Elio Petri. It was recorded in 1968 in two versions for inclusion in the soundtrack of the film by Petri *Un tranquillo posto di campagna*. The violinists were Arnaldo Apostoli, Giulio Cesare Casellato, Silvestro Catacchio, Luigi Muratori, Charles Möench, Monserrat Cervera, Pasquale Sonnino, Dandolo Sentuti, Luigi Vicari, and Franco Tamponi; Bruno Nicolai, conducted. The first version consists of a base

without the final violin solo cadenza keeping, however, the duration of the cadenza as a blank time space. In fact, a second version, now entitled *Distanze*, features the soprano voice of Edda Dell'Orso and percussionist Vincenzo Restuccia in addition to the eleven violins. This time, Dell'Orso fills the space left vacant by the violin cadenza with a vocal improvisation. Ultimately, only fragments of the latter version are heard on the film's soundtrack. Both versions are available for streaming as part of the entire film soundtrack on Amazon.com and other streaming concerns. The original recorded album of Petri's *Un tranquillo posto di campagna* released by General Music, Gm. 33/01-1 offers both versions. A second recording of *Musica per 11 violini* was released as part of the already mentioned LP *Ennio Morricone, Musiche da Camera*, RCA, R1 70761 (2) 1985 with violinists Fulvio Leoffredi, Giuseppe Gabucci, Antonio Leoffredi, Diego Cescotti, Alexandra Stefanato, Alessandro Asciolla, Antonio De Secondi, Arrigo Serafini, Paolo Ciociola, Massimo Quarta, Laura Morelli, and Franco Tamponi, conducting. Ultimately, Outhere Music France, 2017 has released a new rendition of *Musica per 11 violini* in the CD *Cinema per archi—Morricone, Piovani, Rota*, featuring Luigi Piovano as conductor and Archi di Santa Cecilia.

29. Miceli, *Morricone, la musica, il cinema*, 58–59.

Chapter Two

Once Upon a Time Babylon

Rome's Via Tiburtina,[1] the pastoral path followed by visitors, poets, artists, and musicians on their pilgrimage to ancient Villa Adriana and Gian Lorenzo Bernini's fountains in Tivoli's Villa d'Este, was earmarked in 1948 as a junction of the grande raccordo anulare or GRA for short.[2] GRA was a postwar urban renewal project consisting of a 42.4 miles circumference ring-shaped orbital motorway that connected all consular roads in and out of Rome. It was completed in 1951, a time when hordes of commercial real estate speculators eyed—in the frenzy of postwar economic consumerism—the farmland surrounding Via Tiburtina as snatchable from gullible owners.

At the conclusion of World War II, American investments in war-torn Europe according to the Marshall Plan included RCA Records' decision to open an office in Italy. Then, in 1949, Frank M. Folsom, a vice president of RCA Victor since 1942 and a practicing Catholic, was reminded by Pope Pius XII, in the course of a private audience, of an episode that occurred on July 19, 1943: the American Air Forces' bombardment that devastated Rome's neighborhood of San Lorenzo, a crucial railway depot. The Holy Father urged Folsom to devise some form of reparation from the American government to the city of Rome. The Pope suggested the creation of a factory in the very neighborhood of San Lorenzo as an appropriate humanitarian gesture. Folsom, however, proposed the creation of a large manufacturing plant for the production and distribution of audio recordings originally intended for Milan. Folsom's proposal was, in effect, a practical spin-off of an already-made decision conceived not for humanitarian restitution but for lucrative purposes since the cost of producing audio recordings would have been much lower in Italy than in the United States.

The new RCA company, created in 1951, was located at kilometer 12 of Via Tiburtina within easy reach of the GRA junction. RCA Italiana S.p.A., as it was legally known, held 90 percent of the company's shares and the Vatican the remaining 10 percent.

Count Enrico Pietro Galeazzi, Pius XII's fiduciary, half-brother of the Pontiff's personal physician and a friend of powerful New York Cardinal Francis J. Spellman, was appointed president of the new company while Antonio Giuseppe Biondo assumed control of the plant's operations in Via Tiburtina. The original production agenda consisted of manufacturing and distributing on the promising Italian market vinyl records taped in the United States. Then, the surge of a new generation of Italian pop stars, skilled arrangers, and shrewd promoters prompted RCA Italiana to invest large sums of money in talents like the sensational Domenico Modugno, who literally "out of the blue," won the 1958 Sanremo Song Festival with his groundbreaking song *Nel blu dipinto di blu*, aka *Volare*.[3]

However, by the mid-1950s, RCA Italiana's profits plummeted. Losses marred the accounting ledgers and the company headquarters in the United States decided to shut down operations in Italy. An alarmed Pius XII dispatched Count Galeazzi and his young assistant Ennio Melis to the RCA campus in Via Tiburtina for a thorough assessment of the situation. Melis found merits in the enterprise and, late in 1955, received the Pope's nod to proceed with a makeover of all aspects of business. Melis and newly appointed executive manager Giuseppe Ornato guided the destiny of RCA Italiana S.p.A. for the next thirty years.

Ultimately, RCA Italiana closed down in 1985 and its plant and offices remained in a bombed-out-like state of abandon until a generic complex of warehouses serving various commercial concerns emerged from the ashes of a musical Babylon—sad sight for the visitors who travel daily along Via Tiburtina to seek solace in the splendors of Villa Adriana and Villa d'Este.

In a memoir, Ennio Melis recalled that his first order of business at the newly revived music center was to invite onboard young conservatory graduates Ennio Morricone and Luis Enriquez (later known as Luis Bacalov). They created the famous RCA arrangements that connoted a very long string of international successes, songs like *Il barattolo* by Gianni Meccia, *In ginocchio da te* sung by Gianni Morandi, *Sapore di sale* and *Il cielo in una stanza* composed and sung by Gino Paoli, *Il nostro concerto* by Umberto Bindi, *Il mondo* by Jimmy Fontana, and many more hits.[4]

Ennio Morricone's own recollections added a different twist to Melis' account:

> When RCA called me in 1960 to arrange a song by Gianni Meccia entitled *Il barattolo* [The Tin Can], the whole business was on the verge of collapse. It was running out of "oxygen" and, most of all, it was stripped for cash. So, in

preparing the arrangement of *Il barattolo* I used maximum parsimony by recording a simple base consisting of guitar, drum set, bass and a few other instruments. Notwithstanding the constraints of the arrangement whose taping took place during breaks between recording sessions employing larger ensembles, I worked intensely at it and *Il barattolo* became a sensational success.[5] That was exactly what RCA wanted; a total makeover of songs written by celebrities or beginners, anything had to be dressed up to sell, sell, and sell!

My arranging principle was simple: add to the song, good or bad, a sonic structural physiognomy that could work independently of the song itself. A quotation perhaps or anything particular that caught my interest. Later, RCA began to supply me with large quantities of American tapes to be arranged as standard products, a task that artistically resulted in a rather desolate state of affairs. Nevertheless in 1964, *Ogni volta* (Every Time) a song by Paul Anka, defied everyone's expectations by selling 1.5 million copies![6]

Following a quick financial recovery, RCA Italiana diversified its operations. It acquired several large and small record labels aimed at satisfying the bourgeoning market of the single or double 45 rpm disc and the ever-growing jukebox appetite. Also, the new conglomerate published music for motion pictures and enlarged its facilities by adding "Studio A," a huge, state-of-the-art sound stage that served the realization of very ambitious symphonic and operatic discographic productions. In short, the gated campus on Via Tiburtina turned into a musical Babylon; a crossroad of talents, genres, and languages. The RCA Italiana Symphony Orchestra, the centerpiece of the Studio A project, still figures preeminently on the labels of many "classical" LPs.[7]

By 1964, the enormous yet unpredicted success of the soundtrack to the film *Per un pugno di dollari* (A Fistful of Dollars), prompted RCA Italiana to offer Ennio Morricone a five-year contract that included one percent of sale revenues and the commitment, on the composer's part, to produce six LP albums per year. Morricone became, in effect, RCA's arranger-in-chief with powers extending over Rome's major independent recording studios and those of Rai-TV where he was already a well-known figure in their musical palimpsests. Therefore, it came as no surprise when, in 1961, Rai-TV placed Morricone in charge of the music content of a new, musically intriguing television show called *Piccolo Concerto*—A Little Concert.

PICCOLO CONCERTO

The creators of this show, inspired perhaps by the famous Paul Whiteman's *America's Greatest Bands*, offered a rare glimpse inside the Rai-TV sound stage to Italian television viewers like the Columbia Broadcasting System did in the United States with the legendary music makers of the American radio network television series.

Canadian-born Percy Faith and his lush orchestral sound had become synonymous with "easy listening" music throughout the 1960s, a fitting soundscape to the mostly white, suburban, American middle class relaxing at home in front of their television sets. Ennio Morricone was familiar with that type of orchestration because years prior he was asked by colleagues Gorny Kramer and Lelio Luttazzi to orchestrate for them "all'americana," American style that is. One would assume that Morricone was given the opportunity to listen to plenty of LPs by Percy Faith, David Rose, Ray Conniff, and the big bands of Glenn Miller, Harry James, and Stan Kenton, who were among the most popular American arrangers and bandleaders of the period. As a point of reference, Percy Faith's signature pieces for the year 1960 were (1) *Theme from* A Summer Place, after the 1959 film *A Summer Place* scored by Max Steiner, and (2) *The Song from* Moulin Rouge from the 1952 film *Moulin Rouge* scored by Georges Auric. Also, at the end of the decade, Percy Faith's rendition of *Theme from* A Summer Place and *Love Theme from* Romeo and Juliet by Nino Rota from the 1968 film *Romeo and Juliet* directed by Franco Zeffirelli, filled sides A and B of the best-selling disc of the 1960s. In sum, there were enough well-tested ingredients in those American arrangements to entice Morricone to add his own touch to the mix, and so he did.

Piccolo Concerto became Ennio Morricone's ideal laboratory for experimenting with daring and often bizarre arrangements presented in the form of musical entertainment with a touch of intellectual smartness to an eager and growing Italian television audience.

Conceived by journalist Vittorio Zivelli,[8] *Piccolo Concerto* debuted on November 8, 1961, as part of the Rai-TV second television channel inaugurated on November 4. Carlo Savina conducted an orchestra of twelve violins, four violas, four cellos, harp, harpsichord, celesta, vibraphone, winds, brass, percussions, and a cast of instrumental and vocal celebrities featured in each of the six weekly telecasts.

Radiocorriere, the Rai-TV official print mouthpiece for the Italian national broadcasting network, emphasized the birth of this show as one of the most engaging and interesting telecasts that characterized the newly inaugurated second television channel's palimpsest. It consisted of programs of light music rigorously selected from the Italian and international repertoires presented in concert style. Each weekly program, introduced by noted actor Arnoldo Foà, showcased the orchestra conducted by Carlo Savina and well-known soloists like pianist Armando Trovajoli, Franco Chiari on vibraphone, and violist Dino Asciolla among others. A group of audience-favorite singers comprised Nicola Arigliano, Aura D'Angelo, Fausto Cigliano, Daisy Lumini,

Tony Del Monaco, and Jenny Luna. Just imagine *Rumba delle noccioline* (The Peanut Vendor), a 1927 classic by Cuban Moises Simons disguised as a concerto for harpsichord and strings, or Hoagy Carmichael's *Polvere di stelle* (Stardust) arranged for four trombones without the usual intervention of choreographic numbers and/or comedic gags. In this show, the orchestra was the absolute protagonist. An editorial in *Radiocorriere*[9] provided more details:

> A program like Piccolo concerto represents a new type of broadcast for Italian television. Without the participation of dancers, comic actors, and quiz shows, it will be different. Stage director Enzo Trapani has at his disposal the orchestra and some singers, the only nonmusical element is the host Arnoldo Foà, a famous actor. Naturally, to put together a concert of light music American style, including famous songs of the past like Carmichael's *Polvere di stelle* (*Stardust*), Cole Porter's *Night and Day*, the Neapolitan classic *Piscatore 'e Pusillepo* and more, an arranger who could give each song a particular physiognomy and an unusual formal dignity was indispensable. Thus, the choice fell on Ennio Morricone, the young Roman musician (just 33 years old) who has become a sort of "grey eminence" in the world of light music while remaining the preferred musician amongst the most demanding cognoscenti. Graduate in composition under Goffredo Petrassi, Morricone possesses a noticeable curriculum as composer of concert music (his *Concerto per orchestra* was premiered in Venice last year). In his arrangements of popular songs, there is always a novel twist, a delightful citation to please the experts and gain the consensus of the simple aficionados. For example, in the opening program of Piccolo concerto one finds a waltz in swing time orchestrated for four pianos and strings, and *Londonderry Air* treated as a concerto for violin and orchestra with Franco Tamponi as soloist. Carlo Savina, the conductor of Piccolo concerto, possesses a full academic pedigree as well.
>
> Piccolo concerto's first show includes, besides the pieces already mentioned, *The Wrong Note Rag* and *Temptation* while the old Neapolitan standard *Scètate* will be sung by Fausto Cigliano, *Arrivederci . . . ma non addio* by Aura D'Angelo (the young singer who made a sensation at the last Giugno della canzone napoletana) and *The Hot Canary* will be interpreted by Jenny Luna. In the second show (November 15) one will hear the citation of a celebrated motif in Morricone's orchestration of a song, a specialty of his as the audience of the television show *Tempo d'amore* may recall. There, the theme from *Foglie morte* was played by the violins while Fausto Cigliano sang the show's title song.[10] Many listeners are familiar with the recording of another Neapolitan classic, *Voce 'e notte* sung by Miranda Martino which contains an orchestral citation from Beethoven's *Moon Light Sonata*, compliments of Morricone.[11]
>
> For the third installment of Piccolo concerto [November 22], the young Roman arranger has prepared another surprise: a rendition of the famous Neapolitan cabaret song *Spingule frangese* served upon a Rossini flavored background.

As customary, the show includes seven musical selections; four for orchestra and three songs performed by Aura D'Angelo, Fausto Cigliano and Tony Del Monaco. Other delights include *Amorevole* and the celebrated *Marcia dei gladiatori* in waltz time played by eight trombones and tuba.[12]

Programs for the 1961 edition began on November 8 and concluded on December 13. The second installment of the show scheduled for November 15 was announced but cancelled. Furthermore, no program was retrieved pertaining to the fifth installment of Piccolo concerto which would have taken place on Wednesday, December 6.

The success of *Piccolo Concerto* warranted a second edition, which was extended to 12 installments with the addition of more singers and "enriched" by those "distracting" elements so proudly negated in the first edition; choreography, dancers, and comic gags.

Again, here is the preview of *Piccolo Concerto* 1962 as announced in the pages of *Radiocorriere*:

The second edition of Piccolo concerto will begin this week on Wednesday, February 7 on the second television channel realized, more or less, by the same crew that worked on the first edition: Enzo Trapani, stage director, Ennio Morricone, arranger, Carlo Savina, conductor, and Arnoldo Foà, host. However, this time there are some changes: the new series has been extended to 12 installments broadcast in prime time. In sum, Piccolo concerto becomes the main attraction of the second television channel on Wednesday evenings.

Regarding programming, there will be some changes or rather improvements upon the old formula as well: the addition of a *corps de ballet*, a larger participation of both Italian and foreigner singers, and host Arnoldo Foà who will be offering monologues from the poetic and literary repertoire punctuated by a musical background.

The opening show of Piccolo concerto second edition will feature dancers performing *Hora Staccato* arranged by Morricone for percussionists and strings and choreographed by Giorgio Aragno, *Arcobaleno* (*Over the Rainbow*) in an arrangement for multiple harps and orchestra. About the singers: among the Italians, besides Jenny Luna, Nicola Arigliano and Daisy Lumini who starred in the first edition, we will have Milva, Jula de Palma, Miranda Martino, Fausto Cigliano, Sergio Bruni and Gloria Christian. Foreign singers will include Helen Merrill, Charles Aznavour, Peter Kraus, Peter Tavis and perhaps Bobby Rydell, the very young American who relaunched Modugno's *Volare* in the United States and created a discographic sensation with his interpretation of *Sway*.

Helen Merrill, one of the best jazz singers of the moment and prestigious French actor/singer Charles Aznavour are known to our audiences for their participation to several telecasts. It would be good, though, to spend a few words about Peter Kraus and Peter Tevis, little known in Italy. Tevis, who will appear on three shows, was born in Santa Barbara, California 24 years ago.

He started his career as a child in a radio program, joined the Marines, worked as a photo reporter and is now studying English Literature at the University of Iowa. Broadway saw him in some celebrated productions like *Oklahoma*, *West Side Story*, *The Red Mill*, *Hansel and Gretel* (a musical theater version of Humperdinck's famous opera) etc. . . . In Italy, Tevis wrote the lyrics for a song inserted in the soundtrack of the film *Barabbas*.

Peter Kraus, on the other hand, tops the charts of the Austro-German discographic market. We will hear him singing, among other pieces, *Musik, Musik, Musik*, *Oggi per sempre* and *Non ho bisogno di milioni*. Kraus was born in Munich 23 years ago. Son of movie actor Fred Kraus, Peter starred in film at the age of 14, sang in radio shows for the first time in 1956 and took part in numerous productions outside of Germany. Last summer, Peter Kraus and Italian/American singer Connie Francis paired in a television show amidst rumors of their possible engagement. Peter Kraus plays guitar, drums, and piano.[13]

At the closing of the show's second season *Radiocorriere* published the following editorial announcing its termination:

Like all good things, Piccolo concerto n. 2 has come to an end and it will bid farewell. This week's program will be, therefore, a bit special: it will consist of a montage of the most successful numbers of the season in addition to new ballets and many stars like Chet Baker, Renato Rascel, Renato Carosone, Helen Merrill, Gino Paoli, Jenny Luna and Fausto Cigliano. The final number will include the complete rendition of Ennio Morricone's opening title music appropriately entitled *Piccolo concerto* during which, one by one the members of the orchestra will leave their places until a lone violinist and host Foà will bid farewell.

To summarize this second edition of *Piccolo concerto*, the show's purpose was the presentation of an international light music repertoire in an unusually elegant garb based exclusively on music and brief choreographic sketches curated by Mady Obolesky. If the result was positive, the merit goes to the original and intelligent arrangements prepared by Ennio Morricone for Carlo Savina's orchestra and the genial television direction of Enzo Trapani. No doubts, though, merits go to the participating singers, the best on the international scene: Charles Aznavour, Helen Merrill, Peter Kraus, Nancy Sinatra and Peter Tevis among the foreigners; Milva, Jula De Palma, Miranda Martino, Daisy Lumini, Aura D'Angelio, Gloria Christian, Sergio Bruni, Nicola Arigliano, Bruno Martino, Nini Rosso, Nico Fidenco, Fausto Cigliano and the "Swingers" among the Italians.

Many of Morricone's orchestral arrangements have awakened the interest of aficionados and connoisseurs alike. Pieces like *Sonatina di Clementi* in jazz style with Roberto Pregadio soloist at the piano and harpsichord, the arrangement of Gershwin's *It Ain't Necessarily So* with Berto Pisano on double bass, and typewriter and telex machine, *La naja* (based upon military trumped calls), etc. . . . This week we will hear again the *Concerto per radio e orchestra*, *Concerto per silenzi e batteria*, the arrangement of *Hora Staccato* per 25 percussion instruments, *Stornelli italiani* for viola d'amore and lute (respectively played by Dino Asciolla and Giuseppe Anedda), *La biondina in gondoleta* arranged for bassoon soloist (Fernando Zodini), *Giochi proibiti* with Mario Gangi, guitar and many more. The best received choreographic numbers like *La ronde, Tarantella, Fumo negli occhi, Cotton Reel, African Waltz, Darlin' Cora*, etc. will take center stage. The songs selected for the farewell concert are *Sciulddezza bella* (sung by Fausto Cigliano), *Me in tutto il mondo* (Gino Paoli), *Arrivederci . . . è non addio* (Renato Rascel), *Blue Moon* (Jenny Luna and Helen Merrill), *Il mio domani* (Chet Baker, trumpet and voice) and *Gondolì gondolà* interpreted by its author Renato Carosone. The opening selection will be *Let's Face the Music and Dance*, the famous tune by Irving Berlin, which opened the first show of *Piccolo concerto n. 2*.[14]

The repertoire selected by Morricone for the two editions of *Piccolo Concerto* consisted of about 134 arrangements of international and national, well-balanced, spirited, and intellectually stimulating songs, show tunes, and orchestral pieces. The selections, although reflecting the audiences' taste, expanded its cultural boundaries as the idea of "attending" a televised "concerto" (a concert of classical music, that is), albeit "piccolo" (little, cute, friendly) was appealing to an audience who felt intimidated by the "severe" culture of the concert hall. On the other hand, regular concertgoers and connoisseurs did not mind listening/viewing the performances of popular/commercial music tailored in "classical" garb by a gifted professional musician graduated from an important conservatory of music. Thus, *Piccolo Concerto* was a concept and a reality that made everybody happy, a true trans-genre initiative new to Italian audiences not accustomed to the tradition of the Anglo-American "Promenade" and "Pops" concerts.

By the time *Piccolo Concerto* ended its run, Morricone's stature as a musician rose to a level of public acceptability and professional demand that turned him into a sought-after marketable commodity. *Piccolo Concerto* served Morricone as a platform to remind his audience/viewers that arranging and transcribing music was an art as old as music herself. It was constantly practiced by the greatest masters from Bach, Stravinsky, Schoenberg, and anyone in between. Therefore, transcribing/arranging was indeed composing in the most artisanal and professional meaning of the word.

Sadly, there are no extant video recorded sessions of *Piccolo Concerto* but there are some still photographs and the memories of those individuals who were either part of the settings or sat in their living rooms staring at a black-and-white television screen.

For program details pertaining to *Piccolo Concerto* see Appendix 1.

ARRANGING, RE-ARRANGING, AND RE-CYCLING

RCA Italiana wasted nothing bearing Morricone's signature; several of the vocal and instrumental arrangements he prepared for *Piccolo Concerto* were re-arranged and re-recorded subsequently to fit the repertoire of some RCA collections. Other pieces had been arranged for various commercial purposes prior to their *Piccolo Concerto* destination. Such was a clear demonstration of Morricone's polyvalent pursuit of, or obeisance to, all working opportunities made available to him. Morricone's arrangements as well as his film scores were never published in commercial print format; therefore, analytical observations can be made only on aural bases when allowed by the availability of the product of interest through any audio/visual support system.[15] That said, the pages ahead offer some samples of Morricone's "Art of Arranging" by focusing on two collections of Neapolitan songs: *Miranda Martino—Napoli* (RCA Italiana-PML 10334, released in 1962) and *Miranda Martino—Napoli Volume II* (RCA Italiana-FL 30050, released in 1966), followed by two eclectic instrumental curiosities: *Musica sul velluto* (RCA Italiana-PML 10386, released in 1964) and *Arrangements* (RCA Italiana-TPL1-1045, released in 1974), which are deemed, in the context of this book's narrative, representative of the composer's creative contributions to the genre.

VOICES FROM THE ITALIAN RIVIERA AND THE BAY OF NAPLES

When, in 1886, Richard Strauss composed *Neopolitanisches Volksleben*—the fourth and final movement of *Aus Italien*—he thought of *funiculì funiculà*, the Neapolitan song around which the movement pivoted, as a folk tune in the public domain. *Aus Italien* premiered in 1887 and shortly thereafter the composer was sued for plagiarism by composer Luigi Denza, who, with lyricist Peppino Turco, had authored the catchy tune *funiculi funiculà* to celebrate the 1880 inauguration of a cable car service carrying passengers to and from Mount Vesuvius.

Twenty-three years later, composer Alfredo Casella used the same tune in his *Italia, rapsodia per orchestra* op. 11 (1909) with the nudge, this time, of Denza and Turco. In effect, Strauss and Casella were the first classically trained orchestral "arrangers" of a commercial Neapolitan song. They set the path for others to follow.

Raffaele Gervasio (1910–1994), a pupil of Ottorino Respighi and a specialist in composing music for newsreels, arranged forty celebrated Neapolitan songs whose picturesque and lyric/dramatic content were at the core of *Carosello Napoletano* (1953–1954), a film directed by Ettore Giannini designed to bring to the silver screen a colorful spectacle eminently Neapolitan modeled after Vincent Minnelli's *An American in Paris* (1951). The film's cast included actor Paolo Stoppa, a near-debutant Sophia Loren, and Neapolitan singer Giacomo Rondinella. They made *Carosello Napoletano* a masterpiece unjustly overlooked by critics and historians then and now. Furthermore, Gervasio's orchestrations were criticized by orthodox fans of Neapolitan songs because of the lush layers of symphonic patina he added to the simple genuine folksy melodiousness of the Neapolitan songs of old.[16]

Naples, often dubbed the most musical of Italian cities, was the protagonist of another film, *Napoli milionaria* (1950) [*Side Street Story* in the US release], directed by Eduardo De Filippo after his very successful 1945 play. The film, starring Eduardo De Filippo and Totò in a tragic-comic tour de force dense with commentaries on the human condition in post–World War II Naples, was set to music by Nino Rota. In the 1970s, Rota and De Filippo turned both the play and film into the opera *Napoli milionaria*, which premiered at the Spoleto Festival on June 22, 1977. This work, an authentic Italian folk-opera,[17] showed Nino Rota's extreme eclecticism as he combined—pastiche-like music taken from an assortment of film scores he composed for *Napoli milionaria* (1945), *Filumena Marturano* (1951), *Le notti di Cabiria* (1957), *Plein soleil* (1959), *La dolce vita* (1960), *Rocco e i suoi fratelli* (1969), *Le tentazioni del dottor Antonio* (1962), *Toby Dammit* (1967), and *Waterloo* (1970).

Ennio Morricone, well aware of the developments mentioned above, elevated to a higher dimension his arrangements of Neapolitan songs by introducing an array of avant-garde and expressionistic elements that provoked, again, the disappointment of the aficionados anchored to the traditional Neapolitan song aura consisting of a performance practice ranging from the whispered, mandolin titillating ballad/serenade type to the dramatic, heartbreaking, nostalgia-laden invocations of urban exoticism. In sum, all the vital attractions—from the consumeristic/touristic perspective—that made and make Naples a favorite destination; "See Naples and Then Die!" wrote Goethe in the pages of his *Italiensche Reise*.

At the dawn of the Italian economic boom of the 1950s, a strong capitalization of the song, one of Italy's best artistic exports, paved the way for a national song contest that took the everyday life of the nation by storm; the Festival della canzone italiana di Sanremo (Sanremo Italian Song Festival) was born in 1951.[18] Sanremo is a beautiful city in northern Italy, situated on the riviera between Genoa and the Principality of Monaco, a geographical factor that provoked a further cultural rapture in the perennially vulnerable fabric of the country's north–south dichotomy. Neapolitans cried outrage about Sanremo—the city of flowers basking in glamour stealing the "national" song thunder from them. In 1952, the Festival della canzone napoletana (Festival of Neapolitan Song) was created, making the jubilant peninsula revel in a carnivalesque "unifying" rivalry that meshed musical talent, media organizational savvy, and a booming recording industry, parading all over the radio-television waves its stables of songs, singers, orchestras, and top arrangers.

Ennio Morricone's hand was at the ready in both Sanremo and Naples camps, harvesting successes that launched many a singer's career. Morricone's 1960 arrangements of Neapolitan songs written for singer Dino Giacca entitled *O paese d' 'o sole*[19] laid the groundwork that he built upon in the repertoire of Fausto Cigliano's radio show *Tiempe d'ammore* mentioned previously, *Piccolo Concerto*, and in two albums: *Miranda Martino—Napoli* and *Miranda Martino—Napoli Volume II*.[20]

To illustrate this collection, I have selected *Scètate!* a song composed and published in 1887 by Mario Pasquale Costa (1858–1933) with lyrics by Ferdinando Russo (1866–1927) provided with my translation:

> *Si duorme o si nun duorme bella mia, / siente pe' nu mumento chesta voce.*
> *Chi te vó' bene assaje sta 'mmiez'â via / pe'te cantà na canzuncella doce.*
> Asleep or not asleep, my beloved, / Listen for a moment to my voice.
> Who loves you so much stands in the street / To sing for you a sweet little song.
> *Ma staje durmenno, nun te si' scetata, / sti ffenestelle nun se vonno aprì,*
> *è nu ricamo 'sta mandulinata, / scétate bella mia, nun cchiù durmì.*
> But you are asleep, you've not woken up, / These little shutters don't want to open,
> My song on the mandolin is an embroidery, / Wake up my love, don't sleep anymore.
> *'Ncielo se só' arrucchiate ciento stelle, / tutte pe' stà a sentì chesta canzone.*
> *Aggio 'ntiso 'e parlà li ttre cchiù belle, / dicevano: "Nce tène passione."*
> A hundred stars have gathered in the sky, / All to listen to this song.
> I have heard the three most beautiful among them, / They said that "I have a real passion."
> *E' passione ca nun passa maje, / passa lu munno, essa nun passarrà.*
> *Tu, certo, a chesto nun ce penzarraje, / ma tu nasciste pe' mm'affatturà.*
> Mine is a passion that never dies, / The world turns but never my passion.
> You certainly couldn't think of it, / Because you were born to bewitch me.

In this arrangement Morricone captured the atavistic, nocturnal atmosphere suggested by Mario Costa's Mediterranean melody by emphasizing its chromatic contour and evoking leaps of fifths. In fact, the very interval of fifth that propels the melody is heard throughout the orchestral fabric like a perpetual, hypnotic circle that vacillates from instrument to instrument until it forms a web of harmonic ambiguity. In the 1960 arrangement for Dino Giacca, Morricone added soprano Maria Tonini Rigel to the carefully embroidered sonic instrumental texture, and in the more elaborated scorings for Miranda Martino (1963) and the solo orchestral version of 1964/1974, the inimitable voice of Edda Dell'Orso soaring along the violins. See the two albums *Miranda Martino–Napoli, mia bella Napoli* (1960–1965) mentioned above.

Scètate! is a subjective song when performed by a male singer as intended at the time of composition in 1887. However, Miranda Martino's 1963 interpretation presents an interesting case of gendered objectivity highlighted, or ambiguously aggravated, by the intervention of another, albeit wordless, female voice. In sum, the extra-textual voice could be interpreted as the subconscious reflection of the other. It transcends the gender of the object of desire implied by the song's title *Scètate!* (*bella mia*) (Wake Up! [my love.f.]). Morricone's arrangement of this old song recalls stylistic trends of the Art Nouveau (*Stile Liberty* in Italy) of the period, which gave much importance to the ornament to the point of determining the form. In the case of this arrangement, the result evokes a disturbingly beautiful, incantatory, trance-like flavor.

Musica sul velluto is a collection of ten arrangements recorded in installments between 1962 and 1963. They were issued in 1964 as RCA Italiana DYNAGROOVE Recording PML-10386 showcasing "Ennio Morricone e la sua orchestra," an ensemble consisting of twenty-four violins, eight violas, eight cellos, percussions and rhythmic section, keyboard instruments, harp, occasional solo winds, brass, and two vocal quartets. The instrumentalists and vocalists were divided in two halves, placed on each side of the conductor and recorded by multiple microphones set up for obtaining an effect of "natural" stereophony in the spirit of Giovanni and Andrea Gabrieli's antiphonal experiments in Venice's St. Mark Cathedral, a constant in Morricone's thinking.

Musica sul velluto's protracted and costly recording sessions were a special concession, a reward of sort, to Morricone on the part of the RCA management.[21] As an example of the experimental, albeit playful, character of this collection's arrangements, I have selected the opening track.

Parlami d'amore Mariù is a waltz song by Cesare Andrea Bixio with lyrics by Ennio Neri written for the 1932 comedic film *Gli uomini che mascalzoni* (What Scoundrels Men Are!) directed by Mario Camerini. This film, starred Vittorio De Sica who, in a key episode of the film, sang languidly *Parlami d'amore Mariù* to Lia Franca while dancing to the rhythm of a fox-trot. *Gli uomini che mascalzoni* was the first Italian sound film. Its importance was paramount to the development of Italian cinema while the song became legendary.

Morricone arranged this song several times: (1) for singer Tony Del Monaco (November 29, 1961, telecast of *Piccolo Concerto*); (2) for celebrated opera star Ferruccio Tagliavini as part of the anthology *Le canzoni di ieri* (RCA Victor LPM 10106) released in 1962; (3) as a version for solo acoustical guitar played by Alessandro Alessandroni to fill Side B of RCA Italiana PM45-3295 (1964)[22]; (4) as track 1 of *Musica sul velluto* discussed below; (5) finally, the song reappeared in an extremely sophisticated rendition to suit the wordless voice of Edda Dell'Orso in the soundtrack of *Divina creatura* [The Divine Nymph], a 1975 film directed by Giuseppe Patroni Griffi.

Morricone's arrangement of the song included in *Musica sul velluto* features the guitar of Alessandro Alessandroni and vocals by Sergio Endrigo, Gianni Meccia, Michele, Jimmy Fontana, Edoardo Vianello, and Nico Fidenco "ping-ponging" the song's lyrics across the acoustical spectrum.

In March 1974, RCA Italiana issued the LP TPL1-1045 entitled *Arrangements*. It featured "Ennio Morricone e la sua orchestra" in a program consisting of orchestral arrangements of the following songs:

Side 1
  Ciribiribin (Pestalozza-Tiochet); *Smile* (Chaplin); *Spingole Frangese* (De Leva-Di Giacomo); *Fascination* (Marchetti-Larici); *Scétate!* (Costa-Russo)

Side 2
  Lili Kangy (Gambardella-Capurro); *Summer and Smoke* (Bernstein); *Piano piano* (Fontana); *Pippo non lo sa* (Kramer-Rastelli and Panzeri); *Greensleves* (Traditional); *The Pink Panther* (Mancini)

Interestingly, the LP's back cover informed the buyer that the name of Ennio Morricone, firmly established worldwide in the field of motion picture soundtracks, revealed another facet of his talent, one that is perhaps more interesting, but is not as well known. This record proposed to reaffirm Morricone's great name as an arranger. The eleven titles presented songs new and old, including the favorite film music of the time. All firmly established numbers, the LP's blurb said, bore that special Morricone hallmark, a mixture of exciting musical ideas and special instrumental effects.

A particularity of these arrangements was the preeminent use of electronic devices the RCA studios had at Morricone's disposal for experimental and commercial applications. He had become, indeed, the company's most valuable marketing commodity with sales in excess of twenty-five million copies worldwide.

That said, by 1974 Ennio Morricone had curtailed his activity as the arranger of other composers' music, a body of work exceeding five hundred songs, in order to devote himself fully to composing music for motion pictures and concert works. This decision concerned sales at RCA Italiana, thus their attempt to reignite the composer's art of arranging by releasing an album plainly entitled *Arrangements*.

NOTES

1. Via Tiburtina was named after consul Tiberius. It served, in the grand imperial planning, to connect Rome to Pescara on the Adriatic Sea passing through the Apennine mountains of the Abruzzi region.

2. Please note that the acronym GRA corresponds to the surname of Eugenio Gra (1900–1958), chief designer and supporter of the project which, although etched in 1942, was suspended because of the fall of Fascism and the intervening war.

3. To this day, the Sanremo Festival (Festival della canzone italiana di Sanremo) continues to be a televised major national event that engages the Italian people to paroxysmal levels à la par with soccer. In the charming city of San Remo, or Sanremo, on the Italian Riviera, celebrities are created overnight and myths debunked at record speed while Italy sings her glory to the world putting aside the politics of the moment and creating new ones! See Roberto Agostini, "Sanremo Effects: The Festival and the Italian Canzone (1950s–1960s)" in Franco Fabbri and Goffredo Plastino (2014).

4. Ennio Melis, *Storia della RCA: La Grande Pentola*, a cura di Anna Maria Angiolini Melis e Elisa De Bartoli con una nota di Franco Migliacci (Lavagna, Genoa: Editrice ZONA, 2016).

5. It was issued in 1960 as *Il barattolo/Quanta paura*. RCA Italiana 45 CP 71.

6. *Ennio Morricone racconta . . .* (parte prima) in *Colonne sonore*, maggio/agosto 2005. Morricone's quotations are taken from a series of three interviews entitled *Ennio Morricone racconta . . .* he granted to *Colonne sonore*, a journal of film music. See Chapter 1, n24.

7. The ensemble was, in effect, a pick-up orchestra comprising members of Rome's three full-time orchestras: Accademia Nazionale di Santa Cecilia, Rai-Roma, and Teatro dell' Opera, in addition to freelance musicians.

8. Vittorio Zivelli was known for his successful radio rubric *Il discobolo*, a program devoted to the presentation of newly released recordings.

9. Information in this section is drawn from the pages of *Radiocorriere* published in 1961 and 1962. See Rai-TV digital archives available at *Radiocorriere* (accessed February 15, 2018), http://www.radiocorriere.teche.rai.it.

10. *Tiempe d'ammore: Poesie e canzoni napoletane*, a program articulated in six radio broadcast installments beginning April 18, 1961 (on the first channel); thus, a sort of dress rehearsal for *Piccolo Concerto*.

11. See *Il successo Americano di Miranda Martino* 45N 1143 (1961) Side B *Voce 'e notte*. Side A *Just Say I Love Him* (*Dicitencello vuje*) did not involve Morricone.

12. *Radiocorriere* no. 45, novembre 1961, 42.

13. *Radiocorriere* no. 6, febbraio 1962, 38.

14. *Radiocorriere* no. 18, 2 maggio 1962, 38.

15. Rare exceptions are single or collections of favorite themes published in simplified folio format.

16. See Valerio Caprara (a cura di), *Spettabile pubblico: Carosello Napoletano di Ettore Giannini* (Napoli: Alfredo Guida Editore, 1998). On February 3, 1957, Rai-Radiotelevisione Italiana launched a series of clever advertising spots grouped under an allegoric rubric called *Carosello*, clearly inspired by *Carosello Napoletano* insomuch as it was Raffaele Gervasio who composed *Carosello*'s memorable opening jingle which strongly recalled the Neapolitan spirit of the film. *Carosello*'s jingle became part of the Italian popular culture and the symbol of consumerism throughout the 1960s and 1970s.

17. See (1) Myriam Tanant, *Napoli milionaria: Le film*, http://chroniquesitaliennes.univ-paris3.fr; (2) Carlo Montariello, *La 'Napoli milionaria' di Eduardo De Filippo: Dalla realtà all'arte senza soluzione di continuità* (Napoli: Liguori Editore, 2006); (3) Nino Rota, *Napoli milionaria: Dramma Lirico in tre atti di Eduardo De Filippo*, DVD-Festival della Valle d'Itria-Martina Franca, 2012.

18. For a scholarly analysis of the Sanremo phenomenon, see Roberto Agostini, op. cit. For important discussions on the Neapolitan song, see Goffredo Plastino and Joseph Sciorra (Eds.), *Neapolitan Postcards: The Canzone Napoletana as Transnational Subject* (Lanham, MD: Rowman & Littlefield, 2016).

19. *Le classiche canzoni di Napoli* (RCA-KLVP-130).

20. Born in 1933, Miranda Martino was a singer/actress of great talent and versatility who brought the classical Neapolitan song, a specialty of hers, to new heights of popularity and, thanks to Ennio Morricone's arrangements, to a new level of appreciation for a genre steeped in a tradition going back to the seventeenth century. The content of Martino's LPs and some additional tracks were then reissued in 1995 (BMG/RCA 74321-29862-2-EU) and in 2000 as a two-CD set entitled *Miranda Martino–Napoli, mia bella Napoli* (1960–1965)–(RCA Italiana-74321643955), Flashback Series–BMG Ricordi, 2000.

21. This LP was released in 1965 in Argentina under the title *Musica de Terciopelo* (RCA Camden CAL-2945) and in Spain as *Magicos violines* (RCA Victor LSP-10279).

Contents: 1. *Parlami d'amore Mariù*; 2. *You Go to My Head* is John Fred Coots' 1938 song with lyrics by Haven Gillespie recorded many times. The Frank Sinatra/Nelson Riddle rendition of 1946 is probably the closest to the arrangement Morricone made for American singer Helen Merrill in the 1962 edition of *Piccolo Concerto* and for celebrated flautist Severino Gazzelloni in *Musica sul velluto*; 3. *Dove sei Marì?* by Flavio Carraresi is heard in this album played by harpist Anna Palomba, a favorite instrumentalist in Roman recording studios throughout the 1960s and beyond; 4. *Ciao, ciao bambina* (*Piove*) by Domenico Modugno with lyrics by Dino Verdi won the 1959 coveted Sanremo Song Festival and became quickly an international success; 5. *Amorevole* by Vito Pallavicini was a song composed in 1959 by Vittorio Buffoli and Pino Massara to the lyrics of Antonietta De Simone and Vito Pallavicini.

One of Morricone's arrangements was heard first in the album *Gino Marinacci Ensemble—Il jazz in Italia* (Vinyl-EP RCA EPA 30-383-Italy-1960). Then in the 1961 edition of *Piccolo Concerto* and in *Musica sul velluto* featuring Gino Marinacci's jazz flute on both occasions; *6. *Io che amo solo te* by Sergio Endrigo. This arrangement of Endrigo's successful song features Luis Bacalov on piano; 7. *Che cosa c'è* by Gino Paoli. Composed in 1963, this song was arranged multiple times by Ennio Morricone. The version included in *Musica sul velluto* features Anna Palomba on harp, Filippo Settembri on flugelhorn, and Gino Marinacci on jazz flute; 8. *Quando finisce l'estate* by Oreste Vassallo was composed in 1963 to words by Carlo Rossi. Morricone's arrangement in *Musica sul velluto* features the voice of Lydia MacDonald, a member of the vocal quartets involved in the making of this album; 9. *Un solo bacio mi hai dato* is a song composed by Luis Bacalov with lyrics by Rodolfo Carelli. It is heard in this LP performed by solo guitarist Enzo Grillini. Another arrangement was included as Track B of *Rosy* (RCA Italiana PML 1037-1964); 10. *Quando, quando, quando* by Tony Renis, composed in 1961 with lyrics by Alberto Testa, reached the international scene in 1962 thanks to Pat Boone's rendition as *Tell Me When* (lyrics by Erwin Drake). Morricone's arrangements of Renis' song include one made in 1961 for singer Pierfilippi (RCA Italiana/Victor PM45-3057-Italy-1962).

*The arrangement included in *Musica sul velluto* features the voices of Cristina Brancucci and Alessandro Alessandroni from the two participating vocal quartets known as I Cantori Moderni di Alessandroni and I 4+4 di Nora Orlandi.

22. Side A featured trumpet player Michele Lacerenza and chorus performing a dirge-like piece entitled *Il silenzio* (Silence), a meditation on the military bugle call "The Last Post" very reminiscent of the *Degüello* played by Lacerenza in *Per un pugno di dollari* (A Fistful of Dollars) at about the same period. For an in-depth discussion of the origin of *El Degüello*, see Charles Francis Leinberger's "*Degüello*, 'No Mercy for the Losers': The Enduring Role of the Solo Trumpet in the Soundtrack of the Old West," in *International Trumpet Guild Journal*, March 2015: 18–33.

Chapter Three

In the Lion's Den

The origin of the sound that characterized Italian Westerns with the release of *Per un pugno di dollari* (A Fistful of Dollars) in 1964 can be traced back to Morricone's uncredited supplementary version of the main titles cue for *Barabbas*, the 1961 film directed by Richard Fleischer, scored by Mario Nascimbene, and conducted by Franco Ferrara. Morricone's contribution to this film's soundtrack consisted of the elaboration and orchestration, in the form of a Bolero, of Nascimbene's original main titles music cue inspired by the Gregorian chant *Kyrie Eleison*. Morricone's arrangement, lasting about five minutes, was not intended for inclusion in the film's soundtrack but rather for the release of the album which coincided with the premiere of the film.[1]

During the same period, Morricone arranged two abstracts from the well-known American Westerns *Blowing Wild* (1953) with music by Dimitri Tiomkin[2] and the main theme from *The Magnificent Seven* (1960) by Elmer Bernstein. Both pieces were included in the 1961 programs of *Piccolo Concerto* (see Appendix 1). One year later, the programs of the second edition of the show featured Tiomkin's *Degüello* from *Rio Bravo* (1959) and *The Alamo* (1960), a *Square Dance* that later found its way into *Per un pugno di dollari*, and Tiomkin's song *Do Not Forsake Me, My Darling* from the film *High Noon* (1952) (see Appendix 1).[3] More importantly, in 1962, Morricone arranged for American singer Peter Tevis *Pastures of Plenty*, a song made famous by Woody Guthrie in 1941.[4] For the first time, Morricone's score for Tevis employed the full array of natural sounds of anvils, bells, and whip cracks in addition to animal cries and the whistling of Alessandro Alessandroni which were crystallized two years later in the main titles cue of *Per un pugno di dollari*.[5] *Pastures of Plenty*, as arranged by Morricone and interpreted by Peter Tevis, was also featured in the February 28, 1962, broadcast of *Piccolo Concerto* (see Appendix 1). Tevis' successful 45 rpm disc (RCA Victor-Italy PM45-3115) attracted the attention of Sergio Leone who, in 1964, requested that Morricone compose the main titles music cue of *Per un pugno di dollari* by preserving the same sonic apparatus he had used in his arrangement of *Pastures of Plenty*, including the song's short choral "bridge," whose authorship was ultimately credited to Tevis.[6]

Another iconic theme heard in *Per un pugno di dollari* was the *Degüello* (*El Degüello*), a Mexican military dirge-like bugle call that originated in 1836 at the time of the siege and battle of the Alamo. Tiomkin's celebrated *Degüello*, or *El Degüello*, from the films *Rio Bravo* (1959) and *The Alamo* (1960) was used by Leone as temporary track during the filming of *Per un pugno di dollari*. The director, wishing to preserve Tiomkin's evocative atmosphere, asked Morricone to create a musical theme that "resembled" the Tiomkin model. Morricone, then, readapted a tune he had composed as incidental music for a television adaptation of Eugene O'Neill's drama *The Moon of the Caribbees*, which was broadcast on February 18, 1962. There, actress/singer Edith Peters delivered the tune as a lullaby from the bow of a ship.[7] Morricone's new film version, *El Degüello* that is, was scored for solo trumpet, orchestra, and chorus. It achieved unprecedented popularity upon its release on disc following the film's premiere.[8]

It must be added here that, in 1963, Morricone composed, under the pseudonym of Dan Savio, the full soundtrack of *Duello nel Texas* (Gunfight at Red Sands or Gringo), a Spanish/Italian Western directed by Ricardo Blasco. This soundtrack, although conforming mostly to the Tiomkin/Bernstein/Moross stylistic American Western canopy, reveals sparkles of originality, and the song *A Gringo like Me*, sung by Dicky Jones with lyrics by Carol Danell and Tino Fornai, received some attention. In 1965, following the success of *Per un pugno di dollari*, Peter Tevis included this song alongside *Per un pugno di dollari* [title theme] with lyrics by Tevis and *Lonesome Billy*, also with lyrics by Tevis in an album cleverly entitled *Un pugno di . . . West*.[9]

A second Western, *Le pistole non discutono* (*Bullets Don't Argue*), directed by Mario Caiano under the pseudonym of Mike Perkins and scored by Morricone as Dan Savio, was shot in 1964 concurrently to *Per un pugno di dollari*, whose soundtrack—the reader is reminded—at the time of the film's release bore the pseudonym of Dan Savio. The score of *Le pistole non discutono* shows Morricone distancing himself a bit from the classical American Western model in favor of a more advanced approach that ran parallel with Leone's film.[10] *Lonesome Billy*, the film's title song, sung by Tevis to his own lyrics, was not heard in the film. It was, however, issued in pair with *Per un pugno di dollari* as if the latter were to be intended as the film's hypothetical title song.[11]

It would be fair to say that, by 1964–1966, filmgoers, television watchers, and record buyers had become familiar and market-tested about the soundscape Morricone and others following his lead had fully deployed to enhance a cinematic genre—the *Western all'italiana* or Spaghetti Westerns, which was rising quickly to an unforeseen level of international popularity.

The following reflections on Ennio Morricone's involvement with the Italian Western films, directed by Sergio Leone, complement Leone's commentary on his films according to an interview he granted to film critic Francesco Mininni (FM) in Rome in November 1988. It was published in 1989 after Leone's death.[12]

Francesco Mininni: Was the Dollar Trilogy an idea originally conceived as such or did it follow the success of *Per un pugno di dollari* (A Fistful of Dollars, 1964)?

Sergio Leone: It existed since the beginning. Certainly, had the film not been successful, a sequel would have been out of the question. It was a risk I fully accepted at the start since no one else was willing to bet on the film's good outcome.

FM: Are the references to Greek tragedy in *Per un pugno di dollari* explained as citations or are they the bearers of other hidden meanings?

SL: No, there are no citations. The fact is that it is not possible to think of a western without referring to the classics—not only Greek tragedy but also Shakespeare who took practically everything from the classical tragedy. I have always made the case for Homer as the greatest writer of westerns and that his characters are the archetypes of the western genre: heroes like Hector, Achilles, and Agamemnon are the sheriffs, gunmen and outlaws of antiquity.

FM: There are in this film other "erudite" references like Goldoni's *Arlecchino servitore di due padroni* (The Servant of Two Masters).

SL: Certainly, the character interpreted by Clint Eastwood serves two masters while attending to their mutual destruction. This is the commedia dell'arte's scheme derived directly from Plato and Terence.

FM: In this sense though, Eastwood assumes a clear political connotation and his actions emanate a taste of class warfare.

SL: Surely. Not only political but mythical as well. [Eastwood's] is a personage that emerges from nothing and goes nowhere while acting as arbiter between two power-thirsty clans. In the end, such is the essence of my cinema: a fable enriched by links with contemporary reality.

FM: Could one talk of a personage à la Chaplin as well?

SL: Certainly. The gunman without a name puts power in crisis exactly as Chaplin did with irony and a precise destructive consciousness. For me, Chaplin is the greatest genius ever in cinematic art and, without him, we would be doing another profession.

FM: How did you choose Clint Eastwood for the leading role?

SL: I watched him fleetingly in an American television series called *Rawhide*[13] and I thought he was perfect for the role right away. The truth is that I needed a mask more than an actor and Eastwood, at that time, had only two expressions: with the hat and without the hat. No one could have incarnated better the protagonist of my earlier films. The results support my choice.

FM: Violence was a novelty in *Per un pugno di dollari*. Was it a breakaway from the romantic tradition of western films?

SL: Yes. But it does not mean that violence was treated gratuitously for its own sake. Violence in my film has political connotations. It does not mean that in American films people did not die; they died badly in long takes, thus preventing the public from absorbing the idea of death. Death, on the other hand, must represent real fear, which can only be achieved through physical evidence. The dying character must scream, the noise caused by a gunshot must be amplified, blood must be seen, one must understand the physical damage caused by the penetration of a bullet. It is realism yes, but critical realism with a precise point of view. Kubrick, speaking about *A Clockwork Orange* said that it was a moral fable. I can say the same thing about my films. They are fables which cannot be represented with goodness. Why are Disney films employing real actors ugly? Because one becomes aware since the very beginning that the fable is not realistic, that there is something artificial and banally spiced up. Cartoons, on the other hand, are immensely exceptional. A fable must be more realistic than the chronicle, it must involve emotionally the listeners/viewers and, why not scare them through the representation of violence. Therefore, there is no complacency in my films but a precise moral intent. It is important to know that gun shooting causes certain effects on the human body, otherwise, anyone can get hold of a gun thinking that nothing is going to happen. Shooting someone in the leg means amputation, not a body falling silently in long take. Is there complacency in the chronicle? I refer here to the fact per se not to anyone's speculation. In sum, my representation of death is a cerebral fact not a visceral one, with the warning that reality hides behind the fable.

The main titles cue, a three-minute and 16-second animated cartoon sequence, could be interpreted as Leone's homage to the fabled world of Disney not without a pinch of paradoxical humor since real actors appear on screen immediately past the main titles. The first in order of appearance is Clint Eastwood riding a mule. He has no name; however, toward the end of the film the caretaker calls him Joe or just a generic Joe. Superimposed on Joe's image one hears a male chorus rhythmically chant the words "with the wind" and a rapidly descending five-note scale played by a soprano recorder underscoring Joe's gaze from under his hat like a sort of Harlequinesque nose thumbing.

The main titles music cue consists of three and a half measures of easy-going, soft "horse music" played on an acoustic guitar similar to the arrangement of *Pastures of Plenty* mentioned previously. The opening music ushers in a whistled melody based on the interval of fourth A-D, an anticipation, perhaps, of the film's positive attitude veiled by a teasing touch of irony as the protagonist (Eastwood), has entered the dusty scene riding not a horse but a mule like a Sancho Panza dropped from Cervantes' pages.

The cue's main theme in D minor consists of six measures and three variants each landing on the Tonic (D), on the Dominant (A), again on the Dominant but one octave higher (A^1), and finally on the Tonic (D). The second part of the cue introduces a minor second mordent pungently plucked on electric guitar—a sonic rock 'n' roll novelty that cast on the viewer a mnemonic thematic spell that lasted until the end of the film and beyond. Then, a rhetorical "bridge," blatantly chanted by the male chorus accompanied by strings and urged on by the traditional Western galloping rhythm, moves gradually toward an ever more emphatic tripartite coda.[14]

Aside from the incisive sound of the electric guitar, Morricone enhances the palette of this cue with quasi-extra musical elements like the nagging descending five-note scale played by the soprano recorder, the sound effect of the whip crack heard on the strong beat every other measure, the striking of the anvil on the second beat, and the ringing of a bell on the first weak beat which contribute to establishing some tonal and rhythmical irregularities.

Another cue of interest begins with a series of bell strokes preceding the reprise of the main title music and some fleeting fiddling until it is followed by ominous martellato strokes played on the piano. Then, *El Degüello* theme, played on the English horn, is heard for the first time. This theme is heard multiple times during the film as it underscores murderous acts and/or allusions to the intention to kill. Ultimately, it is heard preceded by the great shootout, a sequence underscored by a wild, multitracked conflagration of electronically altered sounds played by Francesco Catania on trumpet and modeled after the ending of the Bolero in *Barabbas*. Then, a brief, elegiac athematic string piece introduces *El Degüello* magnificently played by Michele Lacerenza on trumpet accompanied by the full orchestra and male chorus. This final cue is, indeed, iconic and destined to remain a vital part of Morricone's artistic film music legacy.

Following the unexpected success of *Per un pugno di dollari*, Leone and Morricone embarked upon a second film, *Per qualche dollaro in più* (For a

Few Dollars More, 1965). In the meantime, the composer completed the scoring of two Westerns directed by Duccio Tessari: *Una pistola per Ringo* (A Pistol for Ringo) and *Il ritorno di Ringo* (The Return of Ringo), both released in 1965, concurrent with the second Leone Western.

As obliquely implied by its title, Leone and Morricone's second film was larger in length and budget than its predecessor and so the new score reflected both the surprising success of *Per un pugno di dollari* and the increased finances put at the composer's disposal for the realization of a more ambitious soundtrack which rotated, this time, around three protagonists: Monco (Clint Eastwood),[15] Colonel Mortimer (Lee Van Cleef), and El Indio (Gian Maria Volontè). However, director and composer assigned the film only two principal themes following the scheme adopted for *Per un pugno di dollari*, namely the main titles cue identifying with Monco and *La resa dei conti* (Sixty Seconds to What?) underscoring both Mortimer and Indio since they shared the same heavy psychological burden: the possession of identical carillon pocket watches whose provenance demanded vendetta on the part of Mortimer and death on the part of Indio.

Nevertheless, the new score, cast in D minor, like that of *Per un pugno di dollari*, is enriched by other important cues like *Il vizio di uccidere* (The Vice of Killing) and *Addio colonnello* (Farewell, Colonel!), which account for a total of about forty-eight minutes of music, including eighteen minutes of incidental material.

Granted that Monco and Indio shared the same idiosyncratic characteristics as Joe and Ramon in *Per un pugno di dollari*, notwithstanding the death of the latter, the novelty in the new film was the presence of Colonel Mortimer, a different kind of personage whose intentions were not venal—he did, in fact, renounce his portion of the bounty in Monco's favor. He was fully satisfied with the vindication for Indio's brutal rape of his sister and the killing of her husband on their wedding night (the carillon pocket watch was in possession of Mortimer's sister when she was raped by Indio and died by a self-inflicted gunshot). Thus, the heartfelt sentimentality of the cue *Addio colonnello* (Farewell, Colonel!) offered both composer and spectator an opportunity for evading a soundtrack otherwise filled with hoofing, dust, shooting, whip cracks, anvils, Jew's harps, and bells.

Thanks to a more generous production budget and, consequently, higher expectations, Morricone used an orchestra engorged with lush string sound and a full chorus. Moreover, Colonel Mortimer was ultimately the bearer of another gentle, almost fairy tale–like sonic device: the carillon, a musical pocket watch whose sound, generated by the glockenspiel and the celesta, challenges the protagonists' narrative as well as the spectators' in regard to the timing of shooting in key moments of confrontation. If such soft treatment of the score was certainly aligned with Morricone's arrangements of much commercial music of the period, the composer made great use of his avant-garde "toolbox" of dissonant, strident, frightening instrumental combinations when constructing several pivotal dramatic moments, including Indio's drug-induced hallucinatory spells—an ironic twist on employing rationally constructed music to underscore the irrational, a rather *tout court* procedure in film music.

The defining characteristic of *Per qualche dollaro in più* consists of the essential role assumed by the music, at least from a narrative and symbolic point of view: the soprano recorder for Monco, the Jew's harp for Mortimer, and the carillon for Indio. As already observed, the thematic structure of this film follows the scheme adopted by the main titles cue of the first film, including the human whistle, now an expected sound device in the Italian Western together with a new sonic component, the Jew's harp and its ambiguous tonal instability. Otherwise, the spectator hears some pretty familiar sounds—electric guitar, elegantly deployed percussion instruments, male voices in unison, and more.[16]

The other main theme, *La resa dei conti*, referred to in English as "Sixty Seconds to What?" brings on the scene none other than Johann Sebastian Bach's *Toccata and Fugue in D minor* (BWV 565) and the mighty sound of the organ, another example of musical gentrification already symbolized in the soundtrack by the sound of the carillon and its mechanical counterpoint. In sum, this extroverted, objective second main theme is set in clear contrast to the subjectivity of *El Degüello* in *Per un pugno di dollari*.

Other Western films scored by Morricone following *Per qualche dollaro in più* include: *La resa dei conti* (The Big Gundown) directed by Sergio Sollima (1966),[17] *Un fiume di dollari* (The Hills Run Red) directed by Carlo Lizzani (1966) and signed by Morricone as Leo Nichols, *Navajo Joe* by Sergio Corbucci (1966) also signed by Morricone as Leo Nichols, and *Sette pistole per i MacGregors* (Seven Guns for the MacGregors) directed by Franco Giraldi (1966).

Let us return now to the Leone and Mininni conversation and read more about the third film in the series:

> *FM:* *Il buono, il brutto, il cattivo* (*The Good, the Bad and the Ugly*, 1966) is undoubtedly the most complete of your three westerns.

> *SL:* Absolutely. It is the story of three men who, through the background of the War of Secession, follow the traces of a treasure while fighting their own private conflicts. In my films, big and small history always cross each other. This film's idea emanated from Chaplin's famous harangue that concluded *Monsieur Verdoux*.[18] An assassin's self-defense: Verdoux who confessed to his crime by declaring himself an amateur when compared to the massacres organized by the powerful men of his time. Such represented indeed the greatest *J'accuse!*

It is similar to the episode in which Tuco faces the massacre at the bridge of Legstone, a scene inspired by Emilio Lussu's war story *Un anno sull'altipiano* (A Soldier on the Southern Front).[19] People have detected Keatonian elements in this film and that pleases me. In sum, it is the most complex and complete episode of the Dollar Trilogy with which I reached in full the picaresque tone that represented my main objective. Furthermore, the film includes a sequence, the so-called Triello, which became source of great satisfaction. Imagine that students at the University of Los Angeles examine this sequence frame by frame as an example of montage.

FM: You seem to feel particular affection for the character Tuco in *Il buono, il brutto, il cattivo*.

SL: True. Tuco represents, like Cheyenne later, America's contradictions and partially mine as well. Gian Maria Volontè was interested in interpreting the role, but I thought he was the wrong choice. He would have turned Tuco into a neurotic personage while I needed an actor with a natural comic talent; thus, my choice fell on Eli Wallach mostly known for his dramatic roles. Wallach possessed something of Chaplin that many did not understand. He was perfect indeed for the part of Tuco.

FM: Did you experience production vicissitudes with your early films?

SL: Many with *Per un pugno di dollari*. A producer even told me that film shooting could have begun as soon as Tognazzi and Vianello were free from previous commitments.[20] You can imagine the parodies that would have ensued from such participation; however, some thought that the film was already a parody. I produced myself all the other films; thus, the problems went away. Following the international success of the film, I was given carte blanche regarding all matters until I began thinking about *Once Upon a Time in America*. I wanted to do this film immediately after *Il buono, il brutto, il cattivo*, but the producers were concerned about high costs and, above all, they preferred to strike when the iron was still hot and continue with the westerns. Therefore, since assured success counted more than possible failure, I waited for seventeen years before I could bring to fruition the project closer to my heart.

FM: What about your preferred western?

SL: The Man Who Shot Liberty Valance (John Ford, 1962), no doubt. It is clearly more for a question of themes than style. It is the film in which Ford contradicted himself for the first time by showing the true face of the West and leaving behind his traditional optimism. Ford embraced a more realistic and therefore pessimistic vision by showing the other side of the myth.

In substance, *Il buono, il brutto, il cattivo* (*The Good, the Bad and the Ugly*) is a film even more ambitious than its precedent, totaling some three hours in duration and spanning from the most truculent of infanticides to Italian-style comedy and anything in between.

The soundtrack contains more cues than the preceding two films; however, aside from the main titles music cue whose length is two minutes and 15 seconds and the episode when Tuco (Wallach) searches for Blondie (Eastwood) which extends to two minutes and 39 seconds, the soundtrack contains an overabundance of cues never longer than 40 seconds and an ample role assigned to functional cues as long as five minutes and 35 seconds, like the episode during which Tuco drags Blondie across the desert.

The structure of this film's main titles cue appears even more fractioned than that of its predecessor; nevertheless, it contains another indelible mark of Morricone's inventiveness: the imitation of the coyote's cry, which infuses the cue with a sort of primordial imprint within a simplistic framework. This cue consisted of two semi-phrases whose contrasting characters alternate and integrate with each other four times, each posing the question through different harmonic resolutions underscoring the film's narrative. They are: the twangy electric guitar; the coyote's cry, obtained by recording slightly off sync two tracks of a "choking" male voice; the soprano recorder; the human whistle; and the bass ocarina. In sum, besides the usual array of *object trouvés* and electronically altered vocal concoctions in his third score, Morricone paid attention to certain aspects of experimental music he was involved with at the time. Take, for instance, the cue *Il forte* (The Fort), a piece of intense meditative quality written in madrigal style infiltrated by mundane, military barracks bugle calls that denoted Ennio Morricone's—and perhaps Sergio Leone's—desire to seek intellectual challenges in these cues whose expected tradition had been established by the international success of the first two films.

L'estasi dell'oro (Ecstasy of Gold), the most remarkable cue of the score, is of large proportions and ambitious both in scope and application. It begins with ostinato arpeggios played by the piano—a sonic device familiar in Morricone's later scores—which urge the entrance of the English horn with a melodic interval of a fifth, a rather simple yet spatial opening that stretches the melodic panoply—a Morricone method already detected in *Musica per 11 violini* described in Chapter 1—then once the English horn completes its exposition, Morricone introduces a new "voice," a literal human voice that from this point onwards made a tremendous impact on the composer's vocabulary: the voice of Edda Dell'Orso, a soprano leggero whose three-octave range was endowed with such flexibility that no genre was ever out of bounds. She became the favorite "vocal instrument" of Italian cinematic composers for decades to come, including her husband, composer/producer Giacomo Dell'Orso.[21] *L'estasi dell'oro* constitutes a milestone in Morricone's career. It began to advance that synthesis of two musical types; the "applied" and the "absolute" that Morricone wanted to materialize throughout his career. It transcended Sergio Leone's cinema.

The Triello, a term created to define the showdown among three contenders as a suitable replacement of *El Degüello*, appears at about 170 minutes into the film and lasts four minutes and 27 seconds. Noticeable in this cue is the use of the first thematic unit played by the trumpet heard after one minute and 36 seconds of introduction before the three protagonists finally draw their guns. This suspenseful introduction gives way to a series of incidental music fragments already heard in the previous two films, thus connoting the trilogy with a strong sense of cyclical homogeneity and contributing to the establishment of a metanarrative common to the whole Italian Western project.[22]

In total, Ennio Morricone scored thirty-seven Italian Western films, including:

- *Per pochi dollari ancora* (For a Few Extra Dollars) by Giorgio Ferroni (1966).
- *Un fiume di dollari* (The Hills Run Red) by Carlo Lizzani (1966).
- *Sette donne per i MacGregors* (Up the MacGregors) by Franco Giraldi (1967).
- *Faccia a Faccia* (Face to Face) by Sergio Sollima (1967).
- *I crudeli* (The Hellbenders) by Sergio Corbucci (1967), signed by Morricone as Leo Nichols.
- *Da uomo a uomo* (Death Rides a Horse) by Giulio Petroni (1967).
- *Corri, uomo, corri* (Run, Man, Run) by Sergio Sollima (1968).
- *E per tetto un cielo di stelle* (A Sky Full of Stars for a Roof) by Giulio Petroni (1968).
- *Il grande silenzio* (The Great Silence) by Sergio Corbucci (1968).
- *Il mercenario* (The Mercenary) by Sergio Corbucci (1968).[23]

ONCE UPON A TIME . . .

The year 1968 was particularly busy for Ennio Morricone; he scored more than twenty films, wrote important concert works, ended Sergio Leone's Dollar Trilogy but not the director's Italian Western saga insomuch as *C'era una volta il West* (*Once Upon a Time in the West*) is considered the crowning jewel of the genre. Some critics have opined that this film marked the beginning of a hypothetical Once Upon a Time Trilogy comprised of *C'era una volta il West* (*Once Upon a Time in the West*), *C'era una volta la Rivoluzione* (*Once Upon a Time . . . the Revolution*), and *C'era una volta in America* (*Once Upon a Time in America*). That is an attractive thought, no doubt, but misaligned with the sequential order of the making of the three films, which came full circle many years later in 1984 with the belated release of *C'era una volta in America*.

Leone broke new ground with *C'era una volta il West*, a grand cinematic fresco depicting the construction of the railroad system that linked the East and West coasts of the United States, the necessary development of underground water wells, the consequent erection of new towns, and the network of communication that connected the "conquered" west to the rest of the country. However, was Morricone ready to compose new Western music in the midst of perhaps the busiest time of his career? Morricone's unshakable professionalism, loyalty, and work ethic encouraged both composer and director to take on a new Hollywood challenge. The composer began by taking stock of certain lowbrow stylistic characteristics firmly entrenched in the Dollar Trilogy and added to the new film score a hefty sixty minutes of fresh musical material, including operatic allusions, psychological portraitures, and gentrified musical statements aimed at pleasing his fans and consolidating his success.

My reflections on *C'era una volta il West* (*Once Upon a Time in the West*) begin with a return to the Mininni and Leone interview:

FM: Harmonica, Jill and Cheyenne, protagonists of *C'era una volta il West* [*Once Upon a Time in the West*], were each assigned a musical theme but not Frank, why?

SL: Because Frank's narrative is part of Harmonica's; they represent the two faces of the man, so it would have been difficult to differentiate them musically. A reason why Frank is introduced accompanied by a different arrangement of the harmonica theme is that the man becomes his own interlocutor, the other side of the coin. So, one cannot exist without the other. When Harmonica kills Frank, he leaves the scene as if he had died as well at the moment. He lost the object of his vendetta, which was also the scope of his existence.

FM: The harmonica seems to represent his destiny.

SL: Not only, you know the harmonica produced no notes. I like those sounds as they belong perhaps to the realm of noise. Speaking of which, when *C'era una volta il West* was in the mixing phase, I realized that the first two reels scored by Morricone did not work as I had envisioned. So, I eliminated the music in favor of just the noise track: the weathervane, the wind, the grasshoppers, the squeaking wood, the flopping of the birds' wings. When Ennio saw the film's cut he was unaware of my choice and at the end of the two reels he approached me and said: "Do you know that this is the best music I have composed?" Years later, an assistant of George Lucas' inquired about the noise track in those first two reels. He thought we were from another planet when he learned that the noise track had not been preserved. In America they save everything; how dull!

FM: What about your relationship with the music and therefore with Ennio Morricone?

SL: I have said again and again that Morricone is the best scriptwriter of my films. I could not imagine going to the set without Ennio's music readily available. Even actors used to direct recording, like Henry Fonda, Charles Bronson and Robert De Niro, found themselves disoriented at first about my method of shooting directly with the music. Then, when I tried to please them by eliminating the music, they insisted that it be reinstalled. Music helped them to penetrate the characters and the atmosphere of the film. Every musical theme represents a character, and Morricone, after I explained analytically the film's narrative to him, was able to capture perfectly the spirit and the characteristics. At the time of *C'era una volta il West* we experienced problems with Cheyenne because Ennio did not fully understand my vision of the character. So, the theme he played for me was not to my liking. Noticing his disappointment, I explained to him again that the character of Cheyenne had to represent America in all her contradictions, which Ennio already knew about. Then, aware that he needed to visualize the personage through something already seen and known, I asked whether he had seen Walt Disney's *Lady and the Tramp*. He had seen it. "Well," I said, "Cheyenne is the tramp." He sat at once at the piano and played those notes which became Cheyenne's theme. A propos of music played during filming, I learned that Kubrick, after speaking with me, did the same with *Barry Lyndon* (1975). Evidently the system works.

Although *C'era una volta il West* begins with an unsettling, Cage-inspired opening sequence consisting of undetermined, diegetic, environmental sounds, the somewhat avant-garde stance of the 11-minute introduction wanes as soon as the main titles music cue begins to unfold with the appearance of the "Man with a Harmonica" (hereafter Harmonica [Charles Bronson]) underscored by his very distinctive theme, followed by Frank's allusive theme incisively plucked on the electric guitar and the echo of gunshots.

The *concréte* sounds heard in the introduction are heard again followed by a rifle shot whose provenance points to a location identified in the film as Sweetwater and the appearance there of Maureen McBein humming and then singing *Oh Danny Boy*, a reminder about the not-too-distant Irish roots of the family. Finally, this episode, listed in the film's cue sheet as "The Massacre of the McBeins," includes Frank's allusive theme, the mass shooting, the arrival on the scene of Frank (Henry Fonda), and the implied killing of the

Figure 3.1. **Harmonica's Theme.** Graphic rendition created by author.

In the Lion's Den 59

Figure 3.2. Frank's Allusive Theme. Graphic rendition created by author.

surviving McBein boy punctuated by the ringing of a death knell. Half a minute later, the sound of a diegetically implied, saloon-style piano playing and the noisy hustle-bustle background take us to the train station of Flagstone where we see Jill (Claudia Cardinale) checking the clock while the main titles music cue, now identified as *Jill's Theme* unfolds in full. We are about thirty minutes into the film.

The "dusty" tonality of D minor that saturates the Dollar Trilogy soundtrack gives way in this new film to the sunny key of D major through a melodic theme in 12/8 played in parallel thirds on the harpsichord. It oscillates like a pendulum on the Tonic pedal sustained by violas, cellos, and basses. Both the character and sonority of this opening statement bring quickly to mind the melancholy notes from the carillon watch heard in *For a Few Dollars More*—a sign that Morricone had not fully disengaged yet from past films or that he detected, perhaps, character similarities between the rape victim pictured inside the watch held by El Indio and Jill McBein, a former New Orleans prostitute turned a redeemed, strong woman. The harpsichord-plucked memory theme is soon dispelled by a sweeping interval of sixth played by the violins which gives life to a commanding operatic gesture humanized by the soaring soprano voice of Edda Dell'Orso. This musical sweep sets the tone for the whole soundtrack. One may wonder whether Morricone and Leone intended to transform Jill into a modern-day Minnie of *La fanciulla del West* as the composer's popularity was beginning to approach Puccini's. Meanwhile, the sweeping sound of four French horns and the full choir round out the presentation of the sunny, picturesque soundscape of *C'era una volta il West*.

Jill's stop at La Posada on her way to Sweetwater brings Cheyenne (Jason Robards) to the scene and with him a short theme heard for thirty seconds.

Figure 3.3. Jill's Theme. Graphic rendition created by author.

Then we hear the dialogical integration of Harmonica and Frank's themes and the very important ensuing dialogue between Harmonica and Cheyenne which concludes ambiguously, with Harmonica playing his theme emphasizing its very narrow half steps that sound almost like quarter tones. This tonal nuance prompts Cheyenne's warning: "Watch those false notes" and Harmonica's response: "Like so?" as he sardonically plays "false" notes even more emphatically than before.

Upon her arrival at Sweetwater, Jill views and buries the bodies of the McBein family (her family, we learn, since she and McBein had secretly married in New Orleans), underscored by *Jill's Theme*. Then, Jill looks at herself in the mirror, underscored, again, by her theme followed by incidental Copland-like music based on the carillon motif. Ten seconds later, Jill hears someone at the door and says: "Who is there?" Harmonica's theme is played, this time without "false notes." It stops and resumes followed by Frank's motif played dirge-like on the English horn as the first sixty minutes of the film reaches a conclusion.

Frank and Harmonica's themes constitute two aspects of material set to contrast the music of the main titles (*Jill's Theme*). In fact, they represent both Harmonica and Frank through a series of differentiations highlighted by the use of sound distortions from an electronically modified harmonica and a particularly pungent electric guitar.

Two-thirds into the film's narrative, Leone, perhaps for casting reasons, introduces a love scene between Jill and Frank. The episode, lasting five solid minutes, is engulfed by Morricone's music combining the carillon motif and *Jill's Theme* magnificently played by Dino Asciolla on the viola.

Morricone underscores the convoluted narrative surrounding the character of Norton (Gabriele Ferzetti), the crippled railroad magnate, and his interaction with Frank, his strongman, with permutations of both Frank and Harmonica's themes evidenced during a showdown between the two characters resulting in Frank's death punctuated by the sound of bells as heard near the beginning of the film when Frank orders the McBein boy to be killed.

The electronically altered themes of Harmonica and Frank near Norton's stopped train underscore the agonizing death of Norton. Meanwhile at Sweetwater, Cheyenne's theme is heard again as it marks Cheyenne's peaceful death and the departure from the scene of Harmonica who had witnessed it.

The end credits music cue showcases *Jill's Theme* in all its "From the New World" Dvořák-inspired splendor.

Morricone scored three Western films following *C'era una volta il West*: *Tepepa* (Blood and Guns) directed by Giulio Petroni (1969), *Un esercito di 5 uomini* (The Five Man Army) directed by Italo Zingarelli as Don Taylor (1969), and *Vamos a matar, compañeros* (Compañeros) directed by Sergio Corbucci (1970).

Morricone possesses tremendous ability to handle multiple genres, styles, and human relationships with many individuals, including intellectuals with whom he forged lifelong friendships—from Bernardo Bertolucci, Marco Bellocchio, and Gillo Pontecorvo to Pier Paolo Pasolini and Elio Petri. On the other hand, his status as a composer of concert music—a genre Morricone always referred to as "absolute music" of the post–Petrassi generation—remained solid, although some streaks of commercialism (i.e., Capitalism), began to elicit some criticism in the Italian/Roman intellectual milieu that, in the 1960s, "required" that one subscribe to a Leftist ideological stance.

Morricone made considerable financial gains in the 1960s. Twenty-five million copies of recordings bearing his name were sold worldwide by the end of the decade. He provided well for his growing family, now including sons Andrea (b. 1964) and Giovanni (b. 1966). They moved to a sprawling estate near the town of Mentana about 29 kilometers northeast of Rome, then the family moved back to the city in the very fashionable suburban oasis known as EUR.[24]

The year 1966 brought *La battaglia di Algeri* (The Battle of Algiers), a milestone in Morricone's career as a film composer strongly involved in Pontecorvo's militant discourse on social justice. Additionally, he dedicated a precious amount of time to the tryout score for *The Bible* (1965–1966), a film by John Huston produced by Dino De Laurentiis. For a variety of reasons, Morricone's score never made it to the film. Ultimately, it was Toshiro Mayuzumi who composed the film's soundtrack.[25]

The following is a list of Morricone's film contributions during the period under scrutiny: 1964–1968.

1964

- *E la donna creò l'uomo* (Full Hearts and Empty Pockets) by Camillo Mastrocinque
- *I due evasi da Sing Sing* by Lucio Fulci
- *I Malamondo* (Malamondo) by Paolo Cavara
- *I maniaci* by Lucio Fulci
- *I marziani hanno dodici mani* (The Twelve-Handed Men of Mars) by Castellano and Pipolo
- *Prima della rivoluzione* (Before the Revolution) by Bernardo Bertolucci

1965

- *Altissima pressione* (Highest Pressure) by Enzo Trapani
- *Gli amanti d'oltretomba* (Nightmare Castle) by Mario Caiano
- *Idoli controluce* by Enzo Battaglia

- *I pugni in tasca* (Fists in the Pocket) by Marco Bellocchio
- *Menage all'italiana* (Menage Italian Style) by Franco Indovina
- *Non son degno di te* by Ettore Fizzarotti
- *Se non avessi più te* by Ettore Fizzarotti
- *Slalom* (Snow Job) by Luciano Salce
- *Thrilling* by Carlo Lizzani, Gian Luigi Polidori, Ettore Scola

1966

- *Agent 505—Todesfalle Beirut* (Agent 505: Death Trap in Beirut) by Manfred Köhler
- *Come imparai ad amare le donne* (How I Learned to Love Women) by Luciano Salce
- *El Greco* by Luciano Salce
- *La battaglia di Algeri* (The Battle of Algiers) by Gillo Pontecorvo
- *Mi vedrai tornare* by Ettore Fizzarotti
- *Svegliati e uccidi* (Wake Up and Die) by Carlo Lizzani
- *Uccellacci e uccellini* (The Hawks and the Sparrows) by Pier Paolo Pasolini
- *Un uomo a metà* (Almost a Man and Half a Man) by Vittorio De Seta

1967

- *Ad ogni costo* (Grand Slam) by Giuliano Montaldo
- *Arabella* by Mauro Bolognini
- *Dalle Ardenne all'inferno* (Dirty Heroes) by Alberto De Martino
- *Diabolik* by Mario Bava
- *La Cina è vicina* (China Is Near) by Marco Bellocchio
- *L'harem* (Her Harem) by Marco Ferreri
- *La ragazza e il generale* (The Girl and the General) by Pasquale Festa Campanile
- *L'avventuriero* (The Rover) by Terence Young
- *Le streghe*—Episodio *La terra vista dalla luna* (The Witches—an episode from *The Earth as Seen from the Moon*) by Pier Paolo Pasolini
- *Matchless* by Alberto Lattuada
- *O. K. Connery* by Alberto De Martino

1968

- *Comandamenti per un gangster* by Alfio Caltabiano
- *Escalation* by Roberto Faenza

- *Fräulein Doktor* by Alberto Lattuada
- *Galileo* by Liliana Cavani
- *Grazie zia* (Come Play with Me) by Salvatore Sampieri
- *H2S* by Roberto Faenza
- *La bataille de San Sebastian* (Guns for San Sebastian) by Henri Verneuil
- *L'alibi* by Adolfo Celi, Luciano Licignani, Vittorio Gassman
- *La monaca di Monza* (The Lady of Moinza) by Eriprando Visconti
- *Partner* by Bernardo Bertolucci
- *Roma come Chicago* (Bandits in Rome) by Alberto De Martino
- *Ruba al prossimo tuo* (A Fine Pair) by Francesco Maselli
- *Scusi, facciamo l'amore?* (Listen, Let's Make Love) by Vittorio Caprioli
- *Teorema* (Theorem) by Pier Paolo Pasolini
- *Un tranquillo posto di campagna* (A Quiet Place in the Country) by Elio Petri

Giù la testa or *C'era una volta la Rivoluzione* (Duck You, Sucker!—A Fistful of Dynamite—Once Upon a Time . . . the Revolution) was born a problematic film bearing intriguing alternate Italian and English titles that revealed uncertainties too pronounced for an international film that was expected to match, in the film industry and the public imagination, the fabled allusions of *C'era una volta il West*.

Duck You, Sucker! was not an appealing English translation of the Italian *Giù la testa*. *A Fistful of Dynamite* appeared like a lame tentative to connect the film to *A Fistful of Dollars*, and *Once Upon a Time . . . the Revolution* was too naïve a title for a worldwide audience whose expectations from both Sergio Leone and Ennio Morricone had grown to be very high. So, the negativity provoked by such a predicament became a thorny affair for Leone, who in 1989, the year of his death, deemed it necessary to respond to Francesco Mininni's questions about the film in somewhat defensive terms:

FM: Is it difficult to consider *Giù la testa* a western?

SL: No, in fact it is not a western at all. It represents a new frontier, new horizons to be discovered. Think about a detail: my duels take place always in a circular space like an arena or a circus if you will. There is a similar situation in *Giù la testa* but at the beginning to serve as background for the private violence of Steiger toward Maria Monti. In other words, the stories of the West end there at the beginning of *Giù la testa*, thus, foreshadowing the beginning of something new.

FM: Besides giving life to the flourishing of the Italian western, your films inaugurated a comic trend in the culture of the western as represented by Terence Hill and Bud Spencer. Critics say that such a trend was born by chance and that

Lo chiamavano Trinità[26] was supposed to be a serious, normal western but it seems improbable upon watching it.

SL: It seems improbable indeed, but it is the truth. As you know, these comic westerns are characterized by the absence of people being killed. Well, in the early adventures of Trinità we have at least six people dead. When I worked with Terence Hill in *Il mio nome è Nessuno* [My Name Is Nobody], it was he who told me the whole story. Following the first screening, Enzo Barboni, the director, was confused by noticing the public was in stitches, with laughter; he could not understand that reaction being convinced that he had realized just another western. In fact, he thought that commercially the film was heading toward disaster. Then the success, the consciousness, the slaps on the face, the rugby and all those accessories that determined the fortune of the series. However, the first film was not really a comical western at least in the authors' intentions. Brilliant, exaggerated, lightly humorous perhaps, but comical certainly not.

FM: Among your productions, *Il mio nome è Nessuno* is undoubtedly the most significant. Why did you not direct it personally, preferring to pass it along to Tonino Valerii?

SL: Because with *C'era una volta il West* I was done with the genre. Although *Giù la testa* has been mistaken for a western, it is in reality a film of adventures taking place at the time of the Mexican Revolution. On the other hand, I was very fond of *Il mio nome è Nessuno* as a concept; therefore, I decided to entrust the film's directorship to Valerii who was my assistant in *Per qualche dollaro in più* and then turned director upon my suggestion. It was a good decision although he had, at times, difficulties in synthesizing with my wishes, thus, the noticeable lack of balance in some episodes.

FM: Il mio nome è Nessuno shows some truly Leonian scenes. Did you direct them?

SL: I confess, I did it! The entire beginning, so similar to that of *Il buono, il brutto, il cattivo*; the duel in the Indian cemetery recalls that in *Per qualche dollaro in più*, the clash between Beauregard and the wild bunch, and the fake final duel were directed by me personally. I must say, without false modesty, that those are the most memorable scenes of the film. I believe that the burlesque aspect of the film and those connected to the Trinità series have been underlined too emphatically.

FM: Did you intend to say a conclusive word about the Trinità films?

SL: Yes, it was a rather polemic film in this sense. Directors involved with the comical western needed to understand that they could direct the films they did because of Fonda, Ford, and my work. I felt responsible for introducing the Trinità genre to the public. After *Il buono, il brutto, il cattivo* the public became spoiled; I would say it acquired bad habits due to an enormous amount of despicable films that followed to the point of total saturation. When a title like *Se incontri Sartana digli che è un uomo morto* [If You Meet Sartana Pray for Your Death] is mocked by the public as *Se incontri Sartana digli che è uno stronzo* [If You Meet Sartana, Tell Him He Is a Piece of Shit], it means that the author has been unmasked and that the genre has lost credibility. Thus, the success of Trinità was a sort of vindication on the part of the public.

The ambiguous nature of this film presented Morricone with opportunities to apply compositional experimentation; and he gladly did so starting with the main titles music cue sequence identified as *Invenzione per John*, a "learned" musical term. At first hearing, this cue sounds like the most conventional piece of the film's soundtrack; however, it is the result of an elaborate scheme, the *Invenzione* (invention), that generated the fabric of the film's soundtrack.

The main titles cue, *Invenzione per John*, is divided in two segments; the first segment consists of four measures of steady quarter notes playing A minor chords in 3/4 time that pave the way for a thematic cell consisting of the interval E-B. This cell is treated like a motto as it assumes different functions in connecting various fragments within the same piece and/or different themes. For instance, in the main titles, the interval/motto expands into the G minor triadic intervals E-G-B followed by the note B reiterated one octave higher (see Figure 3.4).

Segment 2 in B flat major is introduced by Alessandro Alessandroni's familiar whistle dispatched with a bubbly, nonchalant mood. It assumes a leitmotiv function in reference to the combined characters Juan/Sean, that is to say, Juan Miranda (Rod Steiger) and John/Sean Mallory (James Coburn) whose names' alliteration Juan/Sean is then vocalized by a falsetto male quartet provided by I Cantori Moderni di Alessandroni. They sing *Scion—Scion—Scion* along the triadic arpeggio E-G-B (see Figure 3.5).

Figure 3.4. Main Titles: Segment 1. Graphic rendition created by author.

Figure 3.5. **Main Titles: Segment 2—Part 1.** Graphic rendition created by author.

Thereafter, segments 1 and 2, moving at the rhythm of a jazz waltz à la Bacharach, generates the central theme, a soaring melodic arch infused with abstract serenity more in the spirit of Johann Sebastian Bach's *Jesu, Joy of Man's Desiring* (from Cantata 147) than from any dramatic foreboding feelings. This central theme is performed by a full string orchestra joined by the voice of Edda Dell'Orso (see Figure 3.6).

In all, Morricone begins this film with a piece that is conventional and enigmatic at the same time since it is never heard in its entirety until the soundtrack's end. It eludes, early on, a sense of conclusion and questions the rationale behind its inclusion in the soundtrack in the first place.

The film's second important cue is *Marcia degli accattoni* (March of the Beggars). It consists of an almost five-minute parade of Juan Miranda's ragtag entourage, actually his relatives, who grow in number as the march progresses in a grotesque fashion. Morricone scores this cue by deploying a full arsenal of sounds produced by homemade instruments and anything that could reflect the bizarrely assorted vestiaries and looks of the marchers including, not the proverbial kitchen sink, but the sinket or sin-ket, a primordial synthesizer the composer had grown fond of.[27]

One could say that in this *Marcia degli accattoni*, Morricone paid homage to his own main titles music cue to Pasolini's *Uccellacci e uccellini* (The

Figure 3.6. **Central Theme.** Graphic rendition created by author.

Figure 3.7. Marcia degli accattoni (Beggars' March). Graphic rendition created by author.

Hawks and the Sparrows) and to Carlo Rustichelli's famous *Marcia di Brancaleone* from Mario Monicelli's film *L'armata Brancaleone* (For Love and Gold) both released in 1966. Furthermore, Morricone mocked Mozart's *Eine Kleine Nachtmusik* K.525, adding to the episode an extra layer of cartoonish flavor, perhaps (see Figure 3.7).

The extended cue, known as either *Messico e Irlanda* or *Mesa Verde*, is fully based on selected modules drawn from *Invenzione per John*. According to Sergio Miceli, who had the opportunity to study Morricone's complex schemata, the manuscript consisted of some thirty modules of various lengths and instrumentation. They were recorded separately, then deployed in any combination by superimposition and mixing—an engineering feat Morricone exploited for years to come in crime/horror film scores, especially in Dario Argento's Animal Trilogy surveyed in Chapter 4.

This combinatorial method, a legacy from his avant-garde background, was detected in *Musica per 11 violini* of 1958 and its application to the soundtrack of the film *Un tranquillo posto di campagna* directed by Elio Petri ten years later, albeit in a modified version as noted in Chapter 1. At any rate, Miceli sampled several modules and their applications in his discussion of the matter.[28]

This film ends with a huge bloody explosion that causes the death of Sean Mallory, the Irish revolutionary who had traveled to Mexico to help the Mexicans in their fight against the Germans occupiers. Mortally wounded, Sean dies in a cave where he sought refuge. Before exhaling his last breath, Sean engaged in a reverie about a hopeless love triangle that was perhaps the cause why he had left Ireland in the first place. The scene, filmed in slow motion, is about two young men taking turns in kissing a young woman accompanied by Morricone's gorgeous main titles music unfolding now in its entirety. This moment is veiled by magical sadness and nostalgia, foreshadowing the "kissing" final episode of *Nuovo Cinema Paradiso*, one would think.

Memories are what cinema thrives on and Sergio Leone's next film *C'era una volta in America* (Once Upon a Time in America) validated that assumption as the film's long gestation had begun before *Giù la testa* to conclude in 1984, a time when the idea behind the film, itself a story about memories, had, in effect, become a memory. Leone explained:

FM: What is *C'era una volta in America* (*Once Upon a Time in America*)?

SL: It is an homage to things I always loved, the American literature of Chandler, Hammett, Dos Passos, Hemingway, and Fitzgerald in particular. Personages who, when I got to know them, were forbidden in Italy. I read them clandestinely in Fascist Italy, thus, like all things forbidden, they assumed a greater meaning than their effective value. Second, it is the most complete reconstruction of the America I followed and dreamt about for years, America of contradictions and myths. Finally, it is a reflection on theatrical representation, on the visual arts. It is not by mere coincidence that the film begins and ends in a Chinese theatre: the public attending a Chinese theatre is to shadow plays as the public of a movie theatre is to film. There is a symbiosis between them and us. It is a double screen, in fact, it is a public looking at another screen.

FM: The screenplay of *C'era una volta in America* required five years of work and, even so, it lacks complete unity, there are some obscure episodes in it.

SL: Originally, the film lasted four and a half hours, so, I needed to eliminate something during the definitive montage. I have no regrets. As a matter of fact, I think it improved the film. That mystery, that sense of vagueness, those little skips in the narrative are all part of the story; I would say that they are essential to it. Are memories, on the other hand, always precise, impeccable, unchangeable? Telling ten times the same story is like telling ten different stories.

FM: The irony that accompanies all of your films seems to have been pushed aside in *C'era una volta in America*.

SL: It could not have been otherwise. The gangsters are no longer frontier gunmen; they have grown and that type of irony one finds in the film is typical of those personages. Reason why the irony found in *C'era una volta in America* refers most of all to sex: times have fatally changed.

FM: *C'era una volta in America* is clearly the film you love the most.

SL: I always said that my films travel through the filter of time. Therefore, the last is the one I love the most. I would say though that I love the least *Per un pugno di dollari* not because my love cooled off with the passing of time but because it is simply remote from my present way of thinking. Love for my films decreases according to a temporal scale with one exception; *Giù la testa*, a film I cannot quite place well. I love it intensely because it took much anxiety, doubts, and desperation out of me. At a certain point I thought about abandoning it and I credit my wife for giving me the strength to bring it to its conclusion. I cannot afford not to love *C'era una volta in America*. It represents the summation of my career regarding content and, above all, style.

FM: Robert De Niro's smile at the conclusion of the film has been defined as the most beautiful smile in the history of cinema. Do you wish to talk about it?

SL: How can one explain the smile of the Mona Lisa? I wanted to end the film as an open work so each viewer could interpret the ending according to his sensibility. *C'era una volta in America* could be intended as a flashback—a story remembered by an aged Noodles upon visiting the places of his youth. Also, it could be possible that Noodles never left the opium den (opium being a drug that obliterates memory while triggering a vision of the future), so, the film is the dream of a drug addict. That smile is the emblem of such ambiguity.

FM: What is America according to you?

SL: It is the place of contradictions. I have always said that whoever wishes to know America and does not have the time to study it in depth, should spend a week at Disneyland. Then, he will understand taste, ingenuity, and the thousands of contradictions of the American people capable of decreeing at the same time—the successes of *Mary Poppins* and *Deep Throat*. These are the nuances that led me to discover America as the locus of my cinematic adventures without counting the mythical image provided by the Hollywood cinema of the 1930s and 1940s, a period that led the dreams of all those of my generation and beyond.

FM: There is a recurrent theme in your films: the ending friendship due to destiny or betrayal. Evidently, this is something very close to your heart.

SL: It is part of my life. Even if not according to the films, I have also endured many friendships which despite all good intentions got to an end. Furthermore, I am an only child and I have always felt the absence of a brother to love. In sum, it is a theme that belongs to me fully.

FM: Flashback is a device you employ frequently.

SL: Time is always the great protagonist of my films; it changes the course of things. How many good ideas etched during youth have turned into nothing, how much hope has been dispersed. Only stubborn individuals like Noodles can believe that the passing of time changes nothing even when evidence proves to the contrary. And then, I wanted to do something new, so the flashback in western movies was a novelty.

FM: There are in your films some technical constants like the upward movement of the dolly, I gather.

SL: And downward most of the time. Think of the sequence in *C'era una volta in America* when aged Noodles returns to the Lower East Side and telephone Moe. How can one describe a character who, after having disappeared for thirty years, returns to one of his dearest friends (who thinks you are dead) and within a phone call is able to synthetize the entire past? The only valid option is not to let the viewer listen in to their conversation: mystery of the Word. Then, if all this is not observed from an abstract, impersonal point of view (the camera never enters Moe's place or Noodles' phone booth, it observes from outside), it cannot be credible. So, when Moe invites his clients to leave the premises and returns to the telephone, the camera comes down like a guillotine and frames the past. Here technique becomes thematic or, better yet, poetry.

For a film as important and financially committed as *C'era una volta in America*, Morricone refrained from any type of experimental music, old or new. The result was one of the best and most traditional film scores of the 1980s that comprised exemplary pages on the interactivity between music and structural narrative. Take, for example, the long scene in which an older Noodles returns to Fat Moe's (Larry Rapp) place and reviews the old pictures of the dead friends hanging on the wall. Following a whispered *ppp* entrance of *Deborah's Theme*, we notice numerous implicit points of synchronization very important for the director since the music was written before the shooting. It reveals the melodic-harmonic evolution between music articulations and camera movements, something that would have been difficult to re-create during montage. In the development of this scene, Noodles, feeling the urgency to revive his past, enters a lavatory and, looking through a peep hole, observes, as he used to do when a boy, the very young Deborah (Jennifer Connelly) practicing dance to the sound of a gramophone. The passage from *Deborah's Theme* to the song *Amapola* to which Deborah danced[29] is quasi-magical as it shifts from non-diegetic to diegetic not only in Noodles' psyche but ours as well, a condition dictated by continuous flashbacks and flashforwards that make the chronology of this exceptionally long film at times challenging to follow (see Figure 3.8).[30] In fact, one could argue that the whole film was a reverie experienced by the aged Noodles and his young self in the opium den.

At any rate, another good example of cinematic chronological transference is provided by the *Cockeye's Song*, a motif that Cockeye (William Forsythe), the youngest member of the gang, breathes into a toy pan flute. It is heard first in one of the earliest scenes with music set in 1932 when Noodles was about

Figure 3.8. Deborah's Theme. Graphic rendition created by author.

Figure 3.9. Cockeye's Theme (Childhood Memories). Graphic rendition created by author.

to leave the city for the time being, but it is heard again forcefully evoked by Zamfir's pan flute and Edda Dell'Orso's voice during Noodles' visit to the tombs of his friends (see Figure 3.9).

Commentary, memories, space-temporal signaling, and self-citations seem to come to a fusion in this film through a sort of evolution-involution use of thematic material and the use of technical devices like the interval of sixth, the suspension upon the half phrase, the deep pedal on the Dominant, and finally, the vocalized lines along with the violins all connoting the making of instantly memorable themes: *Deborah's Theme*, *Poverty Theme*, and *Childhood Memories* (or *Cockeye's Song*) (see Figure 3.10).

In fact, it is *Cockeye's Theme* (see Figure 3.9) that represents another remarkable synthesis of music and cinema in Leone's films because it evokes not only nostalgia and languor but the visceral, raw characteristics of the earlier *El Degüello* in *Per un pugno di dollari* as a specimen of confrontational music.

Cinema moves at its own pace while a composer indulges in just-discovered sonorities, despite particular identification and unique partnerships that can make the composer assume the mantle of coauthor. But, let us keep in mind that a composer is, most of the time, an artisan who produces music to fulfill a commission and, in special cases, the artist who clarifies, interprets, and validates the requests. Morricone embodies both roles as evidenced by his success in productions, which around the time of *C'era una volta in America* included *The Thing* (John Carpenter, 1982), *The Mission* (Roland Joffé, 1986), *The Untouchables* (Brian De Palma, 1987), *Frantic* (Roman Polanski, 1988), *Casualties of War* (De Palma, 1989), *Hamlet* (Franco Zeffirelli, 1990),

Figure 3.10. Poverty Theme. Graphic rendition created by author.

Bugsy (Barry Levinson, 1991), *City of Joy* (Roland Joffé, 1992), and *In the Line of Fire* (Wolfgang Petersen, 1993).

As Morricone exited the symbolic Lion's Den (Sergio Leone's directorial sphere), he remained involved for a while in the Spaghetti Western business at times under Leone's influence as producer of films such as *Il mio nome è Nessuno* (My Name Is Nobody), directed by Tonino Valerii (1973), and *Un genio, due compari, un pollo* (A Genius, Two Friends, and an Idiot), directed by Damiano Damiani (1975). Other films include:

- *Il giorno del giudizio* (Day of Judgment) directed by Mario Gariazzo with Claudio Tallino (1971).
- *Il ritorno di Clint il solitario* (The Return of Clint the Stranger) directed by Alfonso Balcázar (1972).
- *J. and S. Storia criminale del Far West* (Sonny and Jed) directed by Sergio Corbucci (1972).
- *La vita a volte è molto dura, vero Providenza?* (Life Is Tough, Eh Providence?) directed by Giulio Petroni (1972).
- *Che c'entriamo noi con la rivoluzione?* (What Am I Doing in the Middle of the Revolution?) directed by Sergio Corbucci (1972).
- *Ci risiamo, vero Providenza* (Here We Go Again, Eh Providence) directed by Alberto De Martino (1973).
- *Occhio alla penna* directed by Michele Lupo (1981).

The latter's title seems ironic. It translates as *Watch your pen!* [Ennio]—an allusion, I would like to think, to Cheyenne as he warns Harmonica to "watch those 'false' notes" in *C'era una volta il West*.

NOTES

1. The first recording of Morricone's arrangement, shortened to three minutes and 40 seconds, was the A-side of the vinyl single RCA Italiana/Victor PM45-3055 (1961). The B-side consisted of the song *Ritorna* by Gianni Marchetti arranged for orchestra and chorus by Morricone. This disc featured "Ennio Morricone e la sua orchestra."

The full-length *Barabbas* arrangement was released as Track B5 in RCA Italiana/ Serie Europa PML 10306 (1961) and as Track A7 in RCA Italiana/Victor MPL-10316 (1962), a compilation album entitled *Musica in Celluloide*. The complete original soundtrack album of the film *Barabbas*, including Morricone's arrangement, was released in the United States by Colpix Records as CP 510 (1962). At about the same time, Morricone programmed his *Barabbas* arrangement in the April 11, 1962, broadcast of *Piccolo Concerto* (see Appendix 1) with Carlo Savina conducting. Ultimately,

Morricone's arrangement was not included in the DRG (USA) 1996 CD version of the film's soundtrack.

2. Probably *The Ballad of Black Gold*, the film's title song, sung by Frankie Laine.

3. This celebrated song was sung by Tex Ritter in the film's soundtrack.

4. This song was based on the Christmas carol *I Wonder as I Wander* collected in 1933 by American folklorist John Jacob Niles. It was arranged later by Benjamin Britten for inclusion in his 1934 collection of *Folk Songs for Medium Voice and Piano* and by Luciano Berio in 1964 as part of his *Folk Songs for Mezzo-Soprano and 7 Instruments*.

5. See RCA Victor-Italy PM45-3115 [1962]—A-side *Pastures of Plenty* [Traditional-Guthrie] and B-side *Notte Infinita* [Cravero-Migliacci-Tevis]. Another Tevis–Morricone recording released back-to-back with the above was RCA Italiana-Italy PM45-3150. It consisted of A-side *Stanotte si* (Tonight) and B-side *Maria*, both from Leonard Bernstein's *West Side Story*.

6. See Sergio Miceli, *Morricone, la musica, il cinema* (Milano: Ricordi/Mucchi, 1994), 112, n4. Meanwhile, Sergio Leone had to settle a legal claim initiated by director Akira Kurosawa regarding some alleged similarities detected between *Per un pugno di dollari* and Kurosawa's *Yojimbo* (1961).

7. Edith Peters was the fifth sibling of the African-American vocal trio known as the Peters Sisters. They had debuted in Italy in a musical by Renato Rascel produced by Garinei and Giovannini. Edith married an Italian television producer and established her acting/singing career in Italy.

8. See RCA Italiana PM 45 3285 (1964). A-side *Per un pugno di dollari* [Michele Lacerenza, trumpet], B-side *Titoli* [Alessandro Alessandroni, guitar and whistling]. Regarding the choice of Lacerenza to record the *Degüello*, Morricone recounted the following:

> Leone and I quarreled regarding the trumpet player; I proposed Michele Lacerenza, a much in demand studio player and an old conservatory mate of mine. Sergio wanted Nino Rosso, better known than Lacerenza for being also a gifted singer with some successful recordings to his credit. I insisted and engaged Lacerenza who was fully aware of the director's disapproval. He cried while playing, I swear, and under the circumstance, he put his soul in it including all the embellishments that made the piece famous. By the way, it appears that Tiomkin had done the same with his trumpet player when recording the scene that precedes the ending of *Rio Bravo*.

Quoted in *Ennio Morricone racconta . . .* a three-part dialogue with the public that took place at the Feltrinelli Bookshop in Milan on March 28, 2004. This very spontaneous dialogue-interview was published by Stefano Sorice, in three installments in the periodical *Colonne sonore: Immagini tra le note*, see Chapter 1, n24.

9. The LP *Un pugno di . . . West*, featuring Peter Tevis, I Cantori Moderni di Alessandroni, and Ennio Morricone e la sua orchestra, was issued by RCA Italiana in two editions: PML-10402 (1965) and S7 (1966). The full soundtrack of *Duello nel Texas* was released for the first time in 2012 as Digitmovies—DPDM005. It contains two versions of *A Gringo like Me* sung by Peter Tevis (Track 1) and Dicky Jones (Track 20).

10. Remarkable in *Le pistole non discutono* is the cue marked "The Indians," which reflects the influence of Leonard Bernstein's score for *On the Waterfront* (1954). This cue could have been the same piece performed in *Piccolo Concerto* under the title *West* (Indian War Dance), see Appendix 1.

11. The songs *Per un pugno di dollari* and *Lonesome Billy* were paired in RCA Italiana single PM45 3352 (1966).

12. In November 1988, journalist Francesco Mininni spoke with Sergio Leone about his Western films. The interview was published posthumously in Mininni's *Sergio Leone* (Milano: Editrice Il Castoro, 1989; 2nd, 1994). The English translation is by the author with Mininni's permission.

13. *Rawhide* was a classic Western series produced by CBS from 1959 to 1965. It made Clint Eastwood a star of the small screen.

14. This bridge section was taken from *Pastures of Plenty* by explicit request of Sergio Leone. It caused an authorship rift with Peter Tevis who apparently had written the "bridge." The matter was honorably settled.

15. The word *monco* is a contraction of *mancino* (left-handed), a characteristic of the personage (Clint Eastwood) who drew his gun unexpectedly with the left arm hidden under his makeshift poncho.

16. A much-ado-about-nothing dispute with singer/author Giorgio Consolini (1920–2012) arose regarding the full paternity of Morricone's main titles music and Consolini's song *Jamaica* (1959). Morricone acknowledged the thematic similarity between the two pieces but pleaded ignorance of Consolini's song.

17. It is of interest to note how the original Italian title of Sollima's film capitalized on the pivotal cue, *La resa dei conti*, heard in *Per qualche dollaro in più*.

18. A celebrated 1947 drama/crime.

19. Emilio Lussu's memoir of World War I was first published in 1938.

20. Leone refers here to actors Ugo Tognazzi and Edoardo Vianello who often performed as a comedic duo.

21. Extended interviews with both Edda and Giacomo Dell'Orso are available in Stefano Torossi's blog *The Sixth Dimension*, accessed January 20, 2018, https://the6thdimension.com/2014/05/22/edda-dellorso-on-life-as-a-vocalist-in-the-1960s-and-1970s-plus-a-look-at-some-of-her-recent-musical-projects/.

22. The Italian Western has inspired a large body of writings. However, the fundamental study in the field remains Christopher Frayling's *Spaghetti Westerners: Cowboys and Europeans from Karl May to Sergio Leone* (London: I. B. Tauris, 1981; 2nd, 1998; 3rd, 2006) and the IFC-Netflix Documentary *The Spaghetti West: A Celebration of the Classic Italian Westerns of the 1960s* (Docuramafilms, 2005).

23. For detailed analyses of the Leone–Morricone partnership, see Sergio Miceli, "Leone, Morricone and the Italian Way to Revisionist Westerns," in *The Cambridge Companion to Film Music*, ed. Mervyn Cooke and Fiona Ford (Cambridge: Cambridge University Press, 2016), 265–93. Also, Charles Leinberger, *Ennio Morricone's The Good, the Bad and the Ugly* (Lanham, MD: Scarecrow Press, 2004).

24. EUR is an acronym standing for Esposizione Universale Roma, a World Fair first conceived by Mussolini to celebrate twenty years of Fascism in 1942. The approximately two-square-mile quarter became an architectural wonderland showcasing

Razionalismo, a modernist style promoted by its chief architect Marcello Piacentini. Mussolini's celebratory dream did not materialize, but the complex was finally completed on time for the 1960 Olympics taking place in Rome.

25. See Sergio Miceli, *Morricone, la musica, il cinema*, 77 n39. It is interesting to note that Morricone's "rejected" score was subsequently used in the films *Il giardino delle delizie* (1967) and *Il segreto del Sahara* (1987). John Huston had initially commissioned Goffredo Petrassi to score this film. For a full account about this controversial soundtrack, see Gergely Hubai, *Torn Music: Rejected Film Scores* (Los Angeles: Silman-James Press, 2012), 71–72. As late as 2010 and again in 2016, Morricone expressed regret for not having been able to score *The Bible*. Also, see Ennio Morricone, *Lontano dai sogni: Conversazioni con Antonio Monda* (Milan: Mondadori, 2010), 119, and Ennio Morricone, *Inseguendo quel suono: La mia musica, la mia vita. Conversazioni con Alessandro De Rosa* (Milano: Mondadori, 2016), 158–59. Same, translated into English by Maurizio Corbella as *Ennio Morricone in His Own Words: Morricone in Conversations with Alessandro De Rosa* (New York: Oxford University Press, 2019), 109–10.

26. This 1970 film, known in English as *They Call Me Trinity*, was directed by Enzo Barboni and starred Terence Hill and Bud Spencer. The score was by Franco Micalizzi.

27. The Syn-ket (Synthesizer-Ketoff) was a portable compact voltage-controlled performing instrument officially unveiled in 1964 at the conference of the Audio Engineering Society (AES) in New York and Los Angeles. It succeeded Paolo Ketoff's proto-synthesizer Fonosynth. See more on Ketoff's electro-engineering pursuits in Chapter 4.

28. Miceli, *Morricone, la musica, il cinema*, 277–81.

29. *Amapola*, a 1920 song by José María Lacalle García, became a standard instrumental and vocal rhumba number in the 1930s performed thereafter by countless artists. In *Once Upon a Time in America*, the song is heard in two instrumental arrangements by Ennio Morricone both emanating diegetically from a phonograph as young Deborah practices her dance steps and, much later in the story, when Deborah, now a celebrity, dances with Noodles accompanied by the lush sound of a string orchestra at a Long Island resort in perfect "Great Gatsby" style.

30. Originally a six-hour film, it was released in 1984, cut to two and a half hours against Leone's will. Finally, it was re-released in a four-hour format in 2012. However, the original film apparently remained in Leone's possession.

Chapter Four
Toward a New Consonance

The whirlwind of activity occurring in the 1960s prompted Ennio Morricone to confront a personal dilemma that pitted artistic integrity against commercial success—a predicament that was to affect his long creative career. It began with the emergence of two unexpected developments: the 1965 Silver Ribbon (*Nastro d'argento*) for Best Score awarded by the National Association of Cinema Journalists to the film *Per un pugno di dollari* (1964) and an invitation on the part of Franco Evangelisti, the gray eminence of Roman avant-garde music, to join Nuova Consonanza, his Darmstadt-inspired association created in Rome in 1959–1960.[1]

Evangelisti's invitation implied Morricone's participation as composer/trumpet player in the Gruppo di Improvvisazione Nuova Consonanza, the performing branch of Nuova Consonanza known as GINC. This ensemble was formed in 1964 in consultation with American composer Larry Austin (1930–2018) who resided in Rome at the time. Austin had been the moving force behind the New Music Ensemble (NME) which he had created at the University of California–Davis in the summer of 1963. When Morricone first performed with GINC in 1966, the group included composers Mario Bertoncini, Walter Branchi, Franco Evangelisti, John Heineman, Roland Kayn, Jerry Rosen, Frederic Rzewski, and Ivan Vandor.[2]

Morricone welcomed Evangelisti's call as an opportunity to reenter the experimental music milieu at a time when the conferring of the Silver Ribbon on *Per un pugno di dollari* had acknowledged his official success and marketability in the world of film music, in addition to his already well-established reputation as the best arranger in the country—factors that confined "serious" composing to the privacy of his studio.

GINC made considerable inroads in the Roman avant-garde community thanks to Franco Evangelisti's perseverance and the staunch support of a circle of connoisseurs who patronized similar initiatives sprouting up throughout the 1960s, like Musica Elettronica Viva (MEV), a group headed by the American Alvin Curran, and various experimental exploits promoted by the young composers residing at the American Academy in Rome and their associates. These artists included pianist/composer John Eaton, clarinetist/composer William O. Smith, pianist Richard Trythall, flautist Karl (Fritz) Kraber, clarinettist Jerry Kirkbride, sopranos Joan Logue and Carol Plantamura, violist Joan Kalisch, pianists Joe Rollino and Paul Sheftel, Quartetto di Nuova Musica (Coen, Sciannameo, Antonioni, Magendanz), and composers John Heineman, Alvin Curran, Frederic Rzewski, Richard Teitelbaum, Allen Bryant, Jeffrey Levine, Joel Chadabe, Jerry Rosen, Larry Moss, Larry Austin, sound engineer Paolo Ketoff, and other expatriates gravitating around the polarizing figure of Giacinto Scelsi (1905–1988).

Following some GINC public performances, Evangelisti eyed, with Morricone's help, the recording industry with the intention of producing and releasing a series of LPs as a means to generate funds. Ultimately, these discs included:

1. *Gruppo di Improvvisazione "Nuova Consonanza."* RCA Italiana MLDS 20243 (1966) [*1]
2. *The Private Sea of Dreams* by Il Gruppo. RCA Victor–LSP-3846 (1967)
3. *The Feed-back*. RCA Italiana, PSL 10466 (1970) [*2]
4. *Improvvisazioni a formazioni variate dei compositori-esecutori*. LP General Music (1973) [*3]
5. *Nuova Consonanza*. Cinevox (Fonit Cetra), Sc 33/14 (1975)
6. *Gruppo di Improvvisazione Nuova Consonanza: Musica su schemi*. Cramps Records–CRSLP 6109; Serie nova musicha–n. 9 (1976)

The LP *Gruppe Nuova Consonanza: Improvisationem* was included in the six-disc box released by Deutsche Grammophon as Avant Garde Series vol. II. 643511 (1969). However, the six discs bore individual covers and were also sold separately. Another LP entitled *Zeitgenössische Musik II* was released under the label Deutsche Grammophon 2536018 (1974). It included works by Berio, Kagel, Zimmermann, Stockhausen, Cage, and GINC.[3]

Aside from Evangelisti's proclamation that improvisatory parameters were to categorically avoid musical familiarities in terms of harmony, melody, or rhythm, strict adherence to his dogma was not always respected. The content of the recordings varies in terms of quality and originality spanning the overt influence of John Cage, mockeries of Stravinsky's *L'histoire du soldat*, and the traps—intentional or not—of the psychedelic sonorities and progressive rock raging at the time. *The Feed-back* turned out to be the only relatively financial success. At any rate, of particular importance is the documentary film *Nuova Consonanza: Komponisten improvisieren im Kollektiv. Ein film von Theo Gallehr mit Mario Bertoncini, Walter Branchi, Franco Evangelisti, John Heineman, Roland Kayn, Ennio Morricone, Ivan Vandor und Frederic Rzweski*. Produced by Hansjörg Pauli in 1967,[4] this film catapulted GINC and its activities onto the avant-garde music scene in Europe and beyond. Moreover, some twenty minutes of GINC's improvisations ended up, fully credited, in Morricone's soundtrack for Elio Petri's 1968 film *Un tranquillo posto di campagna* and *E se per caso una mattina*, a 1972 comedic film by Vittorio Sindoni, whose eclectic soundtrack was selected by the director in consultation with Nuova Consonanza's operative and future president Egisto Macchi.[5]

In conclusion, was Morricone's active participation in Nuova Consonanza and GINC an initial approach, on his part, to reconcile music for the screen and experimental works? Although it may be speculative to draw conclusions at this point, one may note that the composer seized the moment to float a philosophical divide between what he termed "musica assoluta" (absolute music) and "musica applicata" (applied music), a taxonomic prospect which etched the concept of "doppia estetica," consisting, in his case, of two opposite aesthetic points of view running concurrently. There occurred, however, occasional contradictions when some film scores purported trends common to avant-garde music and concert pieces conceded to a complacent tonal approach.[6] A case of quick "remedial transfer" was *Requiem per un destino* (1966), an intriguing work for orchestra and chorus composed for a choreographic representation,[7] originally part of the soundtrack for a film directed by Vittorio De Seta in 1966, *Un uomo a metà* (Almost a Man and a Half a Man), a story about a man's complex psychotic relationship with his mother. The film had been negatively reviewed by the critics at the 1966 Venice Film Festival, although principal actor Jacques Perrin was awarded the Coppa Volpi for best actor.[8] At any rate, the Venetian experience disappointed Morricone. He turned the film's soundtrack into the stage work *Requiem per un destino* though he purged a charming Kurt Weill–inspired tune composed to underscore a love scene.

SUONI PER DINO

If some "serious" composers are prone to angst caused by their success with commercial music, performers are usually less scrupulous as their professional working ethics may prevent them from differentiating, in most cases, between assignments, especially those sheltered by the "underground privacy" of the recording studio. Ennio Morricone was privileged in this respect because he could benefit from the collaboration of the finest classically trained instrumentalists and vocalists available in Rome. Ultimately, the artistry of these individuals became an irreplaceable component of Morricone's scoring trademark—like the contributions offered by conductor Bruno Nicolai, vocalist Edda Dell'Orso, harpist Anna Palomba, trumpet player Michele Lacerenza, violinist Franco Tamponi, flautist Severino Gazzelloni, percussionist Vincenzo (Enzo) Restuccia, guitarists Bruno Battisti D'Amario and Alessandro Alessandroni, Franco De Gemini and his harmonicas, French horn player Filippo Settembri, and violist Dino Asciolla, among others.

The Dino in the title of Morricone's most important concert work of the 1960s, *Suoni per Dino per viola e due magnetofoni*, was Dino Asciolla (1920–1994), a violist of extraordinary talent, versatility, and inspirational appeal who influenced those who worked with him. Asciolla's viola sound was mythical and "human" at the same time—a paradox that reflected the personality of this magnificent artist.

Morricone and Asciolla had known each other well since their student days at Santa Cecilia. So, *Suoni per Dino* was a tribute to friendship and professional kinship that manifested itself also in the form of sublimation of sound technological inter-coding between man and machine. In fact, only distilled allusions to Asciolla's viola sound and the atomized droppings of his bow are heard in this short piece.[9]

Suoni per Dino, composed in 1969 for viola and two tape recorders, calls for a symmetrical stratification of twelve viola lines superimposed upon a base of electronically generated percussive pitches consisting of the interval of the diminished fifth A-E flat, crystallized in a chord-like cluster heard—like a mystical chime—throughout the piece at regular intervals of five seconds.

This prerecorded base, consisting of thirty measures of one second each, is heard fourteen times emanating from a set of speakers. In the first two rounds, the electronic base is heard alone followed by twelve rounds in conjunction with the viola. Each of the twelve viola lines (rounds) consists, like the electronic base, of thirty measures of one second each, so, the duration of the 420 measures forming the piece corresponds to 420 seconds; that is, seven minutes.

After the introductory prerecorded first sixty seconds, the violist plays line 1, reading it upward from the bottom of the score while the first tape recorded (Machine 1) records it and transfers it to the second tape recorded (Machine 2), which plays it back while the violist performs line 2, superimposing it to line 1 and the base. Hence, the stratification process continues until the completion of line 11. Then, Machine 1 fades out and the violist performs line 12 with the support of Machine 2 playing back the strata of eleven lines recorded in the course of the performance, in addition to the prerecorded base heard from the speakers or just the prerecorded base.

The viola's thematic material consists of idiosyncratic instrumental permutations based on the tetrachord A-C sharp-D-B flat provided by the electronic cluster heard in the base.

The instructions for the performative realization of *Suoni per Dino* call for four speakers situated at each corner of the hall and some stage lighting focusing on the violist placed between the two tape recorders. It appears that this work was performed in this fashion at its premiere in the foyer of the Teatro dell'Opera in Rome in 1970 with the cooperation of Paolo Ketoff, the sound engineer mentioned before and discussed further in the pages ahead. Although Dino Asciolla recorded this piece following its premiere, the value of a recorded performance of a work like *Suoni per Dino* is only academic as it defies the "live" and risky interaction between man and machine, a concept rather advanced for the time.[10]

The viola has always intrigued composers; the indeterminacy of the instrument's size and tone quality and the volatility of viola players have given rise to exceptional works, from Berlioz's *Harold en Italie* to the sensational *Sequenza VI* and the consequent *Chemins III* written by Luciano Berio for French and American viola virtuosi Serge Collot and Walter Trampler, respectively. *Sequenza VI* for unaccompanied viola and *Suoni per Dino* are two important contributions to the experimental viola repertoire provided by two Italian composers of the same generation.

After the passing of Dino Asciolla in 1994, Morricone composed a new work, *Ombra di lontana presenza per viola, orchestra d'archi e nastro magnetico "In memoria di Dino"* (1997), which will be discussed in Chapter 6.

SONIC DIMENSIONS AND SHADES OF *GIALLO*

Leaving the 1960s behind, we now observe Morricone's creative meandering throughout the 1970s, a decade particularly challenging for the Italian people, perpetrators and victims at once of the extremely polarized political life whose cultural shifts and significant economic class disparity tore the nation apart to the brink of self-defeatism despite the secular sense of fatalism ingrained in the majority of Italians.

In retrospect, Ennio Morricone seemed to have provided the appropriate "soundtrack" to Italian everyday life as it swung from crisis to crisis before "live" television cameras. Such a hypothetical meta soundtrack unfolded in "coded colors" that symbolized fear of uncertainty, desire for hope, and unquenched thirst for entertainment. Therefore, in marketing cinematic terms, the color red stood for shocking, blood-dripping horror films; black connoted the classic film noir and detective stories of French-American import; and yellow (*giallo*) was the color assigned to sex-filled, typical Italian thrillers inspired by the hundreds of novels published since the 1920s in yellow, soft cover pocket-size books, the *libri gialli*.[11] Furthermore, *giallo* incorporated film sub-genres with colors including pink standing for *neorealismo rosa*— a term whose coinage was attributed to director Luigi Comencini.[12] It was inspired, perhaps, by the romance novels of Jane Fraser/Rosamunde Pilcher (1924–2019) that influenced an array of films showcasing a new breed of female stars like Gina Lollobrigida, Silvana Mangano, Sophia Loren (born Sofia Villani Scicolone), and, later, Claudia Cardinale and Stefania Sandrelli. These new divas felt at home in comedy, sexually provocative plots, and seasonal offerings dished out along streams of easy listening "lounge" music.

Morricone's music thrived in this cinematic rainbow while he attended to the soundtrack needs of some Western films lingering from the previous decade, a handful of politically involved motion pictures, and a few challenging works composed for the concert stage—which will be highlighted in the pages ahead but not before paying homage to an interesting "lesson" from the past.

There is an isolated score hiding in the chronicles of film music; a nine-minute orchestral work entitled *Begleitungsmusik zu einer Lichtspielscene* op. 34, which Arnold Schoenberg composed in 1929–1930. This *Accompaniment to a Cinematographic Scene* had no practical application nor specific destination but the warehouse of Heinrichshofen Verlag, a Magdeburg music publisher specializing in music for silent movies. Schoenberg's work, aside from running against the composer's intransigent ethical principles that his music could not and was not to be shared with another artist's vision, once published, became an entry in the compilation of "indeterminate" pieces known as "Library Music" available for sale or rent, to be used as one saw fit. Schoenberg and music for motion pictures were never to become a viable solution, even when the composer and his family moved to Los Angeles in 1935 where "everybody" was involved with the industry.[13]

Accompaniment to a Cinematographic Scene, scored for flute/piccolo, oboes, 2 clarinets, bassoon, 2 horns, 2 trumpets, trombone, timpani, xylophone, glockenspiel, snare drum, tambourine, cymbals, triangle, tam-tam, bass drum, piano, and strings is divided into three parts: *Threatening Danger—Fear—Catastrophe*, making it ideal music for underscoring expressionist, angst-filled German films or serving as a model for the innumerable soundtracks that accompanied the "horror" films of the late sound era. Ironically, music like Schoenberg's, inherently rational, whether atonal or rigorously serial, served mostly to underscore cinematic characters' irrational fear of the unfamiliar.

Between 1970 and 1976, RCA Italiana produced a series of 45 LPs creating a Library Music collection for multiple applications. Several artists participated in this project, including Ennio Morricone and Bruno Nicolai. They composed, conducted, and recorded 10 LPs dedicated to experimental music for licensing use only, just as Heinrichshofen Verlag had done with Schoenberg's piece. These albums, entitled *Dimensioni sonore, musiche per l'immagine e l'immaginazione*, were first issued in 1972 as a promotional set.[14] The collection included 103 pieces—50 by Morricone and 53 by Nicolai totaling some five and a half hours of music cues boasting abstract, pseudo-scientific, sort of avant-garde alluding titles like *Rifrazioni, Fasi, Proporzionale, Conduzione, Poligoni,* and *Parabola.* Stylistically, these three-to-nine-minute compositions or applicable cues are eclectic fragments of precious glassy sonorities often flowing smoothly to the rhythms of a fashionable, sexy bossa nova or the thorny path of extreme free jazz, catastrophic brass and percussion clashes, and evanescent sound clouds carefully crafted with atonal, non-thematic material. Their origins, intentions, and destination were indeterminate as implied by the series' all-encompassing title, *Sound Dimensions: Music for the Image and the Imagination.*

This RCA Italiana Morricone–Nicolai collection displayed artful combinations of acoustical and electronic elements delivered by cutting-edge technology. In fact, the content of two of Morricone's discs was devoted to instrumental synthetization that evolved into "sampling," a possibility that sound engineers in Rome and elsewhere were probing in depth with the goal in mind to replace non-essential studio musicians with electronically generated sounds very similar to those emanating from their acoustical instruments. In doing so, they perfected the art of "stacking" multiple tracks recorded by just a few musicians, mostly string players or vocalists, making them sound like the full string section of a symphony orchestra or a chorus of hundreds. The engineers at RCA Italiana had access to the most advanced electronic sound generators in Europe furnished by the RCA laboratories in the United States and the services of Paolo Ketoff (1921–1996), a key figure in the development of electronic music and sound synthetization in Rome. Ketoff, a Polish-Italian chief sound technician at RCA Italiana, Cinecittà film studios, Fonolux, and other recording establishments in Rome flourishing between 1957 and 1965, was instrumental in designing many devices for film music production, including dynamic sound compressors and ring modulators, reverb chambers, and plates that enabled sound post-production to establish new standards.[15]

In 1958, Ketoff was commissioned to design and build the Electronic Music Studio at the American Academy in Rome and to bring to functional completion the Fonosynth, his first synthesizer. This machine was used throughout the late fifties and mid-sixties by a number of expatriate American electronic musicians and composers, including Otto Luening, William O. Smith, George Balch Wilson, Richard Trythall, and Alvin Curran. Ketoff's Fonosynth was also widely used by the Italian film industry for special sound effects.[16] In 1963, Ketoff built a successor to his Fonosynth, the so-called Syn-ket (Synthesizer-Ketoff), which consisted of a portable compact voltage-controlled performing instrument officially unveiled in 1964 at the conference of the Audio Engineering Society (AES) in 1964 in New York and Los Angeles.

The ten LPs *Dimensioni sonore, musiche per l'immagine e l'immaginazione* became a rich reservoir of ready-made musical and sound effects, which Morricone, Nicolai, and a host of composers used abundantly in their many "color-coded" film scores. In fact, operative patterns, including prerecorded "scary" sounds alternated with tuneful and smartly orchestrated pieces, began to emerge as functional recipes for scoring dozens of horror/*giallo* films whose quality ranged from "negligible" to "good" amid much indifference and connivance on the part of producers responsible for flooding the market with such products.

THE ANIMAL TRILOGY

Dario Argento's *L'uccello dalle piume di cristallo* (The Bird with the Crystal Plumage, 1970), *Il gatto a nove code* (The Cat O'Nine Tails, 1971), and *Quattro mosche di velluto grigio* (Four Flies on Grey Velvet, 1971) were three films in the "red" category. Morricone's inventive music followed some of the experimental modular patterns heard in *Un tranquillo posto di campagna* (A Quiet Place in the Country) by Elio Petri (1968) and *Vergogna schifosi* (Dirty Angels) by Mauro Severino (1969), two typical psycho-dramas of the period and developed further in *Invenzione per John* (*Giù la testa*, 1971).

Argento's so-called Animal Trilogy added originality, magic, and an elegant patina of surrealism to an otherwise routinely sterile cinematic panorama except when Morricone, always the on-call professional, contributed a memorable tune and a barrage of prerecorded sonic inventions. Films like *Le foto proibite di una signora per bene* (Forbidden Photos of a Lady above Suspicion) by Luciano Ercoli (1970), *Una lucertola con la pelle di donna* (A Lizard in a Woman's Skin) by Lucio Fulci (1971), *Sans mobile apparent* by Philippe Labro (1971), *La corta notte delle bambole di vetro* by Aldo Lado (1971), *Giornata per l'ariete* by Luigi Bazzoni (1972), *Chi l'ha vista morire?* (Who Saw Her Die?) by Aldo Lado (1972), *Cosa avete fatto a Solange?* (What Have You Done to Solange?) by Massimo Dallamano (1972), *Il diavolo nel cervello* (Devil in the Brain) by Sergio Sollima (1972), *La tarantola dal ventre nero* (The Black Belly of the Tarantula) by Paolo Cavara (1971), and *Mio caro assassino* (My Dear Killer) by Tonino Valerii (1972) to name a few, hold to this day cult status thanks to Morricone's engagingly recognizable, albeit formulaic, soundtracks.

The short-lived relationship between Dario Argento and Ennio Morricone, four films in total, including the 1996 *La sindrome di Stendhal* (The Stendhal Syndrome), produced films that crossed or combined the "red" and "yellow" color lines in an effort to create a distinguished hybrid among a multitude of predictable productions. For Morricone, *L'uccello dalle piume di cristallo*, *Il gatto a nove code*, and *Quattro mosche di velluto grigio* constitute an essay in crystallized sonorities created through modular procedures that allowed him to mix into collages prerecorded fragments ideal for underscoring a sophisticated modern-day urban psychotic, yet somewhat naïve, wonderland. In many ways, these Argento–Morricone scores evoke the spirit of a stuporlike implausibility first detected in Nino Rota's music in Fellini's *Satyricon* (1969) and *Il Casanova* (1976).

The fragmented, modular compositions Morricone devised for Argento's Animal Trilogy—and by association for Aldo Lado's *La corta notte delle bambole di vetro* (Short Night of Glass Dolls) of 1971—bring to mind the highly refined concept of "lightness" developed by Italo Calvino a decade later in his *Lezioni americane* (Memos for the Next Millennium). Calvino's literary references ranging from meditations on the particles of dust observed by Lucretius, the poetry of Eugenio Montale's *Little Testament* (1953), to Shakespeare's Queen Mab episode in *Romeo and Juliet* triggered allusions to the music of Hector Berlioz.[17] In short, in his soundtracks for Argento and Lado, Morricone realized a highly intuitive and exceptionally prophetic micro-sonic web that indeed became a point of departure for many film composers of the period who worked in the genre and beyond.

SAMPLING "PINK"

Morricone's soundtracks for films like *Metti, una sera a cena* (Love Circle or One Night at Dinner) by Giuseppe Patroni Griffi, 1969; *L'assoluto naturale* (He and She) by Mauro Bolognini, 1969; *Anche se volessi lavorare che faccio?* (Even If I Wanted to Work What Could I Do?) by Flavio Mogherini, 1972; *D'amore si muore* (One Can Die of Love) by Carlo Carunchio, 1972; bear, along with several dozens more soundtracks, the composer's welltested "sound brand" created in his days as an arranger: the inclusion of serious compositional formal procedures into otherwise commercial assignments spanning from the tonal pointillism characterizing *Metti, una sera a cena*; the "passacaglia" (see the cue ironically marked "Laboriosamente") in

L'assoluto naturale; the melodic dilation of the violins quasi-morphing out of *Musica per 11 violini* evident in *Anche se volessi lavorare che faccio?* (see the cue "Le se ne more"); or the love theme plaintively played by the oboe in *D'amore si muore*.

Yes, the love theme—that essential staple of operas and songs, and by extension films—found in Ennio Morricone a modern-day Orpheus whose melodic gifts have graced the past fifty or so years of film music. The infectious "Love Theme" from Giuseppe Tornatore's *Nuovo Cinema Paradiso* (1988) alone could have justified Morricone's star on Hollywood's Walk of Fame. Yet, he has composed hundreds of beautiful melodies, many of which were turned into successful songs. At this junction though, it will suffice to mention a tune from Carlo Carunchio's *D'amore si muore* (One Can Die of Love). It is a melody drenched in heartbreaking grief for the loss of a loved one. It is played by the most nostalgic of all instruments, the oboe, accompanied by pulsating quarter notes played by the strings in the Venetian Baroque mold favored by Alessandro Marcello in the Adagio movement of his *Oboe Concerto in D minor*, a piece Johann Sebastian Bach admired so much that he transcribed for keyboard. Only a few composers had and have the power to touch millions of hearts with the sounds of a few notes. Orpheus did it in the mythological world; Morricone does it in ours.

Although the moguls of Italian musical theater Garinei and Giovannini offered Morricone the opportunity to compose for the "light" stage, Morricone dodged the possibilities as he did with one operatic tentative as well.[18] However, the comedy film *La cage aux folles* (Édouard Molinaro, 1978) presented the composer with a wonderful chance to show his intelligent, sarcastic, and caustic musical sense of humor in a virtuoso comedic tour de force starring Ugo Tognazzi and Michel Serrault surrounded by a brilliant cast that moves about at the rhythm of a Morriconian version of Youmans' *Tea for Two*, sunlit by an unmistakable French Riviera feel where the story takes place.[19] Furthermore, Tognazzi, the reader may recall, was the protagonist of *Il federale* (The Fascist), the 1961 comedic film directed by Luciano Salce that was Morricone's first official film score, hence, the composer's particular affection for Tognazzi and *La cage aux folles*, a French-Italian film adapted from the 1973 eponymous play by Jean Poiret. The play told the story of a gay couple, Renato Baldi (Tognazzi) and Albin Mougeotte (Serrault), and their fashionable drag club in Saint-Tropez. The club and the couple's gaudy apartment on the floor above it turns into great mistaken identity theater when Renato's son, Laurent (Rémi Laurent), brings home his fiancée, Andréa (Luisa Maneri), and her ultraconservative parents—the father a staunch government official up for reelection—to meet them. Morricone's score is one of the most nuanced he has ever composed in the light vein, extremely well-suited for underscoring the irresistible artistry of Tognazzi and Serrault.

In 1983, just as *La cage aux folles* was basking in its third sequel, a musical version of Poiret's play opened on Broadway with music and lyrics by Jerry Herman. It was a great success, indeed, crowned by a Tony Award the year after. Another film version of the play, the 1996 American production entitled *The Birdcage*, starred Robin Williams and Nathan Lane with songs by Stephen Sondheim. It was also greeted with acclaim.

PASOLINI'S "COLORBLIND" PALETTE

The ten-year relationship between the most controversial Italian literary figure of the 1960s–1970s and a very promising composer blossomed in a climate of mutual respect that never turned into friendship or camaraderie. Ennio Morricone was schooled within the walls of an exclusive conservatory of music, so he treasured outside opportunities for total immersion into the extra musical critical thinking no matter the platform that generated it. Perhaps he viewed Pier Paolo Pasolini as a "different" individual who professed a Marxist view of Christianity, like a sage out of the Renaissance whose complex multifaceted erudition and talents require to be understood and respected with humility and yet circumspection, especially when veering too sharply toward the opaque. On the other hand, Pasolini viewed Morricone the musician as a magical alchemist whose formulae he intuited both musically and aesthetically and, yet, was not able to control at the fullest.[20] However, it was cinema that brought them together in a paradigm clearly outlined by Pasolini and absorbed by Morricone.

The Pasolini–Morricone cinematic collaboration began in 1966 with the film *Uccellacci e uccellini* (The Hawks and the Sparrows) whose opening credits were a creative departure from the customary scrolling of names. It was Pasolini's idea to have the titles of his film, the harbinger of strong class warfare conditions, set to music in the form of a troubadour's ballad sung by Domenico Modugno, then a highly popular figure, accompanied by a nontraditional ensemble consisting of recorder, flute, E-flat clarinet, trumpet, trombone, tuba, tambourine, snare drum, bass drum, triangle, cymbals, bells, castanets, drum set, piano, harpsichord, synthesizer, prepared piano, church organ, male voice (Modugno's), female voice, male chorus, mandolin, acoustical guitar, electric guitar, violin, viola, cello, and bass. An inventive array of instruments and voices very appropriate for setting the quizzical tone of this extraordinary film. Morricone appeared comfortable composing for a genre requiring a dexterous combination of intellectual acumen and sarcastic sense of humor at the service of strong personalities like Pasolini and legendary veteran comic actor Totò (aka Antonio De Curtis), the film's protagonist. The result was a miniature masterpiece, an ode to an archaic, folkish narrative eminently Italian which we encountered again, if on a much-reduced scale, in the music Morricone provided to more of Pasolini's films, including the 1967 surreal fable *La terra vista dalla luna* (The Earth as Seen from the Moon);[21] *Decamerone* (Decameron), whose ambiance Pasolini set in the Neapolitan countryside, thus requiring a music that reflected a local folksiness removed from Boccaccio's Tuscany; *I racconti di Canterbury* (The Canterbury Tales) of 1972; and *Il fiore delle mille e una notte* (Arabian Nights) of 1974.

For *Teorema* (Theorem, 1968), viewed by many as Pasolini's cinematic masterpiece, the director had chosen large portions of Mozart's *Requiem* and another kind of requiem, the poignant elegy taken from an album first released in 1965 by jazz trumpeter Ted Curson—*Tears for Dolphy*, in memory of saxophonist Eric Dolphy who had passed away in June of 1964.[22] Morricone contributed some dodecaphonic fragments for chamber ensemble. The film, enigmatic but solvable as implied by its title, was an almost wordless essay on alienation, self-absorption, sexual awakening, insanity, and liberation all manifested through the behavior of the members of a bourgeois family and a stranger, albeit a visitor (Terence Stamp), who sexualizes them individually, including housekeeper Emilia (Laura Betti).

The strains of Mozart's *Requiem* offer much symbolism. Morricone's "dissonances" serve to underscore the state of confusion of the father (Massimo Girotti), mother (Silvana Mangano), son (Andrés José Cruz Soublette), and daughter (Anne Wiazemsky) entrapped in their bourgeois predicament. However, it is the desolate sound of Ted Curson's *Tears for Dolphy*, recalling Miles Davis' trumpet sound "following" Florence (Jeanne Moreau) as she wanders the streets of Paris in Louis Malle's *Elevator to the Gallows* (1958), that dominates most of the soundtrack and the character of the housekeeper Emilia, the only character in the film capable, because of her proletarian status, of escaping the family's dysfunction but not before having been sexually awaken by the visitor. Emilia returns to her village, performs miraculous acts and requests to be buried alive while shedding tears in a sort of saintly yet laic ecstasy, like a character out of a Fellini film clinging to a nostalgic moment of otherworldly belief.

Salò o le 120 giornate di Sodoma (Salò, or the 120 Days of Sodom) was completed in 1975, weeks before Pasolini's assassination. For this film, Morricone adapted several pieces of various provenance, composed a derivative swing tune called *Son tanto triste* (I'm So Sad) that is heard on and off throughout the picture, and created an original dodecaphonic work for piano performed at the film's end by a pianist who hurls herself out a window upon finishing playing. Morricone dedicated this piece posthumously to the memory of Pasolini. It was entitled *Addio a Pier Paolo Pasolini*.[23]

However, it was in 1995, when composing the soundtrack for the film *Pasolini, un delitto italiano* by Marco Tullio Giordana that Morricone created some of his most compelling elegiac pages in memory of the November 2, 1975, tragic and violent murder of Pier Paolo Pasolini; a superb homage to the memory of a man he admired so much.

A CHERISHED NOTE

While preparing for the release of the first album of *Dimensioni sonore, musiche per l'immagine e l'immaginazione*, Morricone asked Pier Paolo Pasolini, Giuliano Montaldo, Elio Petri, Gillo Pontecorvo, and Sergio Leone to contribute some thoughts about the function of music in film. Pasolini, the ever-eloquent man of letters, provided Morricone with a remarkable text, which the composer preserved as a personal memento that he loved to read in public on special occasions.[24]

Ultimately, a brief quote from Pasolini's text was published in the booklet accompanying the two-LP album *Ennio Morricone un film una musica*.[25] Then, the full text was printed on the back cover of the LP *Morricone—La musica nel cinema di Pasolini*.[26] It is published here in the English translation prepared by the author:

> Music destined for films can be composed before the film's shooting (like the characters' faces and aspects of the *mise-en-scène*, montage, etc.); however, it is only when music is "applied" to the film strip that it becomes film music. Why? Because the encounter and eventual amalgamation between music and image possess essential poetic characteristics, i.e., empirical ones.
>
> I said that music is "applied" to film; it is true when such an operation occurs, say, at the moviola. But, this "application" can be made in various ways, according to various functions. The principal function is, obviously, that of making explicit, clear and physically present the theme or thread of the film be it conceptual or sentimental. But with music, this process becomes irrelevant since a musical motif has the same moving force whether applied to either application. Moreover, its real function is perhaps that of conceptualizing the emotions (synthesizing them into one motif) and sentimentalizing the concepts. Music has, therefore, an ambiguous function which manifests itself only in the concrete act because it is at once logical and emotional. What music adds to the images, or better, the transformation that it works on the images, remains a mysterious fact difficult to explain.

I can say that, empirically, there are two ways to "apply" music to a visual sequence giving it, therefore, added value: "horizontal" and "vertical." The "horizontal application" occurs on the surface along the moving images; it is a linear and sequential process which follows another linear and sequential process. In this case, the added values are rhythmical, offering new, incalculable, strangely expressive clarity to the rhythmical silent values of the already mounted (edited) images.

The "vertical application" (which takes place technically in the same way), besides following the process of linearity and sequential order, presents a new reality: the principle of depth. Therefore, more than through rhythm, the "vertical application" acts on the meaning itself. The values it adds to the established rhythmical values of the montage are, in reality, undefinable because they transcend cinema by bringing it back to reality, where the source of sound has depth based in reality, not just the illusion emanating from the screen. In other words: cinematic images, taken from reality, thus identical to reality—once impressed on the filmstrip and projected on the screen—lose their real depth, thus assuming an illusory stance, analogous to what in painting is called perspective, although infinitely more perfect.

Cinema is flat, and the depth at which the viewer loses, say, a path leading to the horizon, is illusory. The more poetic the film, the more this illusion is perfect. Its poetry consists of giving the viewer the impression of being inside the matter, in a real depth and not in a flat, i.e., illustrative status. The musical source—unidentifiable on the screen but generated from a physical elsewhere—is constitutionally deep and penetrates the flat or illusory profound images on the screen, opening them up to the confused and limitless depths of life.

A LITTLE *GEBRAUCHSMUSIK*

The intellectual cabaret of German-French import flourished in Milan during the rebellious days of *Scapigliatura* and *Futurismo*, the pre- and post-*fin de siècle* literary/artistic movements, then reached major fruition in the 1960s through the satirical theater of playwright/actor Dario Fo (1926–2016) and the music of Gino Negri (1919–1991) and Fiorenzo Carpi (1918–1997), which ran, side by side, with the experimental music exploitations of Luciano Berio and Bruno Maderna.

The undisputed muse of the Italian intellectual cabaret, though, was singer/actress Laura Betti (1927–2004), who extolled the texts of her often politically and provocative songs/acts from major Italian writers such as Ennio Flaiano, Alberto Moravia, Mario Soldati, Franco Fortini, Goffredo Parisi, Camilla Cederna, Giorgio Bassani, and, above all, Pier Paolo Pasolini, with whom she cultivated a very close relationship which included Betti's important participation in several of Pasolini's films.

Pasolini and Morricone were attracted to the cabaret—one as a Brecht in search of his Weill, Eisler, and Dessau; the other in search of a Muse who could inspire and mediate a middle ground between his commercial and serious music. They pursued their searches individually and together without, however, producing the masterpiece of their desire. Here are some attempts:

Caput Coctu Show (1969–1970) for baritone voice, clarinet, trumpet, bass trombone, percussion, guitar, accordion, mandola, and violin. It is a three-section work on texts written by Pasolini in 1966 upon Morricone's request during the making of *Uccellacci e uccellini*. Regretfully, the piece generated a "linguistic" misunderstanding: the composer wished to create a group of works employing street instruments and expressive modes in the *Gebrauchsmusik* tradition but with a decisively present-day Roman popular idiom. The key word, according to the composer's request, was *posteggiatore(i)*, by which he meant those unsolicited street musician(s) one often finds entertaining customers at dining establishments. Pasolini, on the other hand, identified the *posteggiatore(i)* as those unauthorized car-park attendants helping motorists parking their cars in the congested streets of Rome or any Italian large city. *Caput Coctu Show* resulted in the creation of an anomalous composition that required Morricone to bend his music to an unintended text. The seven-minute composition was performed in Rome's Teatro Centrale in 1971 with Bruno Nicolai conducting.[27]

Another work belonging to the cabaret/*Gebrauchsmusik* genre was *Meditazione orale* (1970), a text written by Pasolini upon Morricone's request for insertion in an RCA LP issued in 1970 to commemorate the first centennial of Rome as the official capital of Italy.[28] Pasolini's text, a critique of the city and its inhabitants' historical and social history, was read and recorded by the poet himself. Morricone's preexisting music commentary included, in fact, the beginning and ending of *Requiem per un destino* (1966), the ballet music noted before whose provenance was the soundtrack of the 1966 film *Un uomo a metà*. Finally, I'd like to mention here a 10-minute sui generis work on Pasolini's texts taken from *Lettere luterane* and entitled *Tre scioperi per una classe di 36 bambini (voci bianche) e un maestro (Grancassa)*. A work for 36 elementary school children and a teacher composed between 1975 and 1988. It was performed for the first time in 1989 at the Università degli Studi in Rome and recorded in 1996.[29]

NOTES

1. The founding members of Nuova Consonanza were Mario Bertoncini, Mauro Bortolotti, Antonio De Blasio, Franco Evangelisti, Domenico Guaccero, Egisto Macchi, and Daniele Paris.

2. For a thorough history of Nuova Consonanza, see two volumes by Daniela Tortora entitled *Nuova Consonanza: Trent'anni di musica contemporanea in Italia (1959–1988)* (Lucca: Libreria Musicale Italiana, 1990) and *Nuova Consonanza: 1989–1994* (Lucca: Libreria Musicale Italiana, 1994). Also, see Valerio Mattioli, *Superonda: Storia segreta della musica italiana* (Milano: Baldini & Castoldi, 2016).

3. Currently, most of the content of these hard-to-find LPs can be heard on YouTube, various websites, and on CDs labeled *1 Schema Records SCEB94400; *2 Schema Records SCEB916CD; *3 GDM4402.

4. This documentary is available in its entirety as "Nuova Consonanza Improvisational Collective" YouTube video, 46:50, November 5, 2014, https://www.youtube.com/watch?v=sUXuZoAMPA0.

5. *Un tranquillo posto di campagna* also featured portions of the groundbreaking *Musica per 11 violini* (1958) albeit identified on the soundtrack playlist as *Distanze per 11 violini, voce di donna e percussione*. Franco Evangelisti and Walter Branchi, with Vincenzo Restuccia and Bruno Battisti D'Amario, performed in the soundtrack of *L'istruttoria è chiusa* (The Case Is Closed, Forget It), a 1971 crime drama by Damiano Damiani, and *Gli occhi freddi della paura* (Cold Eyes of Fear) by Enzo Castellani, both with music by Morricone. In addition, Bruno Nicolai, Bruno Battisti D'Amario, Vincenzo Restuccia, and Walter Branchi participated in the Morricone soundtrack for Elio Petri's *Le buone notizie* (Good News) released in 1979.

6. It appears that compositional behavioral patterns belonging to the first category worried Morricone's older film music colleagues like Carlo Rustichelli and perhaps Morricone's family members who voiced concerns about the composer's eventual loss of income caused by the increasingly hostile reception filmgoers gave to his "challenging" music when applied to the soundtracks of mainstream films. Comments of such a nature, albeit affectionately expressed, were hurtful to a composer of Morricone's sensitivity. Regarding Rustichelli's comment, see Silvio Danese, *Anni fuggenti: Il romanzo del cinema italiano* (Milano: Bompiani, 2003), 330.

7. A Rai-TV production of Teatro del Balletto di Roma that took place on June 17, 1967.

8. On the same award ceremony in Venice, Gillo Pontecorvo's *La battaglia di Algeri* (The Battle of Algiers) won the prestigious Leone d'oro (Golden Lion).

9. Dino Asciolla's original performance can be heard in *Ennio Morricone—Chamber Music*, Virgin Records 7567-90996-2-USA-1988 (Track 6). Morricone's one-page score of the work (Paris: Éditions Salabert, 1973) can be seen as Example 5.1 on page 210 of the volume *Ennio Morricone: In His Own Words* (Oxford: Oxford University Press, 2019).

Morricone featured the sensual sound of Asciolla's viola in many arrangements and film scores, including the soundtrack for the Rai-TV 1982 production *Marco Polo*, a major accomplishment directed by Giuliano Montaldo. The work's main titles cue is scored for viola and orchestra, a concert piece, which if properly developed could have turned into a wonderful companion to Berlioz's *Harold in Italy*. *Marco Polo*'s soundtrack was analyzed by Morricone in his *Comporre per il cinema: Teoria e prassi della musica nel film* (Venezia: Marsilio, 2001), 231–36. Unfortunately, the praiseworthy English version of this volume *Composing for the Cinema: The Theory and Praxis of Music in Film* by Ennio Morricone and Sergio Miceli, translated by Gillian B. Anderson (Lanham, MD: Scarecrow Press, 2013), does not include the wealth of musical examples complementing Morricone's analytical observations. A recording of the *Marco Polo* soundtrack was released as LP Fonit Cetra LPX 108 followed by several reissues by other concerns. A two-CD version of the original soundtrack is available through Rai Trade, Ducale, Intermezzo Media FRT 405 (2004).

10. Both live premiere and subsequent recording were supervised by engineer Paolo Ketoff. In 1992, Morricone supervised a performance by violist Maurizio Barbetti in which the viola parts were performed "live" superimposed on prerecorded playbacks; a safe procedure for preventing technical mishaps yet contradictory to the technical/conceptual nature of the work.

11. Publisher Arnoldo Mondadori launched a series of detective/crime stories in 1929. These very popular books, available for purchase at newsstands, were recognizable by their pocket format and the distinctive yellow cover. A connotation that has remained present to this day.

12. Danese, *Anni fuggenti*, 41.

13. Metro-Goldwyn-Mayer and Schoenberg entered into negotiations in 1937 regarding the soundtrack of a film based on Pearl S. Buck's novel *The Good Earth*. No agreement was ever reached and the project was abandoned, notwithstanding a number of sketches penned by the composer for possible development and application to the film. See Sabine M. Feisst, "Arnold Schoenberg and the Cinematic Art" in *The Musical Quarterly*, vol. 83, no. 1 (Spring 1999): 93–113. Also, for a detailed study about Schoenberg in the United States, see Sabine Feisst, *Schoenberg's New World: The American Years* (New York: Oxford University Press, 2011).

14. In 2005, GDM Music s.r.l. released the Morricone–Nicolai collection as a 6-CD box set in a limited edition for collectors. See GDM 2065 (6). Also, the first volume of Morricone's pieces (*Dimensioni sonore* 1) was made available in 2017 as a single CD under the label GDM 2104.

15. Paolo Ketoff's credits for sound production and effects from this period include the films *L'avventura* (1953), *Planet of the Vampires* (1959), *Hercules Unchained* (1959), *Terrore nello spazio* (1960), *La traviata* (1965), *Pane, amore e fantasia* (1965), and *Africa addio* (1966).

16. The Fonosynth is now on display at the Museum of Musical Instruments in Munich, Germany.

17. See Italo Calvino, *Six Memos for the Next Millennium* [The Charles Eliot Norton Lectures 1985–1986—Harvard University] (New York: Vintage Books, 1993).

18. Sergio Miceli writes that in 1985 Morricone was working on the preliminary sketches for an opera in two acts entitled *Il Musicologo*. Although the Teatro Comunale di Bologna expressed an interest, the project was abandoned. See Miceli, *Morricone, la musica, il cinema*, 281–82, n74. A second operatic effort, *Partenope: Musica per la sirena di Napoli*, opera in one act, composed in 1995–1996 upon libretto by Guido Barbieri and Sandro Cappelletto, although listed in the catalogue of publisher Suvini Zerboni, has yet to be performed/staged despite an interest to produce it on the part of the Teatro San Carlo in Naples.

19. Vincent Youmans' song *Tea for Two* was part of the 1925 musical *No, No, Nanette*. *La cage aux folles* had two sequels: *La cage aux folles II* (1980) and *La cage aux folles 3—"Elles" se marient* (1985).

20. There are many studies dedicated to Pasolini's relations to music and to cinema, however, they all sprout from Roberto Calabretto's volume *Pasolini e la musica* (Pordenone: Cinemazero, 1999).

21. This was 35-minute episode from *Le streghe* (The Witches), a film in five episodes produced by Dino De Laurentiis and directed by Luchino Visconti (*La strega bruciata viva*), Mauro Bolognini (*Senso civico*), Franco Rossi (*La siciliana*), Vittorio De Sica (*Una sera come le altre* [starring Clint Eastwood]), and Pasolini.

22. *Tears for Dolphy* was Track B1 of the LP named after it. Recorded in Paris in 1964, this album was released in the United Kingdom and the Netherlands in 1965 and in the United States in 1975.

23. *Addio a Pier Paolo Pasolini* can be heard in the disc GM 73001 (1983) or GM 803072 (1984) performed by pianist Barbara Vignanelli.

24. The reader may appreciate the composer's composure and humility while reading Pasolini's words in the course of a press conference with director Giuseppe Tornatore that took place in Palermo, Sicily, in 1989. This is available as "The Music and the Movies: Morricone Reads Pasolini," YouTube, 6:30, May 1, 2018, https://www.youtube.com/watch?v=18Ok3PmVrZQ.

25. See RCA Italiana DPSL-10599 (2).

26. Pasolini's text was originally published on the back cover of two LP compilations: *Morricone—La musica nel cinema di Pasolini—*General Music—GM 73001 (1983) and *Les musiques des films de Pasolini—*General Music—GM 803072 (1984), in Italian and French, respectively.

27. This piece, however, was never recorded. Sergio Miceli, who had the opportunity to review Morricone's original manuscript, reached the conclusion that Morricone, dissatisfied with the work's outcome, planned to re-score it with the inclusion of archaic sonorities and urban noises to underline the various characters emerging from Pasolini's text. See Miceli, *Morricone, la musica, il cinema*, 227–29.

28. Due to the often-mentioned pairing of Nino Rota and Ennio Morricone in the Italian film music milieu, we add here that Nino Rota was also commissioned a work to celebrate the first centennial of Rome as Italy's Capital City. Rota's contribution was *Roma Capomunni*, a secular cantata for basso-baritono, coro e orchestra on texts by Goethe, Byron, Horace, and Dante selected by Vinci Verginelli.

29. A commercial recording of *Tre scioperi* was issued in 1996 as New Sounds NANS 062X for the series *Percorsi*.

Chapter Five

Scoring Social Justice

Pier Paolo Pasolini's starry orbit included Greek political dissenter, parliamentarian, and poet Alexandros Panagoulis (1939–1976) and his companion, Italian journalist and political activist, Oriana Fallaci (1929–2006). Panagoulis became a much-discussed figure in 1968 after his attempt to assassinate Greek dictator Georgios Papadopoulos. Imprisonment and torture following the attempt created a grave state of affairs that transformed Panagoulis into a hero/martyr in the eyes of the international Left and an "inconvenient" presence among Greece's mainstream politicians. Panagoulis died in a planned fatal car crash on May 1, 1976, days before he was to reveal before Prime Minister Konstantinos Karamanlis a full dossier accusing many current members of the Greek government of flagrant political corruption and collaboration with the past Papadopoulos regime. He was 36-years-old when he died, mourned and remembered by many through the poetry he penned during incarceration.

Panagoulis' first collection of poems, *Altri seguiranno: Poesie e documenti dal carcere di Boyati* (Others Will Follow: Poetry and Documents of the Prison of Boyati), published in Italian in 1972, displayed introductions by Italian anti-Fascist politician Ferruccio Parri and writer Pier Paolo Pasolini. A second collection, *Vi scrivo da un carcere in Grecia* (I Write from a Prison in Greece), published in Milan after his liberation from prison, was also introduced by Pasolini.[1]

The Panagoulis affair was felt throughout the world as a strong symbol of resistance to any form of oppression. His poetry became a universal song of suffering while Fallaci's caustic journalistic prose reignited the spirit of legions of militants of the 1968 generation. Ennio Morricone, already influenced by Pasolini's personality, fell under Panagoulis' spell at a time when the films bearing his musical signature—*La battaglia di Algeri* (The Battle of Algiers) and *Sacco e Vanzetti* (Sacco and Vanzetti)—were launching a powerful accusation against injustice in all its forms and manifestations.

Morricone celebrated Alexandros Panagoulis the best way he knew how: through music and influence in the recording industry. In fact, RCA Italiana agreed to produce and release an ambitious recording project conceived and coordinated by Morricone: *Alessandro Panagulis "Non devi dimenticare" da "Vi scrivo da un carcere in Grecia."* This LP project, started in 1974 and released in 1979, included the recorded voices of Panagoulis, Pasolini, Adriana Asti, and Gian Maria Volontè reading Panagoulis' poignant poems in Italian "surrounded" by spine-chilling sounds curated by Morricone. In addition, Morricone set to music more verses by the Greek poet in the form of four madrigals for six voices and eight instruments entitled *Canti per la libertà* (Songs of Freedom) and a series of *Improvvisazioni melodiche* (Melodic Improvisations) scored for folk voices, instruments, and electronics. This rare RCA disc formed an opus dense with pathos and stimulating power.[2]

The relevance of this little-known Morricone–Panagoulis testimonial resides in the fact that the composer's sense of responsibility toward human acts of injustice manifested itself in a highly subjective artistic contribution free of the restrictions imposed by commissioned application of his music to motion pictures, including instances pertaining to important films that dealt with pressing labor and civil rights issues, like Elio Petri's 1971 *La classe operaia va in Paradiso* (The Working Class Goes to Heaven or Lulu the Tool) and the 1970 (released in 1971) internationally acclaimed *Sacco e Vanzetti* by Giuliano Montaldo. The latter, a tour de force for actors Riccardo Cucciolla (Nicola Sacco) and Gian Maria Volontè (Bartolomeo Vanzetti), brought a 1920s story to the front burner of American life at the crucible of the turbulent 1960s and 1970s urged on by the combative voice of legendary American singer, songwriter, and activist Joan Baez (b. 1941) singing the riveting *Le ballata di Sacco e Vanzetti* and *Here's to You* that Morricone composed to Baez's own lyrics. The words and music *Here's to You, Nicola and Bart / Rest forever here in our hearts* turned into sweeping street chants as they hailed from some historical revolutionary barricades quite in tune with the turbulent cultural and social climates of the late 1960s in America and the rest of the world.

The Sacco–Vanzetti case is still part of American discourse on jurisprudence well over ninety years after the two Italians were executed in the electric chair accused of robbery and murder they did not commit. The Italian immigrant anarchists, Nicola Sacco and Bartolomeo Vanzetti, were the victims of circumstance aggravated by a wave of implacable bigotry and intolerance directed at immigrants and dissenters in America. Sacco and Vanzetti became the scapegoats for an unprecedented political and legal scandal that took the civilized world off guard and reignited in Europe a cause célèbre about something similar that had happened in France at the turn of the twentieth century: the Dreyfus affair that gave rise to a wave of anti-Semitism of unexpected proportions.[3]

The Sacco–Vanzetti seven-year process, a juridical travesty, made the two Italians the center of a criminal case turned passionate public affair of international proportions that ultimately, wrote Moshik Temkin, "contributed to the decision to execute them rather than offer them the exoneration they deserved. Instead, Nicola Sacco and Bartolomeo Vanzetti became martyrs and folk heroes, champions of the oppressed proletariat in the industrial world of their time and the revival of the Communist International in the 1960s and its anti-American stance, made their case the emblem of the violation of the universal principles of justice, class, ethnicity, and radicalism."[4]

JUSTICE, CLASS, ETHNICITY, AND RADICALISM

Whether the representation of the violation of the principles outlined by Temkin was sufficiently reflected in Montaldo's film and the music Morricone composed for it is a question to be carefully pondered at another time and place. Here, it suffices to say that it would be unfair to engage Morricone in the inexorably Marxist political and musical ideologies professed by his contemporaries Luigi Nono, Luigi Pestalozza, Giacomo Manzoni, Claudio Abbado, Maurizio Pollini, and others who fused music and politics into a constant of their lifelong artistic mission.[5] What must be highlighted, though, is the overwhelming commercial success of Baez's songs that prompted some critics to view them as an attempt to make more palatable the violation of the principles mentioned above.[6] In fact, Baez's songs did eclipse the balance of Morricone's soundtrack which contains some truly beautiful instrumental pieces, like the noble Adagio *Speranze di libertà* for oboe and strings that underscores Sacco's meditative stance. That said, one arrives at the paradoxical conclusion that the Morricone–Baez songs, transcending the life of the film, made statements strong enough to evoke the destabilizing spirit necessary to awaken the people's consciousness despite the reservations harbored by some toward the commercialization of the original application of the songs' text and context.

Cinema and recording industry aside, the tragedy of Sacco and Vanzetti inspired lyrical theatrical expressions on two occasions before and after the release of Montaldo's film, its full soundtrack album, and the many releases of Joan Baez's songs.

In 1960, American composer Marc Blitzstein (1905–1964) began composing a three-act opera, *Sacco and Vanzetti*, for the Metropolitan Opera House in New York at the behest of a commission from the Ford Foundation. Blitzstein's untimely death in 1964 prevented the completion of the work. It was finished by Leonard Lehrman (b. 1949) in the late 1990s but remains to be fully staged to this day.[7]

The second instance concerns American composer/conductor Anton Coppola (b. 1917). He approached the Sacco–Vanzetti story from an Italian-American populist point halfway between Puccini and Broadway. Coppola's overdramatization of the human journey of the two Italian immigrant anarchists was, however, careful not to trivialize their suffering.[8]

Blitzstein, an American Jew, and Coppola, the son of Italian immigrants, let their music—Brecht/Weill-inspired for the former and Puccini for the latter—penetrate the contradictory fabric of prejudicial America of the 1920s with the hope that it would signal closure to the victims of injustice and forgiveness to the perpetrators, perhaps!

FIGHTING FOR ALGIERS

On February 25, 2007, the American Academy of Motion Picture Arts and Sciences' 79th Academy Awards Ceremony awarded Ennio Morricone a special Oscar in recognition of his "magnificent and multifaceted contributions to the art of film music." In the course of the ceremony, actress Jodie Foster eulogized those cinema personalities who had passed away the previous year and, in doing so, she paid tribute to Italian director Gillo Pontecorvo (1919–2006).

Forty years earlier, Pontecorvo received the Golden Lion Award at the Venice Film Festival for *La battaglia di Algeri* (The Battle of Algiers), the film that secured him and, by extension, Ennio Morricone a solid place in the annals of cinema history. In 1995, Gillo Pontecorvo, then-president of the Venice Film Festival, awarded Morricone an Honorary Golden Lion in acknowledgment of his successful career in film music. One more reason, I think, that the 2007 Hollywood Oscar Ceremony became an event more meaningful and poignant for an already emotionally charged Ennio Morricone. His acceptance speech, translated into English by Clint Eastwood, bore witness to that.

Morricone's music for films heavily involved with issues of social justice—like Gillo Pontecorvo's *La battaglia di Algeri* (1966), Giuliano Montaldo's *Sacco e Vanzetti* (1971), Roland Joffé's *The Mission* (1986), and Brian De Palma's *Casualties of War* (1989) among others—have never failed to make viewers reflect on the frailty of the human condition, the perennially ignored lesson of history, and the never-ending quest for change, another constant of human nature.

La battaglia di Algeri continues to inspire an ever-growing amount of historical, literary, political, and cinematic criticism dealing with the events surrounding the birth of Algeria as an independent nation in 1962, the growing pains associated with the concept of nationhood emerging from more than a century of French colonial dominance, and the repositioning of Algeria in the politics of the Arab world vis-à-vis the West. To this day, these have remained subjects of fiery debates in the streets, the academic milieu, and in world affairs.[9]

In 2017, a film by Algerian director Malek Bensmail (b. 1966) added a firm weight of information and fresh perspectives on the 1956–1957 events that led to Algerian independence. Bensmail's new film, entitled *La bataille d'Alger, un film dans l'histoire*, was conceived for "instantaneous" media distribution and realized with funds provided by French and Swiss television organizations.[10] This film recaps, reflects, enlarges, and corrects, when necessary, Gillo Pontecorvo, Franco Salinas, and Saadi Yacef's original film and the important documentary *Gillo Pontecorvo's Return to Algiers* on the making of the historical film shot by Pontecorvo in Algiers ten years after the shooting of the original film.[11]

Bensmail's film, a very important work, is a memoir about the Pontecorvo-Salinas-Yacef film. Those who participated in the film as extras or just as bystanders, the scholars who wrote about the events, the politicians who argued their cases and tended to revise the very history they helped create, and present-day young Algerians who struggle to reconcile past and present while hoping for a better future all offer their reflections. Bensmail's film dispenses, purposely I believe, with the most efficacious element to the perpetuation of memory: music, the iconic Morricone–Pontecorvo soundtrack. Instead, Bensmail cleverly wipes out whatever unintended remnants of westernization, that is, colonialism, such music could have revealed to his 2017 audience in favor of the powerful archeological and genealogical underscoring provided by Algerian percussionist Karim Ziad (b. 1966). That said, the shadowy presence of Morricone–Pontecorvo's *Ali's Theme*, albeit electronically distorted, still looms like a faint memory in the background of the critical text articulated by Algerian rappers Diaz and Rabah Donquishoot heard at the end of the film.[12] The rappers' messages are devastatingly powerful as they mythologize their martyr/hero Ali La Pointe, rip apart postcolonial conditions in Algeria and France, rhapsodize about the soul of the Front de libération national and demand to exchange bombers for dreams, sharp words for the silence kept in their hearts, and how only in the name of Liberty would their dead rest in peace. In our souls, the rappers thunder the fire will burn forever, the news will talk about them from the gutter to the Oscars, however, they exhort their listeners: "Bear it or be mad/or wait for a Peace Nobel Prize/ Don't be afraid Brother!"

The Algerian rappers' litany, though, intentionally or not, further contributes to the mythologization of Pontecorvo's original film.

Since the time of its release, Pontecorvo's film became the pondering locus for terrorism and counterterrorism on the part of extreme groups like the Black Panthers in the United States, the Irish Republican Army, counterinsurgency factions in South America, and even the military strategists at the Pentagon who adopted this film as mandatory viewing for the study of specific urban guerrilla combat tactics developed during the Iraq invasion of 2003. French authorities, on the other hand, banned *La battaglia di Algieri* from public screening for a number of years following its acclaimed international debut. Authorities claimed that the film too favorably portrayed the Algerian cause for independence from France.

Pontecorvo's conceptual and directing masterpiece was highly praised in cinematic circles and the music heard on its soundtrack made composer Morricone, known at the time mostly for his music to Sergio Leone's Westerns,[13] assume the mantle of the subliminal deliverer of the film's message. His music soothes the pains caused upon millions of combatants and collateral casualties alike by the colonial project, the revolutions ensued against it, and the counterrevolutions aiming at crushing the uprisings. If the music Morricone contributed to this film served to soften or intensify the representation of suffering, then it must be regarded as a remarkable achievement. In the world of film music, Morricone's *La battaglia di Algieri* and *The Mission* became the models many composers considered when scoring films or documentaries dealing with terrorism and social justice.

Patterns for scoring social justice emerged from this film's soundtrack cocredited to Morricone and Pontecorvo insomuch as the director, an aspiring musician and once a student of French-Polish atonal composer René Leibowitz (1913–1972), contributed motifs and musical details in support of his idea of "symphonic structure" upon which he intended to build a film narrative coherent with actual events and within the social politics taking place in the tumultuous context of the time: the 1960s. Pontecorvo's musical credentials should not be overlooked. The director was not a dilettante. He thought of himself as a "melodist" who needed the essential collaboration of professionals like Carlo Rustichelli, who coauthored the soundtrack of his first success *Kapò* (1959), and Morricone for *La battaglia di Algieri*. That said, the musical relationship between Pontecorvo and Morricone changed beginning with their next two films, *Queimada!* (Burn! 1969) and *Ogro* (Operation Ogro, 1979), whose soundtracks were, ultimately, the sole responsibility of Morricone. *Queimada!*, a fictional anticolonialist film starring Marlon Brando, was enriched by an exotic, jungle-evoking soundtrack anticipatory of the general tone of *The Mission*. Pontecorvo shot the film while using as temporary track a recording of the *Missa Luba*, consisting of the Latin Mass text set to traditional Congolese music by Father Guido Haazen. A highly successful 1958 Philips recording by Les Troubadours du Roi Baudoin was used in several films, including Pasolini's *Il Vangelo secondo Matteo* (The Gospel According to St. Matthew, 1964). So, in the end, Morricone was compelled to compose for Pontecorvo a work whose appeal and purpose rivaled the popular hybridity of *Missa Luba*, the director's first choice.

IN THE NAMES OF BACH AND FRESCOBALDI

In an interview granted to Emmanuel Deonna on January 25, 2019, for *Jet d'encre* (see note 11 for the website link), Malek Bensmail declared that "the aesthetic qualities of the film—the neo-realistic influence, especially the graininess—as well as the music (Ennio Morricone and Johann Sebastian Bach) also contributed to the film's success. *The Battle of Algiers* has thus been able to win over many audiences across frontiers."

It is very telling that Algerian filmmaker Bensmail mentioned Bach in the same breath as Morricone as the former was the coauthor of the music soundtrack instead of Pontecorvo, notwithstanding the fact that Bach's music is heard in the film for only twenty-six seconds consisting of the first four measures of the instrumental introduction to Johann Sebastian Bach's *St. Matthew Passion*. In fact, the brief Bach quotation stops, like a tragic epitaph, before the entrance of the chorus which would have sung Picander's verses *Come, you daughters, help me to lament, / See—Whom?—the bridegroom, see him—How?—like a lamb*, foretelling, in effect, the essence of the story.[14]

What is the meaning of Morricone and Pontecorvo's choice of Bach's instrumental, abstract music for underscoring what was happening on the

Figure 5.1. Johann Sebastian Bach. St. Matthew Passion BWV 244. First four measures from the orchestral introduction to Part 1. Graphic rendition created by author.

screen: an Algerian man's betrayal under duress, who revealed to the French military the location of the hiding place of Ali La Pointe and his three companions?

The breathtaking close-ups of Mahmud, Hassba, Little Omar, and Ali hiding in the dark behind a tiled wall in a house in the Casbah are at the core of the entire film and indeed the entire fight for independence since the Ali La Pointe persona became the story's sacrificial lamb. Did Pontecorvo want to turn Ali into a symbolic Marxist Christ? I believe he did as this was not a novel concept for him. Pontecorvo had planned, in fact, a full film on the subject entitled *I tempi della fine* (Time of the World's End).[15] That said, Pontecorvo was very familiar with Pier Paolo Pasolini's Marxist views of the life of Christ and the use of Bach's *St. Matthew Passion* in the films *Accattone* (The Procurer or The Scrounger, 1961) and *Il Vangelo secondo Matteo* (The Gospel According to St. Matthew, 1964). Plausible reasons then that prompted the use of the Bach quotation at the beginning of *The Battle of Algiers*.

Bach's tragic yet hopeful allusion is heard over a caption that reads "Algiers 1954," the time when the film's events begin to unfold. We hear veiled strains of Bach's music in the organ rendition of the sadness motif at 1:35:17, and, again at 1:46:48 in the form of solemn, subdued orchestral chords all in conjunction with the betrayal of Ali La Pointe. Then, we watch the scrolling of the opening credits dissolving to a camera pan across Algiers from the European quarter to the Casbah, the two gravitational theaters of action of the story, underscored by a fundamental cue Morricone carved out of Girolamo Frescobaldi's *Ricercare cromatico post il Credo*, a thematic cell that morphed into those forms of life—developments and variations—negated to the Bach quotation.[16]

Morricone introduces the Frescobaldi motif in the form of a Bartók-sounding barrage of hammered notes on the low register of the piano reinforced by the double basses. The result is an ostinato that supports the steady advancing, syncopated rhythmic pulsations played by military snare drums, trumpet(s), and winds. The trumpets are heard first as from a distance, then, engaged in military calls fanfare-like with French horns and lower brass responding as their marching crescendo approaches our ears. Meanwhile, the Frescobaldi motif unravels in canonical and augmentation patterns causing asymmetric disruptions aiming at an optical penetration of the cinematic flat screen in order to draw the viewer into a sonic fragmented vortex foreshadowing the story about to unfold as we see on screen French paratroopers storming across the whole field of vision. The military aggressive stance "searching" for Algerian subversive combatants creates a mental audio/visual counterpoint with the fugal intentional structure of Frescobaldi's *Ricercare*.

Figure 5.2. Girolamo Frescobaldi. Ricercar cromatico dopo il Credo from Fiori Musicali, Op. 12 (Venice, 1635). Graphic rendition created by author.

Figure 5.3. Girolamo Frescobaldi. Ricercar cromatico dopo il Credo from Fiori Musicali, Op. 12 (Venice, 1635). **Motif used by Ennio Morricone.** Graphic rendition created by author.

At 7:11 into the film, a voice-over, a reminder of this film's debt to *Casablanca* (1942), calls the viewer's attention to Ali La Pointe, the film's Algerian protagonist.[17] The voice-over recites Ali's police rap sheet while the film scrolls episodes of his troubles with the law and the consequent apprehension that led him to incarceration in the ill-famed Barbareusse detention facility.

There, Ali and other inmates witness the execution by guillotine of an Algerian dissident. The episode determines Ali's fate to become the visceral leader of the Algerian struggle for independence.

A flashback takes us to the close-ups of Ali, Mahmud, Hassba, and Little Omar hiding behind a tiled wall seen at the beginning of the film. We are now at 9:08 into the narrative when we hear for the first time a motif being played on an Algerian flute: *Ali's Theme*.

Figure 5.4. Ali's Theme. Graphic rendition created by author.

This motif, conceived by Pontecorvo and Morricone, is heard several times during the film. It represents not only Ali and the cause he stood for, but the Algerians' mood swings from sad to hopeful inherent into the motif's undulating melodic intervals of major and minor thirds.

The Arab atmosphere created by *Ali's Theme* shifts at 9:21 when Morricone launches an extended dirge-like piece bearing a vaguely Elgarian flavor. It is played by a string orchestra punctuated by the starry, plucking sound of an amplified harpsichord. This theme will be heard time and time again as a quasi-commentary following random acts of terrorism inflicted by the Algerian rebels upon the French and/or the European emigrant community and by the French police/military reaction against their defiance. It is, in effect, the composer and the director's wish to create a common theme of sufferance, a requiem for humanity. Other noticeable applications of this theme occur at 1:35:37–1:36:46 played by a full church organ, and through the end credits played by the solo amplified harpsichord superimposed to *Ali's Theme* in a rather symbolic conciliatory gesture. However, by stark contrast to the starry, plucking sound of the harpsichord we are reminded about the aggressiveness and culpability—should one embrace that point of view—of the French military when we hear at 24:47–26:55 the isolated notes of the Frescobaldi motif angrily plucked/stopped on what sounds like an electric guitar or a dehumanized electronic devise like Morricone's favorite sinket.

The original music of this Morricone–Pontecorvo soundtrack can be divided in three principal motives: the Frescobaldi motif, *Ali's Theme*, and the Requiem. Morricone applies these motives in a variety of ways, semantically and technically, isolated and in combination with routine incidental music ranging from French pastoral neo-classicism like the cue marked *Matrimonio clandestino* (A Wedding Ceremony) at 22:48, film-noir moments, a touch of Respighi's modal *Pini presso una catacomba* at 1:08:55, and a caricatural military march as a sarcastic allusion to the very colonial *Marche Militaire Française* from Saint-Saëns' *Suite Algérienne* op. 60. These and more anthological touches are evidenced by connecting all the cues available in the recording of the complete soundtrack to the chapters listed in the 2004 DVD special edition of the film.[18]

A RAP FOR ALI AND A CHA CHA FOR REBECCA

Notwithstanding the great contribution brought to this film by the Morricone–Pontecorvo soundtrack, even greater importance assumes the diegetic and diegetic-implied music/sounds we hear throughout the film: the sound of the *qraqeb*, or krabebs, consisting of the rhythmical shaking of metal castanets and the pounding of the *tabl*, a large-frame drum hit by wooden sticks often combined with the ululations of Arab women and the Muezzin chanting. The combination of these sounds turns into a tremendous heart pounding emanating from the indigenous collectivity every time the French military retaliate against them. It becomes, indeed, the spinal sound of the entire film. However, *La battaglia di Algeri* represents the story of two cities, two peoples, two religions, and the clear-cut divisiveness between occupiers and occupied and their complex cultural interconnectedness. The Algerian insurgent population is powerfully underscored by the sound panoply mentioned above, but it is, also, the rest of Algiers' residents, the non-military, non-militant, often not even French people who paid a high prize by being blown up by strategically planted explosives. They too have their own diegetic music in this film although not viscerally atavist but superficially, passive, ephemeral whose provenance is a well-visible jukebox surrounded by dancing young people, people chatting at café tables, including a toddler enjoying his ice cream cone; a much-discussed (and censured in some cases) heart-wrenching shot. The music we hear is *Rebecca*, a 1959 hit cha cha performed by Les Chakachas, a Belgian-based group of Latino soul studio musicians singing "Hasta mañana Rebecca / Espero que tú no vas a olvidar." Ironically and tragically, there was no *mañana* for these young people; their lives were taken away in a matter of seconds.

SUNKEN OBOE

It appears that in 1953, Ennio Morricone set to music a beautiful hermetic poem written in 1932 by Nobel laureate Salvatore Quasimodo (1901–1968); *Oboe sommerso* (Sunken Oboe). Morricone's setting, scored for baritone and five instruments (oboe, English horn, viola, cello, and piano), was never performed in public or published. However, one wonders whether a key episode in the film *The Mission*—Father Gabriel playing the oboe "immersed" in a rain-soaked jungle—could have brought to the composer's mind a glimmer of youthful memories.

The Mission, the epoch-making 1986 film directed by Roland Joffé, produced by Fernando Ghia and David Puttnam, and starring Robert De Niro and Jeremy Irons, is an outstanding example of cinematic narrative that crosses cultural and historical boundaries through a vivid depiction of the conflicting worlds of Spanish and Portuguese colonialism in South America, the plight of the Guarani tribespeople, and the Catholic Church's perpetual mingling with politics and quarelling with the liberal-leaning Jesuit Order. Ennio Morricone was particularly involved in writing *The Mission*'s soundtrack. Overwhelmed by a narrative drenched in social unjustice and human cruelty yet permeated by Christian forgiveness, the composer recounted many times how he came to terms with the moral dilemmas he faced when scoring the story—a story that has no winners but self-sacrificing heroes, a story that ends in desolation with the heartbreaking sight of a Guarani child holding a broken violin, apparently asking the world why it needs another holocaust.

The composer was approached by a dear friend of his, Italian producer Fernando Ghia (1935–2005), who asked him to compose the music for a film based on the compelling fate of the San Carlos Mission in the Guarani Iguazú Falls area, one of the thirty utopian, self-governing cooperative communities established by the Jesuits from 1607 to 1768 in territories across Paraguay, Argentina, and Brazil.

Ghia's sources of inspiration were historical as well as empirical: *The Jesuit Republic of Paraguay*, an award-winning documentary film shot in 1978 by the Jesuit priests Robert McCowen and C. J. McNaspy based on a large study by Philip Caraman,[19] was followed by *The Lost Cities of Paraguay*, an evocative book written by the already-mentioned McNaspy and illustrated with splendid photographs by J. M. Blanch, another Jesuit Brother.[20] Also, it was possible that Ghia had knowledge of the classical study by Eberhard Gotheim (1853–1923), *Der christlich-sociale Staat des Jesuiten in Paraguay*, available in Italian translation since 1928,[21] or a well-known theater piece by Fritz Hochwälder, *Das heilige Experiment*.[22] As well, Ghia—an indefatigable world traveler—was surely aware of a large project initiated by a Paraguayan, Argentinian, and Brazilian committee of experts aimed at the preservation of the ruins of the thirty Jesuit missions, eight of which were located in Paraguay, fifteen in Argentina, and seven in Brazil. In fact, a project called "Itinerary of the Missions" had been on the table since the early 1970s. It included all the elements of artistic and natural values to be found in the Jesuit Province of Guayrá.[23] Conjectures aside though, in 1975, Ghia secured the collaboration of British novelist, director, and scriptwriter Robert Bolt (1924–1995) with whom he had worked on several films and television productions and whose screenplay credits included *Lawrence of Arabia* (1962), *A Man for All Seasons* (1966), and *Dr. Zhivago* (1965). Bolt wrote a novel, *The Mission*, and a screenplay that Ghia pitched to Paramount to obtain development money.[24] It seems that in order to persuade Bolt's participation, Ghia invited him to South America to tour the ruins of the great Jesuit missions and the breathtaking falls, which are more than forty feet taller than Niagara Falls. "Bolt sat and stared at them for an hour, until the light was gone," Ghia recalled in a 1986 interview with the *Los Angeles Times.* Then Bolt said, "It's as if for a day God had decided to be a production designer."[25] Although Paramount's executives approved of Bolt's script in the first place, later they withdrew any financial involvement, perhaps doubting the film's commercial viability. While producing other movies, Ghia continued his quest for funding *The Mission*. In 1984, he finally came to an agreement with Goldcrest Films & Television Ltd. of London and with producer David Puttnam, who brought in Roland Joffé as director.

Puttnam had already seen Bolt's script while in Los Angeles in 1977 and had remained deeply moved by its compelling narrative. He and Ghia met periodically thereafter to discuss the realization of the film. Years later, with the film in full production, a series of irreconcilable disagreements between the two men—Puttman based in London and Ghia on location in Colombia—left Puttnam with no alternatives but to step in and take over the whole production, repositioning Ghia to the role of coproducer. During sixteen weeks of shooting on location in Colombia and at the Iguazú Falls, the cast and crew—while dealing with scorching temperature, high humidity, tropical rains, floods, deadly reptiles, infesting mosquitoes, and widespread dysentery—was also plagued by continuous financial contretemps caused by Goldcrest that made the situation in Colombia reach anguishing proportions. Finally, though, the last of Goldcrest's money arrived just before the end of *The Mission*'s shooting.[26]

When *The Mission* finally reached theaters in 1986, the *Times*' Charles Champlin, who had first reported Fernando Ghia's plans for it in 1975, wrote that the Italian producer had told him after the movie's release, "The thing that's important to me is that there should be social commitment. We provide entertainment, but we should also provide food for thought."[27]

In fact, it was this very notion of social commitment brought up by Ghia that left Morricone profoundly overwhelmed and confused after screening the film's rough cut for the first time in London. He recalled:

> I was aware that when I went to London to view the film at Ghia's invitation, Puttnam had already tried to get in touch with Leonard Bernstein for compos-

ing the score, but apparently, his query remained unanswered. However, at the end of the screening I felt so torn by what I saw that I decided against scoring the film. Following some strong convincing on Ghia's part, I accepted the task, immersed myself in reading what I could about the story's historical period and devised a musical scenario based on the mystique of the Trinity. It consisted of three principal thematic "mandatory conditions" provided respectively by the sound of the oboe (as one of the protagonists plays indeed the oboe), the human voice (the Guarani people sing "solo" and choral pieces), and a kind of illusory ethnic music which is heard in combination with the other two components only during the end credits as a collective musical fresco.

Father Gabriel's oboe playing signified that he was the bearer of a specific instrumental post-Renaissance experience connected to its time. So, I had to compose a theme for the oboe that sounded sort of constrained at the beginning, a theme based on the "supposed" notes and embellishments that the apparently "untrained" fingers that Father Gabriel (Jeremy Irons) employed in his oboe playing simulation. I preferred to follow this procedure in order to offer the viewer the illusion of some kind of synchronization especially in the moment when the "frightened" Jesuit priest tried to play surrounded by a large group of suspicious and menacing Guarani. Then, the theme is heard performed with full accompaniment.[28]

This theme, known as *Gabriel's Oboe*, not only generated the melodic and harmonic cells that formed the other themes in the film's soundtrack, but acquired great significance insomuch as Father Gabriel emerged in the film as the true utopian who searched for an impossible coexistence between the opposite factions. He remained and marched with the Guarani toward death

Figure 5.5. Gabriel's Oboe, from *The Mission*. Author's collection courtesy of Sergio Miceli

while holding high the holy emblem of his own faith. Furthermore, his gaze searched for the mortally wounded Rodrigo (Robert De Niro) almost as a priest/soldier alter ego in order to die together. In other words, *Gabriel's Oboe* was no longer a generic message of Christian faith but the musical materialization of a sentiment of love more than civilization.

There have been speculations surrounding the origin, or rather the type, of Baroque oboe repertoire that could have inspired Morricone to compose his oboe theme. The very pragmatic explanation reported in the quote above makes a lot of sense, but one cannot help noticing by pure coincidence a certain sonic resemblance between Morricone's theme and the *Adagio per oboe, violoncello, archi e organo* by none other than Domenico Zipoli (1688–1726), an Italian Jesuit musician active in the missions of South America. This Adagio, a transcription by Francesco Giovannini of one of Zipoli's *Toccate per l'elevazione*, had been recorded by French oboist Pierre Pierlot in the 1970s and was part of a best-selling Erato LP entitled *Le charme du houtbois*. Were Morricone and/or Ghia aware of its existence?[29] On the other hand, one may detect an antecedent of *Gabriel's Oboe* in the main theme of *Il deserto dei Tartari*, a film by Valerio Zurlini made in 1976.

Regarding the liturgical component of his "Trinitarian" set, Morricone pointed out that "in order for me to be historically pertinent to the period in question, I composed *Conspectus Tuus*, a four-part motet in the style of Palestrina. This type of setting would have reflected better the traditions of Church music after the Council of Trento (1545–1563) as imported by the Jesuits into South America."

Figure 5.6. Conspectus Tuus, mm. 1–7 from *The Mission*. Author's collection courtesy of Sergio Miceli.

Another important liturgical four-part composition heard in the film is *Ave Maria Guarani*, first sung solo by a Guarani boy in a poignant scene that took place before an assembly of religious and political notables, then as a choral procession toward martyrdom at the end of the picture. Morricone recalled the following:

> In this film, I had a problem that did not manifest itself right away but little by little without any warning coming from the director or producer. The film takes place in a Catholic Mission of South America in the first half of the eighteenth century. There are some priests who teach music to the Guarani, imparting them what was practiced in Europe at that time. Furthermore, the Jesuit in charge of the mission plays the oboe. There was a liturgical context to consider still connected to the Western tradition but in this case referred to sacred music. Then, for ambiance reasons consideration needed to be given to the music of the Indians, an ethnic music. I wanted to mix the three ideas which I did throughout the film, preferably in pairs; oboe and ethnic music—ethnic music and liturgical choir. Only at the end, I combined all three components, something I had anticipated since the beginning, and thus I did without much struggle—with the idea of interpreting the union of the priests with the Guarani. The technical involvement of the music is similar to the communion between the people. For me, reaching this solution was greatly satisfactory, because it was difficult to find a way so autonomous yet combining the three components.
>
> I would like to point out something else like the Bass Drum that plays out of tempo. I wanted it so as a reminiscence of the cannon shots heard during the battle, however, there is another reason; every time I heard Argentinian or Brazilian music but above all Argentinian that casual (or perhaps was not casual) sound out of tempo was always a constant characteristic. So, I used it as a touch of authenticity.
>
> The fusion of the three themes in the last scene is heard when a little Guarani girl rescues a broken violin from the river before she climbed on a canoe. That "Requiem Glorioso" was dubbed by Fernando Ghia *On Earth as It Is In Heaven*, a verse from *The Lord's Prayer*.[30]

From a technical standpoint this finale turned into an extraordinary achievement that broke new frontiers in the field of film music; the folklike chorus and congas repeating a rhythmic ostinato pattern in 3/8—aspects of which Morricone said he had previously used in the 1974 film *Il sorriso del grande tentatore* by Damiani—superimposed on the motet *Conspectus Tuus* sustained by the strings, thus making it, in effect, an eight-part chorale in 4/4, and *Gabriel's Oboe*, which was recorded separately and then dubbed in the mix for major impact, have remained emblematic in the world of popular culture of anything representing forms of "coming together."

The paramount role of music in *The Mission* becomes clear since its opening scenes; the long shot of the San Carlos Mission that shows Father Ga-

Figure 5.7. Finale, mm. 1–4 from *The Mission*. Author's collection courtesy of Sergio Miceli.

briel imparting a group violin lesson to Guarani children while the Pontifical envoy Altamirano's (Ray McAnally) voice-over "the noble souls of these Indians incline towards music. Indeed, many a violin played in the academies of Rome have been made by their nimble and gifted hands" as he writes his report to the Pope is portentous of things to come. In fact, it is Father Gabriel who communicates with the Guarani above the Iguazú Falls through the sound of his oboe. Then again, Altamirano's voice is heard admonishing that with an orchestra, the Jesuits could have subdued the whole continent.

Finally, we see a dispute taking place in Asunción between Altamirano, the Spaniard Don Cabeza (Chuck Low), and the Portuguese Don Hontar (Ronald Pickup) regarding the partition of the Guarani land. To foster their cause on behalf of the Guarani's freedom, the Jesuits proudly display a youth who sings a melody (the *Ave Maria Guarani* mentioned before), which provokes the following testy exchange between Altamirano and Don Cabeza:

Altamirano: Don Cabeza, how can you possibly refer to this child as an animal?

Don Cabeza: A parrot can be taught to sing, Your Eminence.

Altamirano: Yes, but how does one teach it to sing as melodiously as this?

These examples are sufficient to establish that in *The Mission* music does not appear as common language, but as Sergio Miceli very appropriately stated in *Morricone, la musica, il cinema* (1994), 282–83, it constitutes

> a paradigmatic constant whose potential is developed by Morricone by transforming it into a syntagmatic constant, one unique exchange coin, a vehicle for individual growth and collective spirit applied from time to time to Christian and laic mystiques or both at the same time, in a moment of illusory fusion (a message rendered explicit by Morricone), which in the Jesuits discourse as well as the director's point of view, clearly manifested in the last scene in which a surviving naked young girl collects an object from the water; the frame shows a three-armed candelabra and a violin, but without hesitation she picks up the latter; a demonstration that for her innocent instinct the violin as an object does not betray but could encompass the values of the former, not vice versa.

ALEKOS, ALI, AND GABRIEL

There is no doubt that taken as a whole this film constitutes a great example of idealism, the same ideals perhaps that could explain Morricone's emotional reaction and initial decision not to compose music for the film. Aside from the film's multiple narratives, one could affirm that Morricone found in *The Mission* an unequivocal expression of musical symbolism drenched in idealism that as we know has always accompanied him in each of the genres he dedicated his art to. The decision to give a musical voice to the film was a sort of challenge in attempting a formalization of those semantic values already expressed so efficiently by Joffé.[31]

This chapter, while discussing the music Morricone composed for some particularly special films, focuses on personalities who lost their lives in tragic circumstances. Pier Paolo Pasolini was assassinated on November 2, 1975, by a mob of youngsters at Ostia, Rome's main seaside town. His body was found reduced to a pulp. Nicola Sacco and Bartolomeo Vanzetti were executed on the electric chair on August 23, 1927, before cheering crowds on one side and dismayed people on another; Alexandros Panagoulis was assassinated by his political opponents through a well-orchestrated automobile crash on May 1, 1976; Ali La Pointe's body was blown up by French paratroopers on October 8, 1957; Father Gabriel walked himself to martyrdom, holding high a crucifix, at the hands of the Spanish and Portuguese colonial powers and the Church of Rome. Of course, Father Gabriel was a fictitious character. The real victims of that massacre in the jungle were the Guarani people. Their survivors rebuilt a jungle community that "progress" and industrialization promoted by the governments of Paraguay, Argentina, and Brazil dispersed again and again. The Guarani have no land to call their own, only cherished memories of 1985 when a film crew descended upon them to make a film about them and with them in it. It was the only time in their long history that the Guarani became relevant as a people; video cassettes of their "Mission" are jealously treasured by the now elders, and Ennio Morricone's music rings in their ears—it is their music now![32]

NOTES

1. See *Altri seguiranno: Poesie e documenti dal carcere di Boyati* (Palermo: S. F. Flaccovio, 1972); *Vi scrivo da un carcere in Grecia* (Milano: Rizzoli, 1974). For English versions of the above, see Alexandros Panagoulis, *Collected Poems* (Athens: Papazissis, 2002). Also, see Oriana Fallaci, *Un uomo: Romanzo* (Milano: Rizzoli, 1982) published in English as *A Man* (London: Arrow, 1993). Panagoulis was also the subject of the 1973 documentary by Silvano Agosti entitled *Altri seguiranno* (Others Will Follow) and various docudramas made for television.

2. See RCA LP 31238.

3. French army captain Alfred Dreyfus was convicted of treason for allegedly selling military secrets to the Germans in December 1894. Dreyfus was Jewish.

4. See Moshik Temkin, *The Sacco-Vanzetti Affair: America on Trial* (New Haven, CT: Yale University Press, 2009). Also, see *Sacco and Vanzetti*, a film-documentary

by Peter Miller produced in cooperation with Crawford Communications, Atlanta, GA, 2006.

5. Particularly illustrative of this point are Luigi Nono's masterworks *Intolleranza 1960*, *La fabbrica illuminata* (1964), *Como una ola de fuerza y luz* (1972), *Al gran sole carico d'amore* (1975), and ultimately, the monumental *Prometeo—Tragedia dell'ascolto* (1984–1985). See the recently published anthology *Nostalgia for the Future: Luigi Nono's Selected Writings and Interviews*, edited by Angela Ida De Benedictis and Veniero Rizzardi, with a foreword by Nuria Schoenberg Nono (Berkeley: University of California Press, 2018).

6. Miceli, *Morricone, la musica, il cinema*, 250.

7. For a full account of Lehrman's completion of Blitzstein's opera, see "ljlehrman artist in residence," accessed April 18, 2019, https://ljlehrman.artists-in-residence.com/SaccoAndVanzetti.html.

8. For a discussion of Coppola's operatic effort, see Eugene H. Cropsey, "*Sacco and Vanzetti:* An American World Premiere," *The Opera Quarterly*, vol. 19, no. 4 (Autumn 2003): 754–80.

9. For a comprehensive bibliography on *The Battle of Algiers*, see "The Battle of Algiers—Nicholas Harrison," accessed February 15, 2018, http://www.oxfordbibliographies.com/view/document/obo-9780199791286/obo-9780199791286-0140.xml. See also a study by Alan O'Leary available as "*The Battle of Algiers* at Fifty—Film Quarterly," accessed February 20, 2018, https://filmquarterly.org/2017/01/10/the-battle-of-algiers-at-fifty-end-of-empire-cinema-and-the-first-banlieue-film/.

10. INA (Institut National de l'Audiovisuel), France, and RSI (Radiotelevisione Svizzera di lingua italiana), Lugano.

11. See the following links: (1) "La Bataille d'Alger, un film dans l'histoire-Film-documentaire.fr," accessed March 10, 2019, http://www.film-documentaire.fr/4DACTION/w_fiche_film/51213; (2) "Beautiful Memories of 'The Battle of Algiers'—Jet d'Encre," accessed March 10, 2019, https://www.jetdencre.ch/beautiful-memories-of-the-battle-of-algiers, and *Gillo Pontecorvo's Return to Algiers* in Disc Three (The Film and History) of *The Battle of Algiers*, The Criterion Collection, 2004.

12. The rappers were involved as authors/performers in a 2016 video montage comprising the most salient moments of their anticolonial cause in Pontecorvo's film. There, the rap featured in Bensmail's film is heard extensively. See it at "Donquishoot Ft Diaz—La Bataille d'Alger—2016," YouTube, 5:45, June 9, 2016, https://www.youtube.com/watch?v=66CRPKsuiKg.

13. It appears that Gillo Pontecorvo had seen only *Per qualche dollaro in più*.

14. Picander was the pseudonym of German poet Christian Friedrich Henrici, known for having authored the librettos of Bach's cantatas composed in Leipzig and that of the *St. Matthew Passion*.

15. See Joan Mellen, "An Interview with Gillo Pontecorvo" in *Film Quarterly*, vol. 26, no. 1 (Autumn 1972), 2–10, and other interviews Pontecorvo granted throughout his career.

16. *Ricercare cromatico post il Credo* was published in the collection *Fiori musicali* (Venice, 1635). Originally, it was part of the Offertory from the Mass of the Apostles. The Apostles of Jesus were: Simon Peter, Andrew, James (son of Zebedee),

John, Philip, Bartholomew, Matthew, Thomas, James, Thaddeus, Simon the Zealot, Judas Iscariot, and Matthias. Judas betrayed Christ by revealing his whereabouts to the Roman authorities and then took his own life. Matthias replaced Judas as the 12th Apostle. In this film, the Algerian man who revealed the location of Ali's hideout to the French military shows repentance for his betrayal by attempting to hurl himself out of a window in a desperate screaming fit. Ennio Morricone claimed in many interviews and in his own autobiography (see Chapter 3, n25) that the Frescobaldi motif was a youthful obsession of his; one cannot help noticing the serendipitous application of the symbolism carried by this motif in *The Battle of Algiers*' soundtrack. While a student at Santa Cecilia in 1955, Morricone composed *Variazioni su un tema di Frescobaldi* for 12 instruments; the theme in question was indeed the Frescobaldi motif. In 1976, Morricone used Variation 5, newly orchestrated, in the film by Bertolucci *Novecento* (1900). The cue was identified as *Autunno 1922*. Furthermore, this Frescobaldi motif appears in his important *Gestazione per voce femminile e strumenti, suoni elettronici preregistrati e orchestra d'archi ad libitum* composed in 1980. Ultimately, Morricone dedicated an entire work to the Frescobaldi motif. See *Roma (pensando al "Ricercar Cromatico" di Girolamo Frescobaldi) per soprano, voce recitante maschile e ensemble* (2010), which will be discussed in Chapter 6.

17. Ali La Pointe was the nickname of Ali Hammar (1930–1957), guerrilla leader of the Front de libération national (FLN). He was interpreted in the film by non-professional actor Brahim Haggiag.

18. See the complete Morricone–Pontecorvo film soundtrack available on GDM CD Club 7028 (2005), which includes six tracks missing in the original RCA Italiana LP SP8019 (1966), vis á vis the film's chapters listed in *The Battle of Algiers*, The Criterion Collection, 2004.

19. Philip Caraman, *The Lost Paradise: The Jesuit Republic in South America* (New York: Seabury Press, 1976).

20. C. J. McNaspy and J. M. Blanch, *Lost Cities of Paraguay* (Chicago: Loyola University Press, 1982). Furthermore, it appeared that McNaspy collaborated as a consultant to the making of *The Mission*.

21. Venezia: La Nuova Italia Editrice, 1928.

22. Hochwälder's 1941 very successful play was presented in two made-for-television films in 1966 (Rainer Wolffhardt) and 1985 (Wolf Kaiser). Also, it was translated into English as *The Strong Are Lonely* and staged in New York on Broadway for seven performances in 1953.

23. For details see *The Jesuit Missions of the Guaranis*, an ICOMOS-UNESCO Publication (Buenos Aires: Manrique Zago Ediciones, 1997) and *Il sacro esperimento del Paraguay: Dagli scritti del gesuita Antonio Sepp*, with an introductory essay by Francesco Barbarani (Verona: Cassa di Risparmio di Verona, Vicenza, Belluno e Ancona, 1990). Morricone's autobiography (see Chapter 3, n25) states on page 334 (Italian edition) and 235 (English edition) that he purchased a copy of this book in order to familiarize himself with historical facts. However, the publication date of this book, 1990, makes it an unlikely source of information in the middle 1980s. It was probably Ghia who informed him about Fritz Hochwälder's *Das heilige Experiment* and/or the television films derived from it.

24. Robert Bolt, *The Mission* (New York: Jove Publications, 1986).

25. Quoted by Dennis McLellan in the *Los Angeles Times* of June 11, 2005, under "Fernando Ghia, 69; Italian Film, TV Producer Known Best for 'Mission.'"

26. Andrew Yule, *Fast Fade: David Puttnam, Columbia Pictures, and the Battle for Hollywood* (New York: Delta Publishing, 1989), 151.

27. Quoted by Dennis McLellan in the *Los Angeles Times* of June 11, 2005, under "Fernando Ghia, 69."

28. Ennio Morricone in conversation with the author, May 10, 2013. See Franco Sciannameo, "Ennio Morricone at 85: A Conversation about His 'Mission,'" *The Musical Times*, vol. 154, no. 1924 (Autumn 2013): 37–46.

29. For information on Zipoli see Pedro José Frías, *Memorias del músico Zipoli* (Córdoba: Ediciones Olocco, 1975). Zipoli's *Adagio per oboe, violoncello, archi e organo*, trascrizione di Francesco Giovannini was published in Paris by Costallat in 1964.

30. Ennio Morricone to author, May 10, 2013. Quoted by Sciannameo in "Ennio Morricone at 85."

31. Following *The Mission*, Morricone and Joffé collaborated on films like *Fat Man and Little Boy* (1989), *City of Joy* (1992), and *Vatel* (2000).

32. See two powerful film-documentaries about the plight of the Guarani: *We Are the Indians*, a film by Philip Cox and Valeria Mapelman (Journeyman Pictures, 2007) and *La terra degli uomini rossi* (Birdwatchers), a film by Marco Bechis (Rai Cinema, 2009). Also, Disc 2: Omnibus: The Mission, part of *The Mission*—Two-Disc Special Edition issued by Warner Bros. Home Video in 2003, is highly recommended.

Chapter Six

Legacy

In May and June 2019, oceanic crowds gathered in the Verona Arena, Rome's Terme di Caracalla, and Lucca's Mura storiche to bid farewell to nonagenarian composer Ennio Morricone as he conducted his music in public for the last time.

This series of concerts, intended as a testimonial to Morricone's 60-year "Walk of Fame," concluded on the 29th of June in Lucca, Giacomo Puccini's birthplace—more than a coincidental symbolic gesture considering that, in the popular imagination, Morricone trails Puccini closely.

Giacomo Puccini died in 1924, at nearly age sixty-six, leaving his last opera, *Turandot*, unfinished. The opera, completed by Franco Alfano, premiered in 1926, two years after Puccini's death and two years before Morricone's birth.[1]

Aspects of Puccini's legacy continue to be debated in scholarly circles amid speculations that terminal illness was not the only reason preventing the composer from bringing *Turandot* to completion. Some argue that Puccini's procrastination was caused by concerns he had that the orientation of his predictable stylistic and artistic choices was excluding him from the modernist discourse of the time. He felt an opera composer of his stature could not afford to assume such a problematic stance, hence the *Turandot* impasse.

In 2001, Luciano Berio (1925–2003) brought to light his completion of Puccini's *Turandot*. The new score developed Puccini's modernist streaks that Berio detected in the extant sketches and provided the opera with an open-ended conclusion that musically and philosophically advanced the concept of Puccini's last work. The newly completed *Turandot* then became part of Berio's progressive thinking, and by association, the thinking of many Italian composers of his generation, including Ennio Morricone, Italy's favorite living musician and, again, in the popular imagination, Puccini's heir.[2]

The value of the cinematic and commercial music Morricone composed during the past sixty years is indeed qualifiable and quantifiable by means of cultural analytical methodologies and computational economics. It is the balance of his output, the so-called musica assoluta that remains embroiled in a paradox pitting the Morricone music everybody loves against the Morricone only a few appreciate.

The earlier chapters of this book have pointed out Morricone's aesthetic views of his creative duality and the necessity to divide his music into two categories: "musica applicata" (discrete compositions applied to a particular function such as cinema) and "musica assoluta" (compositions based on continuous coherence of content and form) in addition to works that, by design or coincidence, have fallen somewhere in between.

This chapter, entitled "Legacy," highlights a number of representative works in each category beginning with a panoramic view of the large expanse of the composer's "musica applicata" taking as its flag bearer the 2007 recorded anthology of songs entitled *We All Love Ennio Morricone*, a celebratory homage that followed the American Academy of Motion Pictures' presentation of Oscar for his career achievements in film music.[3]

This considerable recording effort, coordinated by Ars Latina and Sony Classical, involved a legion of artists, audio engineers, and producers who convened from all over the globe for a virtual celebration of Morricone's music, the "musica applicata" obliquely mentioned by the composer in his Oscar acceptance speech, but overlooked by its English simultaneous translation as there was no other type of Morricone's music to globally celebrate but that which he composed for the screen.

WE ALL LOVE ENNIO MORRICONE

The repertoire of this famous collection includes film music cues provided with lyrics and presented as songs that indicate well, in terms of quantifiable popularity, the various stages of the composer's commercial achievements. The program begins with Canadian star Celine Dion singing *I Knew I Loved You* with lyrics by Alan and Marilyn Bergman and orchestral accompaniment arranged by Quincy Jones. The tune of this song is *Deborah's Theme* from the film *Once Upon a Time in America* (1984), which was used in Sergio Leone's film to underscore, through its melodic circularity, the undetermined cinematic passing of time implied by the film's narrative. Opening this celebratory album with this theme is appropriate as it conveys a sense of timelessness to Morricone's walk of fame through songs.

Dion's song is followed by another arrangement prepared by Quincy Jones, this time for keyboardist Herbie Hancock: the main title music including the iconic "coyote's cry" from *The Good, the Bad and the Ugly* (1966). Then, Bruce Springsteen plays on the guitar a rendition of *Jill's Theme* from *Once Upon a Time in the West* (1968), followed by tenor Andrea Bocelli's offer of a change of pace and style singing a retrofitted 1996 recording of *Conradiana*, a song with lyrics by Francesco De Melis and Emma Scoles, orchestrated and conducted by Morricone. This song's provenance is the incidental music composed for the 1996 made-for-Italian-television, three-part series *Nostromo* after Joseph Conrad's novel. It is then the turn of the group "Metallica" to perform "The Ecstasy of Gold," a favorite cue from *The Good, the Bad and the Ugly*, followed by cellist Yo-Yo Ma playing the main theme from Giuseppe Tornatore's 2000 film *Malèna*, a track borrowed from the 2004 CD *Yo-Yo Ma Plays Ennio Morricone* described in the pages ahead.

Now, having achieved a high level of artistry with Ma's contribution, the album aims even higher by reaching the golden point of its remarkable compass: Renée Fleming, one of the greatest sopranos of our time, singing *Come Sail Away*. This song showcases the incomparable voice and sensitivity of the famous soprano in a melody extracted from the orchestral score Morricone composed for the 1990 made-for-television film *Voyage of Terror: The Achille Lauro Affair*, a German-American-Italian-French docudrama about the 1985 hijacking off the coast of Egypt of the "Achille Lauro" Italian cruise ship by a group of Palestinian terrorists and the assassination of the disabled Jewish-American passenger Leon Klinghoffer.[4] This tune, with lyrics by Leonie Gane and Amii Stewart became the song *Come Sail Away* featured in the CD *Pearls: Amii Stewart Sings Ennio Morricone*.[5] It was recorded by Renée Fleming specifically for the *We All Love Ennio Morricone* collection at Sony Studios in New York upon the orchestral base originally recorded by Morricone in Rome. Thus, the particular technological creation of this recorded track—never performed live by Fleming and Morricone together—assumes a rare value.

An instrumental rendition of *Gabriel's Oboe* from *The Mission* (1986), recorded live in 2006 in Tokyo by Morricone, oboist Carlo Romano, and the Roma Sinfonietta, opens the CD's second half followed by the tune known as *Conmigo* from the 1969 successful film by Giuseppe Patroni Griffi *Metti, una sera a cena* (One Night at Dinner or Love Circle), featuring Eumir Deodato at the keyboard. Then, multitalented Portuguese singer/songwriter Dulce Pontes interprets the theme song, borrowing verses by Federico Garcia Lorca, from the film *La luz prodigiosa* (The End of a Mystery, 2003) directed by Miguel Hermoso. Overtime, Dulce Pontes became a featured guest of many Morricone concerts around the world.

Trumpet showman Chris Botti follows Pontes with a version of the celebrated theme song from the 1994 film *Love Affair* starring Warren Beatty and Annette Bening, much admired for their virtuoso performance in *Bugsy* (1991), a milestone film soundtrack mentioned later in this chapter. The next selection, *Je changerais d'avis*, presented by the group "Vanessa and the O's," headed by Parisian artist Vanessa Contenay-Quinones, refreshes the 1968 spirited song entitled *Se telefonando* brought to international success by Italian trailblazing singer Mina. The song, originally written for the 1966 Italian television show *Aria condizionata*, is the oldest selection in the *We All Love Ennio Morricone* tribute. Moving forward, a heartfelt rendering of *Lost Boys Calling* by singer Roger Waters and guitarist Eddie Van Halen pays tribute to one of Morricone's favorite films, *La leggenda del pianista sull'oceano* (The Legend of 1900) directed by Giuseppe Tornatore in 1998, while the haunting sound of the kaval, a Rumanian type of wooden flute, characterizes *The Tropical Variation*, another piece from *Nostromo*.

Track 15 brings us back to the film *Voyage of Terror: The Achille Lauro Affair* with another leading theme song *Could Heaven Be*, originally included, like *Come Sail Away*, in the CD *Pearls: Amii Stewart Sings Ennio Morricone*. It is interpreted here by American operatic star Denyce Graves. This performance, like Fleming's *Come Sail Away*, was recorded in two different places: Ms. Graves' voice at Starke Lake Studios in Orlando, Florida, and the orchestral base conducted by Morricone at Forum Music Village Studios in Rome. The same Roman recording studios hosted a performance by eclectic Japanese violinist Taro Hakase and the Roma Sinfonietta conducted by Morricone performing an "Aria" from the popular 1989 Italian television miniseries *I promessi sposi* (The Betrothed) after Alessandro Manzoni's masterpiece of Italian literature first published in 1840. Morricone provided this miniseries with abundant music composed in Verdi-mannered operatic style as shown by the piece in this anthology entitled *Addio monti* (Farewell to the Mountains), inspired by a famous literary passage in Manzoni's novel.

Finally, no piece could have been more appropriate to close this tribute album than Morricone's beautiful, concise arrangement for piano and orchestra of the "Love Theme" from *Nuovo Cinema Paradiso* (Tornatore, 1988). The composer's "signature" is affixed at the conclusion of the album by pianist Gilda Buttà, a longtime collaborator of the composer.

MORRICONE'S ELUSIVE SONGBOOK

It is important to reiterate that Ennio Morricone was not a songwriter in the great tradition of Irving Berlin, Kurt Weill, George Gershwin, Cole Porter, Robert Sherman, or Stephen Sondheim, to mention a few, nor did he practiced the song as a favorite short form like Nino Rota who could improvise one at the piano at any time. In fact, Morricone authored only a few songs, the many others were adaptations from film and television themes as the reader can see from the titles included in the 1998 and 1999 four-CD collection surreptitiously labeled *The Ennio Morricone Songbook (Canto Morricone)*. This release came as a surprise even to the composer when he spotted and purchased a set at a New York record shop.[6]

Appendix 2 provides an annotated list of the artists and repertoire represented in the four-CD collection. It is a fair cadre of the popularity level achieved by many film cues/songs composed by Morricone from 1962 to the late 1990s and the progress these songs made toward the creation of a commercial musical product that became associated with the "Made in Italy" brand as it was a musical continuum running parallel to the phenomenal attention paid worldwide to Italian cinema, cuisine, design, fashion, architecture, and the automobile industry since the postwar reconstruction years.[7]

Regarding the Morricone songbook, I would like to single out some songs that made a strong impact on the culture of the time and/or were influenced by it. See for instance, *Se telefonando* (vol. 1 #3) composed in 1966 for Mina, the darling of Italian television and jukebox aficionados. The song, programmed in the appealing variety television show *Aria condizionata*, received immediate success and maintained a high position on the viewers/listeners' approval charts season after season. On the opposite spectrum of volume 1, famous opera star Anna Moffo, host of her own show on Italian television in 1964 and 1967, and actress in films criticized for their explicit sexuality, interprets a gorgeous song entitled *In fondo ai miei occhi* (#8). It was extracted from the soundtrack of the film *Menage all'italiana* (Menage Italian Style, 1965) in which Moffo played the role of Giovanna. *Menage all'italiana* was a satirical, quasi-musical comedy about the near impossible chance of obtaining a divorce in Italy at the time, a situation that induced the film's ingenuous male protagonist Alfredo (Ugo Tognazzi) to be married concurrently to eight wives. Ultimately, Alfredo fakes his own death in order to escape from such an impossible situation. At the funeral of the purported Alfredo—a poor devil found dead with an unrecognizable face—the "real" Alfredo, present at the ceremony, flirts anew with his first wife/widow Giovanna (Moffo) amid a rocambolesque series of contretemps.[8]

If the success of several *commedie all'italiana* (comedies Italian style) was not enough, the bombshell of Sergio Leone's *Western all'italiana* exploded in plain air, forever changing the panorama and the history of the traditional American Western.[9] Volume 2 of Morricone's songbook is dedicated in part to songs composed for some of the *Western all'italiana*/Spaghetti Western films or extracted from them quite efficaciously by gifted singers like Peter Tevis, Maurizio Graf, Christy, and Raoul as noted in Chapter 3.

The second half of volume 2 is dedicated to *The Ballad of Hank McCain* (Tracks #11–13) from the film *Gli intoccabili* [The Untouchables] (Machine Gun McCain, 1969), a Las Vegas mobster thriller starring John Cassavetes as Hank McCain, a robber just released from prison, and Peter Falk as mobster Charlie Adamo. Morricone's soundtrack, a prophetic training exercise for Brian De Palma's *The Untouchables* of 1987, presents moments of interest and a forceful ballad heard at key points in the film—*The Ballad of Hank McCain* delivered with much gusto by British balladeer Jackie Lynton. This film, directed by Giuliano Montaldo could not be in starker contrast with *Sacco e Vanzetti*, the masterpiece Montaldo and Morricone worked on next. In fact, the last six tracks of this recording feature *The Ballade of Sacco and Vanzetti* and *Here's to You* sung by Joan Baez, and Georges Moustaki singing *Marche de Sacco et Vanzetti*, a French version of *Here's to You*. The inclusion in this collection of many tracks of the Baez–Morricone songs is a clear demonstration of the immediate popularity they gained since first heard.

Volume 3—The 70s, illustrates a shift in Italian commercial music preferences toward a Brazilian mood strongly advanced by innovative artists like Antonio Carlos Jobim and João Gilberto and his wife, singer Astrud Gilberto, famous for Jobim's iconic song *The Girl of Ipanema* and the consequent bossa nova mania the invaded the pop music world. Tracks #11 and #18 feature Astrud Gilberto in two Morricone songs extracted from the 1971 film *Gli scassinatori* (The Burglars) directed by Henri Verneuil. Other tracks are dedicated to two historical song collections especially arranged for Milva (*Dedicato a Milva da Ennio Morricone*), which includes five songs with lyrics by Maria Travia (Mrs. Morricone). The second anthology was arranged for French singer Mireille Mathieu hailed as the new Édith Piaf. One can detect in Morricone's arrangements a reactionary stance toward the easy-listening, lounge music of Latin American import by contrasting it with a decisively Italianate melodramatic flare.

The fourth and last CD reflects the beginning of the composer's stylistic turning point evident, in terms of soundtracks, in films ranging from *State of Grace* (Joanou, 1990) and *Bugsy* (Levinson, 1991) to *The Hateful Eight* (Tarantino, 2015). Also, this portion of the songbook reveals Morricone's return to the art of arranging that served him so well in the 1960s—this time, though, for the exclusive enhancement of his own compositions. See, for instance, the 1990 remarkable album *Amii Stewart Sings Morricone* from which five tracks are included in the songbook collection.

THE TURNING POINT

The history of film music is replete with details about cues morphing into symphonic or chamber ensemble repertoire pieces. From Erich Wolfgang Korngold to John Williams, John Corigliano, Hans Zimmer, and Danny Elfman, among many others, concert works incorporating or based on thematic material originally intended for films have gained a life of their own thanks to the patronage proffered upon them by famed players like Jascha Heifetz who commissioned and launched the Korngold Violin Concerto and composers/conductor like Bernard Herrmann and John Williams who assembled viable concert suites from the scores of their legendary films.

Morricone appears to have reached a turning point in his film music activity with the scores for *State of Grace* (1990) and especially *Bugsy* (1991), which, aside from including sparse incidental music, consists of a large orchestral cue which is, in effect, a psychological portraiture in the form of a symphonic synthesis of Benjamin Siegel's character known as Bugsy, a real-life mobster boss whose brutality and ambition knew no limits. Yet, Siegel was the visionary who, ultimately, created the hotel-casino Flamingo and made what we know today as the Las Vegas Strip, a phantasmagoric reality that sprouted out of the desert against all odds. The *Bugsy* score made Morricone feel comfortable with the course his film music was taking by achieving a workable creative compromise that blurred his self-imposed distinction between "musica applicata" and "musica assoluta"; it was just Morricone's music.

When around the time of *Bugsy* Morricone began conducting concerts of his best-known film music, his newly acquired level of artistic self-confidence permitted him to offer synthetic samplings of hybrid compositions suitable for large, indiscriminate audiences. Programs performed worldwide by full symphony orchestras, massive choruses, and large technical crews, often at outdoor venues to accommodate audiences of several thousands, were carefully and somewhat didactically organized by genre as shown by the following program offered at the Philharmonie im Gasteig in Munich on October 20, 2004.[10] It consisted of:

Life and Legend
The Untouchables (Brian De Palma, 1986)
Deborah's Theme from *Once Upon a Time in America* (Sergio Leone, 1984)
The Legend of 1900 (Giuseppe Tornatore, 1998)
Nuovo Cinema Paradiso (Giuseppe Tornatore, 1988)

Single Pages
H2S (Roberto Faenza, 1968)
The Sicilian Clan (Henri Verneuil, 1969)
Love Circle (Giuseppe Patroni Griffi, 1969)
Uno che grida amore from *Love Circle*
Maddalena (Jerzy Kawalerowicz, 1971)

Sergio Leone: Modern Film Legends
Cockeye's Song from *Once Upon a Time in America* (1984)
The Good, the Bad and the Ugly (1966)
Once Upon a Time in the West (1968)
Giù la testa (1971)
Ecstasy of Gold from *The Good, the Bad and the Ugly* (1966)
Making Love (*Canone Inverso*) (Ricky Tognazzi, 1999)

Socially Committed Cinema
Investigation of a Citizen above Suspicion (Elio Petri, 1970)
According to Pereira (Roberto Faenza, 1995)
The Working Class Goes to Paradise (Elio Petri, 1971)
Casualties of War (Brian De Palma, 1989)

Tragic, Lyrical, Epic . . .
The Desert of the Tartars (Valerio Zurlini, 1976)
The Mission (Roland Joffé, 1986)

In this setting, the process of stylistic integration is particularly evident in a section of *Canone Inverso* (1999), a film about a love affair between a concert pianist and a violinist for which Morricone composed fragments of a double concerto for piano, violin, and orchestra. This work, decisively cast in a light romantic idiom, shifts sporadically into complex contrapuntal—thus the title—expressionistic mode bringing to mind Alban Berg's *Kammerkonzert* for piano, violin, and thirteen winds (1923–1925). A missed opportunity, perhaps, on the part of Morricone who could have developed this checkered score into a full-length, cohesive concert work. Another piece bearing a strong elegiac character in the Munich program is the substantial cue heard toward the end of *Casualties of War*.

Ennio Morricone has always been a near-professional chess player. Discrete and continuous content-and-form pieces are placed strategically in his programs. Take, for instance, the tune known as *Chi mai* from the film *Maddalena* (1971) that, aside from its original and clever instrumental or vocal syllabication of the melodic theme, becomes de rigueur in programs performed in the United Kingdom as British audiences are very familiar with the tune adopted as title theme for the highly successful nine-episode BBC television series *The Life and Times of David Lloyd George* broadcast in 1981 and rerun many times since. In Prague, a concert performed in the austere Smetana Hall on July 15, 2018, was advertised as a program of "Musica Assoluta" to fit, perhaps, the gravitas imposed by the concert venue. However, according to reports, the repertoire appeared to have alienated part of the "unprepared" audience,[11] notwithstanding the inclusion of music derived from films like *The Bible*, *Bugsy*, *H2S*, *Love Circle*, *Baarìa*, and the television docudrama *Giovanni Falcone, l'uomo che sfidò Cosa Nostra*.[12] That said, the Prague audience was supposed to understand that the presence of stylistic integration was placed there as a gradual introduction to more challenging listening experiences provided by *Vuoto d'anima piena, cantata mistica per flauto, coro e orchestra* (2008), *Sicilo e altri frammenti* (2007), and *Ostinato ricercare per un'immagine* (2009), which completed the balance of the program.

A comparative study of Morricone's concert programs, a task beyond the scope of this book, would probably reveal much data about the programming/marketing strategies adopted by Morricone in the course of the past twenty-five years or so. At this juncture though, I want to conclude the first part of this chapter by focusing on a rather unique exemplar of stylistic integration: the content of a CD entitled *Yo-Yo Ma Plays Morricone*.

YO-YO MA PLAYS MORRICONE

Morricone's walk of fame, aside from the symbolic star with his name etched in the historic sidewalk on Hollywood Boulevard, is surrounded by "stars" each bright enough to obfuscate anything and anybody in their surroundings, albeit in an inherently ephemeral manner. However, it is the very scarce presence of starring personalities whose light radiates mostly from within that is noticeable in Morricone's long career. Opera divas like Anna Moffo, Renée Fleming, Denyce Graves, or Katia Ricciarelli made only cameo appearances; world-famous conductors Riccardo Muti and Antonio Pappano conducted his concert works perhaps on one occasion. So, it is even more remarkable that Yo-Yo Ma, one of the greatest cellists ever, collaborated with Ennio Morricone in the making of a superlative CD unequivocally entitled *Yo-Yo Ma Plays Morricone*.[13]

The program consists of arrangements for cello and orchestra of Morricone's best-known film cues which sound like encores great players bestow upon their audiences following the success of a demanding performance. However, Yo-Yo Ma is known for being a most versatile and adventurous artist. He has performed and recorded with many—exploring uncommon repertoires derived from various ethnographic cultures—so he feels very comfortable with Morricone's whirlwind voyage through favorite films like *The Mission*, cues from the cinema of Giuseppe Tornatore and Sergio Leone, including an idiomatic solo cadenza preceding *Cockeye's Song* (Once Upon a Time in America), and themes from Brian De Palma's *Casualties of War* and *The Untouchables*. The former deserves a commendation as it becomes, in Ma's hands, a powerful elegy that brings to mind great moments in music like Adagietto, Cavatina, and Adagio for Strings. Cues from the film *Moses* and the made-for-television epic *Marco Polo* are revived by Ma in the style of Ernest Bloch's *Schelomo* (1916), a milestone of the cello literature and one of the artist's signature pieces.

The program closes with two gems from an otherwise forgotten film, *La califfa* (Lady Caliph), a 1970 production. One may think of this recorded anthology as a book of cello meditations on Morricone's music and wonder whether Ma was made aware of the composer's intensely expressive movement for cello and orchestra belonging to the *Secondo Concerto per flauto, violoncello e orchestra* (1984–1985), a work I describe in the pages ahead as part of this chapter's intent to provide the reader with thoughts about selected works Morricone composed for the concert hall.

SELECTED CONCERT WORKS

Disregarding chronological order to follow an intuitive sense of discovery, it is helpful to begin an excursion through Morricone's concert music with *Gestazione per voce femminile e strumenti, suoni elettronici preregistrati e orchestra d'archi* (1980),[14] a complicated work, which—without evoking the myth of Oedipus, Freudian theories, or making references to Pasolini's *Edipo Re* (Oedipus Rex, 1967)—requires an introductory note before taking a listen of it.

The work's title appears in print in two iterations as *Gestazione* and *Gesto-Azione*, meaning gestation and gesture-action. *Gestazione* is the title printed in the published score followed by the motto *alla donna-madre nella rabbia ignara* (to the woman-mother in [her] oblivious rage) and the notes B-flat, A, C-flat, B-flat, A, C-flat, which are a permutation of the Frescobaldi motif used in *La battaglia di Algeri* (see Chapter 5). The literary motto, on the other hand, refers to a text written by Emanuele Giovannini, a Morricone protégé, entitled *Nella rabbia ignara*, a story about a man who wishes to return into his mother's womb to become her lover and, consequently, the father of his unborn child, a situation that places man, woman, and child in a perennial state of gestation.

Gesto-Azione appears on the back cover of the LP RCA RL 31650 (1982) as the work's subtitle in reference to its possible theatrical representation. In fact, *Gesto-azione* was presented as a ballet in January 1984, in a version incorporating *Requiem per un destino* (1966) (see Chapter 4) and selected readings from Giovannini's text.[15]

By the time Morricone completed *Gestazione*, the concept of setting to music the birth of the universe, the world, or the human race had illustrious historical precedents, including Morricone's own *Creazione* (Creation) from the trial score for the film *The Bible* mentioned before; the works of Giacinto Scelsi, George Crumb, and György Ligeti, among others; and the *Universe Symphony* by the greatest prophet in modern music, Charles Ives, who left his symphony unfinished because it needed to remain so. At any rate, Morricone's exploration of sound cosmogony as represented in *Gestazione* can be heard, based on the only available recording thus far, as an essay in sonic proxemics envisioned and realized by the composer and sound engineer Sergio Marcotulli at Studio Forum in Rome in 1982.

In fact, *Gestazione* begins with barely perceptible tingling sounds that grow slowly into forming a cosmic drone whose provenance is from as far as the listener's auditory system can detect; however, its acoustical approach gradually reveals signs of forms of life through stuttering phonemes morphing into unified sound bodies punctuated upon reaching their full phase of development by four resounding electronic thuds; a clear allusion to Beethoven's Destiny motto and Ives who quoted it obsessively. This episode ushers in the female voice vocalizing electronically altered sounds created around the pitches of the Frescobaldi motif. The result is an amalgam of spasmodic birth pains and orgasmic pleasure. Then, the instruments join the sonic magma with the solo viola and the solo double bass leading the attack of razor blade–like sounds produced by the string orchestra whose inner dynamics and advancing proximity to the listener's ear become ever more intense until it invades fully the listener's auricular space by provoking an unbearable fit of sonic violence. Then, it begins to retreat, deflate, and vanish into the nothingness it came from. A lone, isolated electronic deaf explosion signals the end of the piece.

In general terms, Morricone's *Gestazione* is a conceptual work that takes the shape of an emotional sonic gesture like a roller coaster with no beginning or ending but a "romantic" climax at the middle point of the gestural arch.

The next piece, *Secondo Concerto per flauto, violoncello e orchestra* (1984–1985), takes us out of the conceptual and more in the realm of the processual in line with *Concerto per orchestra* (1957), now listed in the composer's catalogue as *Concerto per orchestra no. 1*.

Twenty-eight years separate the two concertos with the in-between being a period of time in Morricone's career that fulfilled unpredictably the advice Petrassi gave his student upon graduation. As stated in Chapter 1, Petrassi cautioned Morricone against taking any commitments for two years because something remarkable was going to happen to him in the course of that period, enigmatic advice that Morricone did not fully comprehend at the time. However, he clung to Petrassi's words as if to an indispensable life vest to float upon the perilous waters he was about to navigate.

Almost three decades later, Morricone dedicated his *Secondo Concerto* to Goffredo Petrassi as he had done in 1957, with the preceding *Concerto per orchestra*.[16] Stylistically though, these concerti could not be more different: massive the first, evanescent the other, based on the juxtaposition of the minimal thematic essence rotating around three pitches: A, B-flat, C-flat (B-natural), which correspond, again, to the Frescobaldi motif discussed before and the unusual instrumental ensemble of 3 oboes, 3 clarinets, 3 bassoons, 3 French horns, 3 trumpets, 3 trombones, a trio of harp, celesta, marimba, 12 violins I, 12 violins II, 12 violins III, and another group of three including 15 violas, 13 cellos, and 10 basses. These elements foreshadow numerological perplexities while creating a sonic panoply that allow the solo flute and cello to weave, Escher-like, textured patterns of refined and intriguing quality. The result is a 26-minute piece that, although flowing in one continuous movement, shows a division into three sections. In fact, section one, marked *Liberamente mosso*, is scored for flute and orchestra amounting to a huge solo cadenza that showers the listener's ears with a "liquified" concentration of Berio's *Sequenza I* (1958), Petrassi's own *Concerto per flauto e orchestra* (1960), Maderna's *Musica su due dimensioni* for flute and electronics (1958) and *Serenata per un satellite per flauto e suoni elettronici* (1969), which all bear the imprimatur of flautist Severino Gazzelloni (1919–1992), the foremost master of the instrument at the time, especially in avant-garde music circles.

Liberamente mosso had a predecessor in some manuscript sketches for flute and harpsichord composed in 1980 and a successor in *Cadenza per flauto e nastro magnetico* (flute and electronics), which Morricone composed and dedicated to virtuoso Roberto Fabbriciani in 1988, then a rising star in the flute world.[17] This section of *Secondo Concerto* reaches some of its more delicate sonorities between measures 458 and 472 through a concerted dialogue between flute and the trio of harp, celesta, and marimba. See measures 458 to 462 in the following example.

Then, it fades into a metrically spaced distribution of the pitches B-flat, A, C-flat, B-flat, A, C-flat followed by a triple piano pedal on the note A which paves the way for the inconspicuous entrance of the solo cello.

Figure 6.1. Secondo Concerto per flauto, violoncello e orchestra, mm. 458–462. Ennio Morricone (Suvini Zerboni, 1991). Courtesy of Edizioni Suvini Zerboni.

The second section, marked *Liberamente*, scored for solo cello and orchestra, is an extensive, dramatic soliloquy delivered from a hypothetical Hamletic platform considering that, according to Sergio Miceli, the concerto's original manuscript bore the title É! (It is!) in confirmation or rebuttal of something the composer did not wish to make public.[18]

In fact, the third section of the concerto, a five-minute, fast virtuosic drive featuring both soloists, engages them in a game of dialogues between themselves and with other solos or groups in the orchestra as shown in Figure 6.2. Midway through the movement though, the solo instruments cease their agonistic dialogue and converge into a univocal orchestral crescendo and accelerando culminating in an avalanche magically stopped by a speared fortissimo; a forceful affirmation of the É! mentioned before as a fist pounding with which Ennio Morricone wanted to assert his presence in the Italian milieu of contemporary music.

That said, let us remind ourselves that *Secondo Concerto* was composed to celebrate Petrassi, so perhaps he was the É! in question.

If *Secondo Concerto*'s É! may leave us perplexed, *UT* in the title of next piece is an exemplar of clarity. *UT per tromba in Do, timpani—grancassa e orchestra d'archi* (1991) is, by all means, a concerto for trumpet in C. Its title *UT* refers to the first of the Latin syllables *Ut, Re, Mi, Fa, Sol, La, Si* placed at the beginning of each line of the first stanza of Guido of Arezzo's Hymn to St. John the Baptist as a mnemonic device to learn the tones of the scale.[19] *UT* bears the dedication *A mio padre, a Francesco Catania, a Mauro Maur e a tutti i miei amici trombisti*, meaning his father (Mario Morricone), colleague Francesco Catania, the work's commissioner Mauro Maur, and all of his trumpet-playing friends. A restricted circle, unless Morricone meant to say that all trumpet-playing were indeed friends of his.

Mario and Ennio Morricone played trumpet in various dance club bands in Rome during the postwar years and Ennio fulfilled the requirements for a trumpet degree at Santa Cecilia; Ennio continued to perform on the trumpet

Figure 6.2. Secondo Concerto per flauto, violoncello e orchestra, mm. 579–683. Ennio Morricone (Suvini Zerboni, 1991). Courtesy of Edizioni Suvini Zerboni.

for as long as his arranging and composing activities permitted. It was expected of him to compose a concerto for his instrument in a style that was not only eminently idiomatic but approachable, despite its advanced modernist challenges.[20]

UT is a piece lasting slightly over fifteen minutes played without interruptions but clearly divided in sections: the opening five minutes establish the "physical," almost aggressive, presence of the solo instrument emerging from stretches of hallucinatory sounds provided by the string orchestra and mysterious touches of timpani and bass drum. Then, the strings settle into the familiar Morriconian static pedal mode preparing the solo trumpet to soar in a quasi-blues improvisation ending with a very brief cadenza at about eight minutes from the start of the piece. *UT* ends with another slow section characterized by the transformation of the static pedal mode into a lunar luminous soundscape provided by the strings employing some extended techniques. Here the solo trumpet indulges in a series of enunciations recalling moments from Ives' *The Unanswered Question* (c. 1908).

The lyrical intervention of a solo violin joined by the solo trumpet at twelve minutes and 28 seconds joins the two solo instruments engaging in a most delicate dialogue disappearing slowly into silence, thus concluding this section of an attractive trumpet concerto despite the lack of a brilliant finale expected in a solo concerto aspiring to enter the contemporary trumpet concerto repertoire. That said, we have to come to grips that composing a full-fledged trumpet concerto was not, perhaps, the composer's intention. His intention was, though, to compose two more concertos for orchestra.

Composed in 1991, *Terzo Concerto per chitarra classica amplificata, marimba e orchestra d'archi* belongs to the chamber orchestra repertoire since it requires a string ensemble of only 3 first violins, 3 seconds, 2 violas, 2 cellos, and 2 double basses. It is a guitar concerto with marimba obbligato more than a double concerto as the guitar is assigned indeed a more preeminent role including a solo cadenza borrowed from an early work *Quattro pezzi per chitarra* composed for Mario Gangi in 1957.[21]

The idea of a modern guitar concerto—delicate, transparent, and somewhat echoing exotic flavors of Iberian provenance—attracted several composers beginning with the Spaniard Joachím Rodrigo (1901–1999) who achieved international fame with his *Concierto de Aranjuez*, composed in 1939 for guitar virtuoso Regino Sainz de la Maza, and *Fantasía para un gentilhombre* (1954), written for the great Andrés Segovia. Also, Segovia inspired another milestone of the guitar concerto repertoire—the *Concerto in D* by Mario Castelnuovo-Tedesco (1895–1968), composed in 1939 under particular circumstances. Castelnuovo-Tedesco's guitar concerto was, in fact, the composer's farewell to his beloved Tuscany before emigrating to California in order to escape the "enforcement" of racial laws enacted by the Italian government against its own citizens of Jewish descent.

Rodrigo and Castelnuovo-Tedesco's very popular guitar concertos and the tenacity of world guitar virtuosi headed by Segovia inspired several composers to write in the genre including the Italian Ennio Porrino (1910–1959), a well-known moderate modernist composer of Sardinian heritage active in Rome. Porrino's *Concerto dell'Argentarola per chitarra e orchestra* (1953), written for Roman guitarist Mario Gangi, was a work Ennio Morricone had knowledge of as Gangi was indeed a popular, versatile player and a dear friend of his.[22] In fact, as stated above, Gangi was the dedicatee of *Quattro pezzi per chitarra* whose second piece, *Allegro scherzoso*, became the guitar cadenza heard in *Terzo Concerto*.

The marimba as a solo instrument inspired Italian-American composer Paul Creston [Giuseppe Guttoveggio] (1906–1985) to write a very attractive concerto for marimba and orchestra (1940) that quickly became a marimba player's favorite, together with a more recent concerto for marimba and strings (2005) by neo-melodic French composer/percussionist Emmanuel Séjourné (b. 1961).

Morricone's inventive pairing of marimba and amplified guitar in a rather advanced scoring makes for an enticing divertimento featuring the marimba as the bearer of sounds and visions from faraway lands and the resonant fingernails plucking sounds of the classical guitar enhanced by the microphone without sounding "electric"—an axiomatic description since the art of playing acoustical and electric guitar is not mutually exclusive in the musical profession, especially in the practice and culture of the recording studio.

Quarto Concerto per organo, 2 trombe, 2 tromboni e orchestra "Hoc erat in votis" (1993) is an imposing undertaking "embossed" with the gravitas of the Horace locution in its title. Horace's phrase, "This is what I prayed for," thanking Maecenas for the gift of a villa, was invoked by Morricone as an implicit dedication and expression of gratitude toward the Istituzione Universitaria dei Concerti (IUC), the concert institution sponsored by Rome's Universitá degli Studi "La Sapienza" that commissioned the work in celebration of the 50th anniversary of the IUC's founding.[23] The special spirit of *Romanità* imbued in Morricone's *Quarto Concerto* comes even more to the fore if traced back to the Conservatorio di Musica Santa Cecilia and the presence there of Fernando Germani (1906–1998), world famous organist, professor, Vatican organist, luminary in Morricone's eyes, and a proud fellow *Romano de Roma* (Rome's Roman).[24]

In 1926, composer Alfredo Casella (1883–1947), an adopted Roman, was commissioned by Philadelphia retail magnate and philanthropist Rodman Wanamaker to write an organ concerto to be performed in New York at the

Wanamaker Department Store's famous organ. Casella's *Concerto romano per organo, 3 trombe, 3 tromboni, archi e timpani*, op. 43 was premiered on March 11, 1927, at the Wanamaker Auditorium by organist Charles-Marie Courboin with the composer conducting. This work, dedicated to celebrated painter, sculptor, and printmaker Felice Casorati and inspired by the Roman Baroque architectural wonders, was published in Vienna by Universal Verlag in 1928. A letter from Universal to Casella dated September 4, 1928, confirmed that copies of *Concerto romano* had been forwarded to Pablo Casals and Fernando Germani at the composer's request.[25]

On March 21, 1929, Germani performed *Concerto romano* in Rome with Casella conducting. That was a time when all things Roman in music were highly popular: Ottorino Respighi's *Fontane di Roma* (1916), *Pini di Roma* (1924), *Vetrate di chiesa* (1926), *Feste romane* (1928), and even some foreign homages like *Roman Sketches* (1916) for piano by the American Charles Griffes[26] and *Castelli romani* (Piano Concerto No. 2, 1919–1920) by the Austrian Joseph Marx.

Fernando Germani continued to perform *Concerto romano* throughout his career as late as August 27, 1972, at the Accademia Chigiana in Siena for the commemoration of the 25th anniversary of Casella's death.[27]

This preamble means to invite an aural comparison between Casella's *Concerto romano* and Morricone's *Quarto Concerto*, two works composed sixty-seven years apart in idioms certainly distant from each other's and yet linked by instrumental idiosyncrasies and cultural commonalities emanating from the ghosts of Germani's organ, the Conservatorio, Rome's "La Sapienza," and the "air" of the Eternal City with all the churches and bells and organs so vitally important to Ennio Morricone and his music.[28]

Concerto romano begins with *Sinfonia*, a brief introduction consisting of a modal chant played in unison by cellos and double basses echoed, responsorial-style, by trumpets, trombones, and timpani. Then, the entrance of the organ begins in a contrapuntal feast of (Roman) Baroque splendor. The second movement, *Largo*, counterbalances the two orchestral factions: strings at one side versus three trumpets, three trombones, and timpani at the other. The strings play a very somber melody in unison, while the brass respond in choral syllabic fashion until the organ makes its presence known with a delicate *ricercare* played on the high register of the instrument, followed by an orchestral contrapuntal fanfare driven by the steady beat of the timpani. A slow march evolves into a large texture from which a solo violin emerges with much lyricism. *Cadenza e Toccata* form the concerto's finale pitting in the initial phase of the cadenza organ against the orchestra in a thunderous recitative-like dialogue, then the toccata unleashes the organ, or rather the organist's hands and feet, across the manuals and pedals culminating in an aggressive attack in Rachmaninoff/Paganini style that gives way to an extended coda, which includes a very suggestive use of the angelic *vox humana* stop in the midst of a pandemonium.

Dedicated to organ virtuoso Giorgio Carnini, Morricone's *Quarto Concerto* is scored for organ, two trumpets, two trombones, and orchestra, offering in principle the same sound apparatus as Casella's *Concerto romano*.[29]

Like many works by Morricone, *Quarto Concerto* begins with a long pedal of gargling sounds and melodic sprinklings emerging from all sides of the sound spectrum and growing to become a continuous frothing amalgam. At about five minutes into the piece, organ, trumpets, and trombones engage in a virtuoso fragmented, quasi-skirmish dialogue that concludes three minutes later. Then, the initial pedal gives life to a new extended slow, flat, frozen section enlivened by sporadic intervention of the organ with "scary" yet very poetic, evanescent, and lush sonorities at the same time creating a neo-impressionistic soundscape. Similar to *Concerto romano*'s, the organ cadenza of *Quarto Concerto* is flanked by trumpets and trombones, then joined by the strings in preparation of the virtuoso tour de force finale which lasts about five minutes. The work disintegrates into nothingness until a Stentorian pizzicato of the double basses signals its end.

It seems that Morricone's *Quarto Concerto per orchestra* or "Concerto per organo" as he at times refers to it, sounds like music full of inner energy submerged in the static waters of a laguna, in contrast to the chiseled, marble architectural aspiration of *Concerto romano*. And yet one represents the evolution of the other.

Ombra di lontana presenza per viola, orchestra d'archi e nastro magnetico (1997) is a 19-minute piece clearly divided in two parts. Part one consists of an expanse of spectral sonorities anticipating the entrance of the viola's nostalgic melody based on the notes C-flat, B-flat, G, a descending paraphrase of the Frescobaldi motif, which, in this instance closely resembles a turn of phrase heard in Stravinsky's Berceuse from *The Firebird*. This motif is heard again at the conclusion of part one, biding a symbolic farewell amid a flurry of agitated feathery sounds to someone who is no longer there. Then, in part two, the same theme joins a blurry diaphony which reveals itself to be *Suoni per Dino* with all its stratifications as originally recorded by Dino Asciolla (see Chapter 4). Morricone's is an interesting case of rewriting that brings to mind, in terms of viola repertoire, Luciano Berio's *Sequenza VI* (1968) for unaccompanied viola rewritten as *Chemins III* (1973) for viola and orchestra and provided by the statement, "Nothing one does is ever finished." In the case of *Ombra di lontana presenza* (Ghost of a Faraway Presence), whose overall effect is desperately moving, even morbid for some, we are indeed in the presence not of a ghost but of a concert work by Ennio Morricone we can call a masterpiece.

Vetrate di chiesa (Church Windows), four orchestral panels, three of which are preexisting as *Tre preludi sopra melodie gregoriane* for piano (1919), was as close as Respighi came to compose a fourth Roman tone poem he could have called *Chiese romane*. But, selecting three or four Roman churches to describe in sounds would have been a problem because there are hundreds of beautiful churches in Rome—all drenched into the history of Christianity and the history of Rome's everyday people.

The *Chiesa del Gesù*, the first Jesuit church to be built in Rome between 1568 and 1584, was under the spotlights on June 10, 2015. The occasion was the world premiere of the much-waited for *Missa Papae Francisci* composed by Ennio Morricone for that particular church and in honor of Pope Francis.

The title of this mass is daunting since *Missa Papae Francisci* (2015) and *Missa Papae Marcelli* (1562) can be misunderstood as two sides of the same papal musical coin. Ennio Morricone and Giovanni Pierluigi da Palestrina have many things in common besides being Romans. Regardless of whether Pope Francis and Pope Marcellus II shared the same worldviews, I find relevant to this context that Morricone composed *Missa* inspired by the severity of the Palestrina model but departed, for the finale, closely toward Pope Francis (Jorge Mario Bergoglio from Buenos Aires, Argentina), the first Jesuit pope.

Missa's finale *Ad Maiorem Dei Gloria* makes a drastic musical shift from the arcane to the familiar. The very familiar, in fact, *On Earth as It Is in Heaven* from the film *The Mission*, a film about a Jesuit Mission near the Iguazú Falls in the Amazon rainforest disputed by the Spanish, the Portuguese royals, the Guarani tribe, and the Jesuit priests (see Chapter 5). Pope Bergoglio was the man who understood their human and religious drama more than anyone, so, Morricone's homage was more than pertinent. The Pope did not attend the premiere of the work but received the score from the hands of the composer—a very moving moment, the composer has reported on many occasions.

Stefano Cucci, a well-known musician, scholar, and a very close collaborator of Morricone, dedicated a large portion of his book *Lontane presenze . . . L'universo poetico di Ennio Morricone* (2018) to *Missa Papae Francisci. Anno 200° a Societate Restituta*.[30] Regarding the questionability of the finale, Cucci suggests that since the *Agnus Dei* concludes so satisfactorily the liturgical portion of the Mass, the finale appears as an extraneous body to the rest of the composition, something the composer wanted to add onto the premiere performance for "practical reasons." However, *Missa Papae Francisci* could be purged of the added finale, restoring the organic and coherent structure of the composition. Then, in his descriptive analysis of the work, Cucci goes on to say:

> Yes, although the choral writing is substantially the same as that used in the cinematic version, the part sung in the film by the folk [untrained] voices acquires a more epic character when executed by the [trained] mixed chorus, which enhances, furthermore, the timbrical and rhythmical articulation of the voices. Through a different orchestration, Morricone modifies and somehow "purifies" the writing in the wind section and condenses the parts of organs and strings in a counterpoint that interacts constantly with the choral masses, notwithstanding the loss [in the new score] of the characteristic sound of the original like the woodwinds, violins and violas. Here Morricone assigns the principal theme to the French horns.
> This page concludes Morricone's work triumphally and only history will be able to establish whether this piece [the Finale] will have the honor to remain as part of the extraordinary sonic architecture of the *Missa*.[31]

The highly evocative video-recording of the world premiere of *Missa Papae Francisci* conducted by the composer is the best documented source to draw proper conclusions about what has been stated above.[32]

I conclude my reflections on the music of Ennio Morricone with some thoughts about a little-known chamber work entitled *Roma (pensando al "Ricercar Cromatico" di Girolamo Frescobaldi) per soprano, voce recitante maschile e ensemble su un testo di Valentina Morricone* (2010).[33]

Rome (Thinking about Frescobaldi's "Ricercar Cromatico"), scored for soprano, male speaking voice, flute, oboe, clarinet, piano, violin, viola, and cello, is based on the poetic text, *Roma*, written by Morricone's granddaughter Valentina. The work is Morricone's synthesized homage to his beloved city. It takes the form of a series of six notes: A, B-flat, C-flat, F-sharp, F-natural, E—the Frescobaldi motif—representing the musical essence of the city. Like the mundane Lupa Capitolina, the iconic medieval bronze statue of the she wolf, or the acronym SPQR (Senatus Populusque Romanus), the emblem of the ancient Roman Republic embossed, to this day, on any piece of Roman municipal work, for Morricone, the Frescobaldi motif became the equivalent of a personal signature.

When asked about his acquaintance with the Frescobaldi motif, Morricone replied vaguely claiming that the motif had gotten somehow impressed in his mind during his student years. It is possibly so, since a Frescobaldi revival was initiated in Rome by organist Fernando Germani who published a new edition of Girolamo Frescobaldi's *Opera XII (Fiori musicali di diverse composizioni: toccate, kirie, canzoni, capricci e recercari)* for Rome's Edizioni

De Santis in 1936. The *Ricercare cromatico* that so much impressed young Morricone was included in that cherished publication.

Of the numerous applications of this motif beginning with the unpublished *Variazioni su un tema di Frescobaldi per 12 strumenti* (1955), I find it significant that Morricone had chosen it as the locus of meditation for one of his last works written in collaboration with a young member of his beloved family.

Roma begins with a hushed exposition of the Frescobaldi motif commented upon by a brusque, rapid descending sextuplet echoing Beethoven's cello "muttering" quadruplets in the *Adagio ma non troppo e semplice* of String Quartet in C-sharp minor op. 131. *Roma*'s eight-measure introduction leads to the entrance of the soprano singing the note A as a long, double piano—wordless and with the mouth semi-open—while other instruments continue to weave a sound web joined by flute, oboe, and clarinet. They play rhythmically dilated arabesques created from the pitch permutations of the Frescobaldi motif (see Figure 6.3).

This section ends with a clustered pedal of piano and strings, followed by an extended fleeting instrumental Allegro which explores the possibilities of the Frescobaldi motif until a new intervention of the soprano puts order to chaos by enunciating the Frescobaldi motif in augmentation (see Figure 6.4).

Figure 6.3. Roma (pensando al "Ricercar Cromatico" di Girolamo Frescobaldi) per soprano, voce recitante maschile e ensemble, mm. 20–22, Ennio Morricone (Suvini Zerboni, 2010). Courtesy of Edizioni Suvini Zerboni.

Figure 6.4. Roma (pensando al "Ricercar Cromatico" di Girolamo Frescobaldi) per soprano, voce recitante maschile e ensemble, mm. 53–55, Ennio Morricone (Suvini Zerboni, 2010). Courtesy of Edizioni Suvini Zerboni.

Again, fast contrapuntal virtuoso instrumental writing comes to a screeching halt, ensuing a pedal with the indication *da qui alla fine un rallentando continuo* (continuous rallentando from here to the end). The piano's clustered chords create then a support for the male speaker to read Valentina Morricone's poem while the instruments delicately highlight the many nuances contained in the text. This 9-minute work ends with a last, whispered reiteration of the Frescobaldi motif (see Figure 6.5).

I would argue that this brief, intimate work represents the essence of the Roman composer more accurately than the glamorous Walk of Fame star engraved in the sidewalk of Hollywood Boulevard, a place far away from his beloved home in the earth of Rome.

Figure 6.5. Roma (pensando al "Ricercar Cromatico" di Girolamo Frescobaldi) per soprano, voce recitante maschile e ensemble, mm. 147–152, Ennio Morricone (Suvini Zerboni, 2010). Courtesy of Edizioni Suvini Zerboni.

NOTES

1. The world premiere of *Turandot* took place in Milan at La Scala on April 25, 1926, with Arturo Toscanini conducting. However, the maestro concluded the performance with the "Death of Liù," according to Puccini's completed score. Alfano's ending was included in all subsequent performances and Toscanini's baton was passed to Ettore Panizza after the third performance. Toscanini never conducted *Turandot* again.

2. Luciano Berio's Finale of *Turandot*, published by Ricordi in 2001, was premiered as a stand-alone piece in concert format on January 24, 2002, at the Festival de Musica de Gran Canaria (Las Palmas, Canary Islands) and later in Amsterdam also conducted by Riccardo Chailly.

3. See *We All Love Ennio Morricone*. Produced by Ars Latina/Sony Classical 88797-06590-2 (2007).

4. The *Achille Lauro* hijacking and the Klinghoffer case polarized the world press and public opinion for a long time. Following the theatrical release of the film *Voyage of Terror: The Achille Lauro Affair*, American composer John Adams composed a controversial opera on the subject entitled *The Death of Klinghoffer*, which premiered

at La Monnaie/De Munt in Brussels, Belgium, on March 19, 1991. Thereafter, Adams' opera, with libretto by Alice Goodman and stage direction by Peter Sellars, made the rounds of the main opera houses.

5. See RCA BD 74808 (1990).

6. This anecdote was reported in the three-part article *Ennio Morricone racconta . . .* (parte seconda), a cura di Stefano Sorice in *Colonne sonore* (gennaio 2005), see Chapter 1, n24. The four CDs were produced by Bear Family Records distributed by BMG as BCD 16244 AH—*Canto Morricone*, vol. 1; BCD 16245 AH—*Canto Morricone*, vol. 2; BCD 16246 AH—*Canto Morricone*, vol. 3; BCD 16247 AH—*Canto Morricone*, vol. 4.

7. See Renato De Fusco, *Made in Italy: Storia del design italiano* (Roma-Bari: Edizioni Laterza, 2007; 2nd edition, 2010); Franco Fabbri and Goffredo Plastino (Eds.), *Made in Italy: Studies in Popular Music* (New York: Routledge, 2014); and *Cinema Collection: I 30 capolavori della musica da film italiana*—CAM 64223—30-CD boxset (2013).

8. One can admire the artistic versatility of this great opera singer and violist Dino Asciolla (uncredited) by listening to Track 8 *In fondo ai miei occhi* from the film soundtrack of *Menage all'italiana* (1965), reissued in CD format as GDM 4405.

9. For an accurate survey of cinematic *commedie all'italiana*, see Andrea Bini, "The Birth of Comedy Italian Style" in *Popular Italian Cinema: Culture and Politics in a Postwar Society* (Flavia Brizio-Skov, Ed.) (London: I. B. Tauris, 2011), 107–52. For the subject in a larger context, see Peter Bondanella, *Italian Cinema: From Neorealism to the Present* (New York: Continuum, 1995).

10. See EuroArts *Morricone Conducts Morricone*—DVD 2054698, directed by Giovanni Morricone and produced by Helmut Pauli (2006).

11. See "Ennio Morricone—Prague 2018—Prague Proms . . ." accessed March 15, 2019, https://soundtrackfest.com/en/articles/ennio-morricone-prague-2018-prague-proms/.

12. Morricone's trial score for John Huston's film *The Bible*, discussed elsewhere in this book, included only one piece entitled *Creation* to which the composer added *The Tower of Babel* in order to form a diptych for concert use only.

13. *Yo-Yo Ma Plays Ennio Morricone*. Yo-Yo Ma, cello, and Roma Sinfonietta Orchestra conducted by Ennio Morricone. Produced by Ennio Morricone for Sony Classical SK93456 (2004).

14. Edizioni Suvini Zerboni, Milano, 1982; LP-RCA RL 31650 (1982).

15. For Giovannini's full text see his book *Nella rabbia ignara* (Roma: Remo Croce Editore, 1983).

16. The dedication heading *Secondo Concerto* reads "*Dedicato a Goffredo Petrassi per il suo ottantesimo compleanno.*" The work is published by Edizioni Suvini Zerboni, Milano, 1991.

17. *Cadenza* is published by Edizioni Suvini Zerboni, Milano, 1991. It can be heard as Track 1 of CD 3, part of the four-CD set compilation entitled *Io, Ennio Morricone*, Milan 198 791-2 (2002).

18. See Miceli, *Morricone, la musica, il cinema*, 310–15.

19. Guido of Arezzo (c. 990–1050) is credited as the inventor of modern musical notation.

20. *UT* is published by BMG Ariola, 1991, and recorded by Mauro Maur, trumpet with the Orchestra Sinfonica Abruzzese, conducted by Flavio Emilio Scogna on the CD RCA 74321 17516-3 (1993).

21. *Quattro pezzi per chitarra* (1957). Edizioni Suvini Zerboni, Milano, 1988. See the CD *Ennio Morricone—Chamber Music*, CDVE Virgin Records, 1988; Bruno Battisti D'Amario, guitar. *Terzo Concerto per chitarra, marimba e orchestra d'archi* can be heard as Track 2 of CD 4, part of the four-CD set compilation entitled *Io, Ennio Morricone*, Milan, 198 791-2 (2002). Giovanni Senènca, guitar; Marco Bagarini, marimba; with Benedetto Montebello, conducting.

22. Porrino named his guitar concerto after the *Argentarola* islet in the Tuscan Archipelago.

23. See Q. Horatius Flaccus (Horace), *Satires* II, 6.

24. *Romano de Roma* (Rome's Roman) is an expression referring to the traditional saying that an individual whose Roman ancestry goes back seven generations can call him/herself Rome's Roman. Fernando Germani used to practice his organ in the privacy, so he thought, of the Sala dei Concerti, the concert hall located on the ground floor of the Conservatorio di Musica Santa Cecilia. Although measures were taken to make sure Germani worked undisturbed, students—Morricone included and others in later times—managed to crawl through spaces surrounding the concert hall to listen to the maestro practicing or any of the great performers rehearsing in the hall.

25. See *Catalogo Critico del Fondo Alfredo Casella* (Francesca Romana Conti and Mila De Santis, a cura). I. Carteggi; II. Scritti, Musiche, Concerti (Firenze: Leo S. Olschki Editore, 1992).

26. Griffes orchestrated *The White Peacock*, the first of his *Roman Sketches*.

27. Piero Bellugi conducted the Orchestra del Maggio Musicale Fiorentino. Furthermore, on September 20 of the same year, organist Wijnand van de Pol performed *Concerto romano* in Rome's Chiesa di S. Ignazio with the Orchestra dell' A. M. R. conducted by Miles Morgan.

28. Here are the links to two listening possibilities: Casella's *Concerto romano* Tracks 5–7 of CD 2, part of the two-CD set from the Signum label entitled *Expressionismus*, SIG X121-00 (2002); Martin Schmeding, organ, and the Brandenburgisches Staatsorchester Frankfurt, conducted by Christoph Campestrini. Morricone's *Quarto Concerto per organo, due trombe, due tromboni e orchestra* can be heard as Track 3 of CD 4, part of the four-CD set compilation entitled *Io, Ennio Morricone*, Milan, 198 791-2 (2002); Giorgio Carnini, organ, with Carlo Rizzari, conducting.

29. *Quarto Concerto* was premiered on November 15, 1994, at the Aula Magna of the Universitá degli Studi "La Sapienza" in Rome with the Orchestra of the Rome Opera House conducted by Flavio Emilio Scogna. Giorgio Carnini was the organist.

30. See Stefano Cucci, *Lontane presenze . . . L'universo poetico di Ennio Morricone* (Lucca: Libreria Musicale Italiana, 2018).

31. Cucci, *Lontane presenze*, 92–93.

32. See "Missa Papae Francisci," YouTube, 34:01—June 12, 2015, https://www.youtube.com/watch?v=jECzxt6gngk.

33. *Roma* is published by Edizioni Suvini Zerboni, Milano, 2010. It was commissioned by the Campus Internazionale di Musica di Latina on behalf of Festival Pontino 2010.

Appendix 1

Piccolo Concerto 1961 and 1962 Programs

November 8, 1961 (1)

Singers:
Aura D'Angelo
Jenny Luna
Fausto Cigliano

Leonard Bernstein: *The Wrong Note Rag*
From the 1953 Broadway show *Wonderful Town*

Nacio Herb Brown–Arthur Freed: *Temptation*
Published in 1933, this song was brought to success by Bing Crosby in 1934

Mario Costa–Ferdinando Russo: *Scètate!* [Fausto Cigliano]
A very evocative Neapolitan song composed in 1887 by Mario Pasquale Costa with lyrics by Ferdinando Russo

Renato Rascel–Pietro Garinei and Sandro Giovannini: *Arrivederci . . . e non addio* [Aura D'Angelo]
A 1961 Rascel success following his 1959 international hit *Arrivederci Roma*

Paul Nero: *The Hot Canary* [Jenny Luna]
The Hot Canary was written and first recorded by Paul Nero in 1949 performing it on the violin

Jerome Kern–Deborah Fields: *Waltz in a Swing Time*
A celebrated Fred Astaire/Ginger Rogers dance routine from the 1936 American RKO musical comedy film *Swing Time*

Anonymous: *Londonderry Air* [Franco Tamponi, violin]
A famous tune from Northern Ireland transcribed by many a virtuoso including violinist Fritz Kreisler. It was also heard in the 1938 British romance film *The Londonderry Air*

November 22, 1961 (3)

Singers:
Aura D'Angelo
Fausto Cigliano
Tony Del Monaco

Cole Porter: *Night and Day*
From the 1932 musical *Gay Divorce* starring Fred Astaire

Charles Dumont–Michel Vaucaire: *Nulla rimpiangerò* [Aura D'Angelo]
A cover to Édith Piaf's classic *Non, je ne regrette rien* brought to success by Milva in 1962

Julius Fucik: *Marcia dei gladiatori* (Entrance of the Gladiators)
A military march composed in 1897

Enrico De Leva–Salvatore Di Giacomo: *'E spingule frangese* (Safety Pins) [Fausto Cigliano]
A celebrated Neapolitan cabaret song written in 1888 by Enrico De Leva and Salvatore Di Giacomo

Vito Pallavicini–Vittorio Buffoli and Pino Massara: *Amorevole*
A hit song recorded by Mina in 1959

Gianni Marchetti: *La pioggia va in su* [Tony Del Monaco]
This song, performed by Tony Del Monaco, occupied Side A of RCA PM45-3002 (1961). Side B contained *La tua stagione* (from the film *La voglia matta* directed by Luciano Salce). Also, it was included in the anthology *Musica in Celluloide* RCA Italiana—PML 10316 (1962) B6

Stan Jones–Pinchi: *I cavalieri del cielo* (Riders in the Sky)
This tune, composed in 1949, was based on the ballade *When Johnny Comes Marching Home* brought to fame in 1942 by Morton Gould who included it in his orchestral fantasy entitled *American Salute*

November 29, 1961 (4)

Singers:
Aura D'Angelo
Fausto Cigliano
Tony Del Monaco

Felipe Pertichela: *Danza messicana del cappello* (Mexican Hat Dance)
Pertichela's *Mexican Hat Dance* was one of the many popular colorful fiesta songs and dances of Mexico featured in films, radio, and television

Giorgio Fabor–Gian Carlo Testoni: *Nè stelle nè mare* [Fausto Cigliano]
Fabor's *Nè stelle nè mare* was a 1959 Sanremo success sung by Fausto Cigliano

Harry Warren: *Orchidee al chiaro di luna* (Orchids in the Moonlight)
Warren's *Orchids in the Moonlight* was a tango danced by Fred Astaire and Ginger Rogers in their first film *Flying Down to Rio* (1933)

Gaetano Donizetti–Raffaele Sacco: *Te vojo bene assaie* (I Love You Very Much) [Aura D'Angelo]
A celebrated Neapolitan song whose music is attributed to Gaetano Donizetti

Cesare Andrea Bixio–Ennio Neri: *Parlami d'amore Mariù* (Speak to Me of Love, Little Mary) [Tony Del Monaco]
A song by Cesare Andrea Bixio with lyrics by Ennio Neri sang by actor Vittorio De Sica in the 1932 comedic film *Gli uomini, che mascalzoni* (What Scoundrels Men Are!) directed by Mario Camerini

Dimitri Tiomkin–Paul Francis Webster: *Ballata selvaggia* (Blowing Wild)
Blowing Wild was taken from the eponymous 1953 film starring Gary Cooper

George Gershwin: *Fantasia Gershwin* [Armando Trovajoli, piano]
Medley of Gershwin's tunes arranged for piano and orchestra

December 13, 1961 (6)

Singers:
Daisy Lumini
Fausto Cigliano
Nicola Arigliano

Daisy Lumini–Tritono: *Il gabbiano* [Daisy Lumini]
Il gabbiano was a Lumini recording success together with *Tante piccole cose* on RCA Camden 45CP 106

Mario Pagano–Franco Maresca: *Lucente* [Fausto Cigliano]
Lucente was a Neapolitan song by Franco Maresca and Mario Pagano brought to success by Dino Giacca in 1960 (RCA PM45-3018-Italy)

Carlo Donida–Mogol: *Romantico amore* [Nicola Arigliano]
Romantico amore, lyrics by Mogol and music by Carlo Donida, was recorded by Nicola Arigliano in 1961 on the Columbia SCMQ 1475 single paired with *Mister Amore* by Bruno Martino

Angelo Giacomazzi: *Cuban cha cha cha*
A 1960 cha cha by Angelo Giacomazzi

Raymond Scott: *La trombettina* (The Toy Trumpet)
Raymond Scott, pseudonym of Harry Warnow of cartoon music fame, was the author of this captivating piece

Gino Paoli–Mogol: *Il cielo in una stanza*
Il cielo in una stanza, composed by Gino Paoli in 1960, became an instant success sung by Mina. It was presented here in orchestral version under the authorship of Mogol (Giulio Rapetti) and Toang (Renato Angiolini) as Paoli was not yet a member of SIAE (Società Italiana Autori e Editori), thus, he could not collect royalties

Elmer Bernstein–Leo Chiosso: *The Magnificent Seven*
Titles music from the 1960 eponymous film

February 7, 1962 (1)

Singers:
Gloria Christian
Fausto Cigliano

Daisy Lumini
Peter Tevis

Irving Berlin: *Let's Face the Music and Dance*
A song written in 1936 by Irving Berlin for the film *Follow the Fleet* introduced by Fred Astaire

Tomás Méndez: *Cucurrucucú paloma*
Méndez's *Cucurrucucú paloma* was a 1954 song favorite by many singers. It was also featured in several films

Grigoras Dinicu: *Hora staccato*
Grigoras Dinicu, a Roma violinist and composer, achieved international fame in 1932 when Jascha Heifetz recorded and published his own transcription of *Hora staccato*, a Romanian hora-style piece written in 1906

Riccardo Morbelli–Giuseppe Rampoldi: *La sedia a dondolo* [Daisy Lumini]
Giuseppe Rampoldi's *La sedia a dondolo* (The Rocking Chair) was a 1942 happy-go-lucky typical Italian tune of the period. It was made famous by singer Dea Garbaccio

Dimitri Tiomkin: *Degüello*
Degüello, a Mexican military march with trumpet solo, has appeared in many versions made famous through films like *Rio Bravo* (1959) and *The Alamo* (1960). Morricone used it abundantly in his Westerns, thus, one could assume that this arrangement was a very early tryout version

Gaetano Lama–Libero Bovio: *Silenzio cantatore* [Fausto Cigliano]
A 1922 Neapolitan sea-inspired song

Harold Arlen–E. Y. Harburg: *Arcobaleno* (Somewhere over the Rainbow)
Celebrated song from the 1939 film *The Wizard of Oz* starring Judy Garland

Anonymous: *Danny Boy* [Gloria Christian]
A version with lyrics of the Northern Ireland folk tune *Londonderry Air*

Wayne Shanklin: *Jezebel* [Peter Tevis]
The song *Jezebel* was written by Wayne Shanklin and was first released by Frankie Laine in 1951

February 14, 1962 (2)

Singers:
Nicola Arigliano
Fausto Cigliano
Bruno Martino
Milva
The Swingers

Léo Daniderff: *Je cherche la Titina* (*Je cherche apres Titine*) [The Swingers]
French composer Léo Daniderff's 1917 foxtrot-shimmy tune became famous after Charlie Chaplin sang it in his film *Modern Times* (1936)

Ernesto De Curtis–Eduardo Nicolardi: *Voce 'e notte* [Fausto Cigliano]
Classical Neapolitan song composed in 1903

Harry James: *Black Bottom* [The Swingers]
Black Bottom Dance goes back to the 1920s. The authorship attribution to Harry James is a possible reference to *Black Bottom Stomp*, a Charleston made popular by Paul Whiteman and later by Jelly Roll Morton and his Red Hot Peppers band

Roger Bernstein–Alex Alstone: *Symphonie* [Milva]
The song *Symphonie* was composed by Alex Alston, first released by Fred Adison and his orchestra in 1945, then it was included in the repertoire of major singers like Frank Sinatra with lyrics by Andrè Tabet and Roger Bernstein

Narciso Yepes: *Giochi proibiti* (Forbidden Games) [Mario Gangi, guitar]
Giochi proibiti was a guitar solo of unestablished provenance performed by guitar virtuoso Narciso Yepes in the 1952 French film *Jeux interdits* directed by René Clément

Gian Piero Reverberi–Franco Franchi: *La notte* [Bruno Martino]
Reverberi's *La notte* was a song made popular by Mina in 1960

Fred Brooks: *Darlin' Cora* [The Swingers]
Darlin' Cora was a song by Fred Brooks that became a signature piece of Harry Belafonte in 1959

Melle Weersma–Lulli: *Serenata sentimentale* [Nicola Arigliano]
Weersma's *Serenata sentimentale* was a 1938 foxtrot popular over the Italian radio waves

Cole Porter: *Can-Can* [The Swingers]
Cole Porter's 1953 Broadway musical *Can-Can* was released as film in 1960 starring Frank Sinatra, Shirley MacLaine, and Maurice Chevalier. The music was arranged and conducted by Nelson Riddle

February 21, 1962 (3)

Singers:
Charles Aznavour
Nico Fidenco
Jenny Luna
Helen Merrill
The Swingers

Carlo Alberto Rossi: *Stradivarius*
Carlo Alberto Rossi, composer and music publisher, wrote *Stradivarius* in 1953 as an instrumental piece for pianist-composer Armando Trovajoli

Gorni Kramer–Pietro Garinei and Sandro Giovannini: *Non so dir ti voglio bene*
This was a 1957 song brought to success by Jula De Palma

Anonymous: *Square Dance*
An American western country song and dance with ad hoc "calls." It was used in numerous Western movies and radio and television shows

Nico Fidenco: *Audrey* [Nico Fidenco]
Audrey occupied Side B of a 45 RPM RCA Victor (1962) arranged and conducted by Luis Enriquez (Bacalov). Side A included *Moon River* by Henry Mancini from the 1961 film *Breakfast at Tiffany's* starring Audrey Hepburn

Jerome Kern–Oscar Hammerstein II: *Old Man River*
The song *Old Man River* was taken from *Show Boat*, Jerome Kern's 1927 musical turned into films in 1936 and 1951

Carlo Alberto Rossi–Ugo Calise: *Non è peccato* (*Nun è peccato*) [Helen Merrill]
A 1959 Neapolitan song by Carlo Alberto Rossi

Victor Young–Edward Heyman: *When I Fall in Love*
When I Fall in Love (1952) from the film *One Minute to Zero* starring Robert Mitchum and Ann Blyth, was brought to success by Nat King Cole

Richard Rodgers–Lorenz Hart: *Lover*
A charming waltz by Richard Rodgers from the film *Love Me Tonight* (1932), then successfully recorded in 1948 by guitarist Les Paul

Charles Aznavour: *Sur ma vie* [Charles Aznavour]
A 1956 signature song by the celebrated Armenian-French singer-composer Aznavour

February 28, 1962 (4)

Singers:
Nancy Sinatra
Fausto Cigliano
Jula De Palma
Peter Tevis

Jerry Livingston–Mack David and Al Hoffman: *Chi-baba chi-baba* (My Bambino Go to Sleep)
A 1947 lullaby immortalized by Perry Como

Amilcare Ponchielli: *Like I Do* (from the *Dance of the Hours*) [Nancy Sinatra]
Like I Do was a song written in 1962 by Dick Manning for Nancy Sinatra after Ponchielli's *Dance of the Hours*

Duke Ellington: *Sophisticated Lady*
Duke Ellington's 1932 jazz standard

Eduardo Di Capua–Salvator Rosa: *Michelemmà/Vulimmo pazzià* [Fausto Cigliano]
The origins of this song are controversial as the verses were attributed to sixteenth-century painter/poet Salvator Rosa and the music was published in 1840 under the name of Guillaume Louis Cottrau, a French composer and music publisher residing in Naples. This has gone through several variants and authorial attributions

Muzio Clementi: *Sonatina* [Roberto Pregadio, piano and harpsichord]
An arrangement by Morricone of the first movement of Clementi's *Sonatina* op. 36, no. 1

Gino Paoli: *Senza fine* [Jula De Palma]
A 1961 success that launched the extraordinary career of author/composer/singer Gino Paoli

Anonymous: *West* (Indian War Dance) [Arnoldo Foà, narrator]
Joseph Engleman's *Indian War Dance* was composed originally as incidental music in silent films. It was published in 1927

Woody Guthrie: *Pastures of Plenty* [Peter Tevis]
Pastures of Plenty by Woody Guthrie (1941) was based on the folk song/Christmas carol *Wonder as I Wander*

Richard Adler–Jerry Ross: *There Once Was a Man*
Richard Adler's song was taken from the 1954 Broadway hit *The Pajama Game*. The 1957 film version starred Doris Day and John Raitt

March 7, 1962 (5)

Singers:
Fausto Cigliano
Nicola Arigliano
Miranda Martino
Charles Aznavour
The Swingers

Nico Fidenco–Gianni Marchetti: *Legata a un granello di sabbia* [The Swingers]
A 1961 success of the popular author/composer/singer

Anonymous: *O' Guarracino*
Famous seventeenth-century Neapolitan tarantella

Galt MacDermot: *African Waltz*
African Waltz was first released in 1956 by Galt MacDermot and his Trio

Alessandro Cicognini–Gian Bistolfi: *Una romantica avventura* [Miranda Martino]
Una romantica avventura was heard in the eponymous 1940 film by Mario Camerini

George Gershwin: *It Ain't Necessarily So* [Berto Pisano, double bass]
From *Porgy and Bess* in an arrangement for double bass and orchestra

Giovanni D'Anzi–Alfredo Bracchi: *Il maestro improvvisa* [Nicola Arigliano]
A popular 1941 song brought to success by Alberto Rabagliati and the Trio Lescano

Oscar Strauss: *La ronde*
Theme song from the 1950 film *La ronde*

Charles Aznavour: *Tu t'lassez aller* [Charles Aznavour]
Another signature song by the celebrated Armenian-French singer/composer/actor

Richard Rodgers: *Dove e quando* (Where or When)
From the 1937 musical *Babes in Arms*

March 14, 1962 (6)

Singers:
Helen Merrill
Jula De Palma
Peter Kraus
Sergio Bruni
The Swingers

Dimitri Tiomkin: *Mezzogiorno di fuoco* (High Noon) [The Swingers]
Title theme from the 1952 film starring Gary Cooper and Grace Kelly

Vincenzo De Crescenzo–Sergio Bruni: *O' cappotto* [Sergio Bruni]
Sergio Bruni's 1961 discographic success

Kenneth Alford: *Colonel Bogey* [The Swingers]
Colonel Bogey was a British march composed by Kenneth J. Alford. Part of it was used by Malcolm Arnold in the 1957 film *The Bridge on the River Kwai*

Norbert Glanzberg–Jean Constantin: *Tu mi fai girar la testa* (*Mon manège à moi*) [Jula De Palma]
Mon manège à moi was a great 1958 success song by Jean Louis Constantin sung by Édith Piaf

Anonymous: *Stornelli* [Dino Asciolla, viola d'amore, and Giuseppe Anedda, lute]
No details about this repertoire have been retrieved

Bernie Baum–Stephen Weiss: *Musik, musik, musik* [Peter Kraus]
A 1950 song which could have been inspired by Peter Kreuder's tune by the same title written in 1939 for the German musical film *Hallo, Janine!* starring Marika Rökk

Kurt Weill: *Speak Low*
Speak Low was introduced by Mary Martin and Kenny Baker in the Broadway musical *One Touch of Venus* (1943)

John Fred Coots–Haven Gillespie: *You Go to My Head* [Helen Merrill]
J. Fred Coots' 1938 *You Go to My Head* was recorded many times. The Frank Sinatra/Nelson Riddle 1946 rendition was probably the closest to Morricone's version

Richard Rodgers: *People Will Say We're in Love* [The Swingers]
Richard Rodgers' *People Will Say We're in Love* was taken from the musical *Oklahoma* (1943)

April 4, 1962 (7)

[Broadcast of March 21 program preempted because of a soccer game]

Singers:
Nicola Arigliano
Aura D'Angelo
Fausto Cigliano
Gloria Christian
The Swingers

Ennio Morricone: *Balletto per silenzi e batteria* [Joe Bennett]
An original work by Morricone

Angelo Francesco Lavagnino: *Canzone di Lima* [The Swingers]
Angelo Francesco Lavagnino's tune *From the Incas to the Uru* (*Canzone di Lima*) was taken from the 1955 film *L'impero del sole* directed by Enrico Gras and Mario Craveri

Romero Alvaro: *No Jazz* [Nicola Arigliano]
No Jazz was a tune written in 1948 by legendary Romero Alvaro

Ennio Morricone: *La naja*
La naja was a fantasy on military calls inspired by the Italian compulsory service identified in slang as naja, a Venetian contraction of the word tenaglia (pliers)

Cesare Andrea Bixio–Cherubini: *Violino zigano* [Aura D'Angelo]
Cesare Andrea Bixio's *Violino zigano* was heard in *Melodramma*, a 1934 film directed by Giorgio Simonelli

Jerome Kern–Mogol: *Fumo negli occhi* (Smoke Gets in Your Eyes)
Jerome Kern's *Smoke Gets in Your Eyes* was taken from the 1933 musical *Roberta*

Gaetano Lama–Libero Bovio: *Reginella* [Fausto Cogliano]
A celebrated Neapolitan song written in 1917

Anonymous: *Carnevale di Venezia*
A popular folk tune upon which many composers have written virtuoso variations

Pablo Beltrán Ruiz: *Chi sarà* [Gloria Christian]
Quién será was a 1953 mambo song by Pablo Beltrán Ruiz revived in 1961 by Mina as *Chi sarà*

Juan Y. D'Lorah: *La cucaracha*
La cucaracha was a traditional Spanish/Mexican folk song adapted by Juan Y. D'Lorah and heard in the 1934 film *La cucaracha* directed by Lloyd Carrigan

April 11, 1962 (8)

Singers:
Jula De Palma
Gloria Christian
Sergio Bruni
Nicola Arigliano
The Swingers

Morton Gould: *Pavana* [The Swingers]
Pavane is the second movement of Morton Gould's *American Symphonette No. 2* (1938)

Lelio Luttazzi–Giulio Scarnicci: *Souvenir d'Italie* [Jula De Palma]
A successful 1955 song by Lelio Luttazzi written for Jula De Palma

Harold Arlen–Johnny Mercer: *Blues in the Night*
Harold Arlen's *Blues in the Night* (1941) was recorded many times as a jazz instrumental piece or with lyrics by either Johnny Mercer or Ted Koehler. It was first heard in the 1941 film *Blues in the Night* directed by Anatole Litvak

Louis Prima: *Sing, Sing, Sing* [Gloria Christian]
Louis Prima's classical 1936 jazz standby

Anonymous: *La tarantella*
Possibly the same source that inspired Rossini and, consequently, Respighi and Britten in their homages to Rossini

Nino Fiore–Antonio Vian: *Suonno a Marechiaro* [Sergio Bruni]
A success at the 1958 Sanremo Festival

Richard Rodgers–Lorenz Hart: *Falling in Love with Love*
Rodgers' tune from the musical *The Boys from Syracuse* (1938)

Di Ceglie–Gian Carlo Testoni: *La barca dei sogni* [Nicola Arigliano]
From the great 1961 soundtrack of the film *King of Kings* directed by Nicholas Ray with music by Miklós Rózsa

Mario Nascimbene: *Barabbas*
This selection could have consisted of the Bolero which Morricone arranged for the 1961 release of the LP to coincide with the opening of the film *Barabbas* directed by Richard Fleischer and starring Anthony Quinn

April 18, 1962 (9)

Singers:
Daisy Lumini
Fausto Cigliano
Peter Tevis
Miranda Martino
Peter Kraus
The Swingers

Gianni Meccia–Franco Migliacci: *Il barattolo* [The Swingers]
This 1960 song marks Morricone's debut as an arranger at RCA

Victor Young–Peggy Lee: *Johnny Guitar* [Daisy Lumini]
A song from the 1954 film *Johnny Guitar* directed by Nicholas Ray and starring Joan Crawford

Eduardo Alfieri–Salvatore Palomba: *'O lampione* [Fausto Cigliano]
A Neapolitan song written by Eduardo Alfieri for Fausto Cigliano

Anonymous: *Jamaica Farewell* [Peter Tevis]
Jamaican Farewell was one of Harry Belafonte's great hits, part of the 1957 album *Calypso*

Domenico Modugno: *Notte di luna calante* [Miranda Martino]
A popular 1960 ballad by an innovative author/singer

George Gershwin: *The Man I Love* [Filippo Settembri, flugelhorn]
The 1924 song by Ira and George Gershwin arranged for flugelhorn and orchestra

Robert Katscher–Geza Herczeg: *Wenn die Elisabeth . . .* [Peter Kraus]
Austrian composer/entertainer Robert Katscher reached international success in 1930 with this song whose full title in English reads: *If Elisabeth Did Not Have Such Nice Legs*

Robert Maxwell: *Ebb Tide* (*Bassa marea*) [The Swingers]
Celebrated tune by composer/harpist Robert Maxwell first recorded in 1953

Frank Churchill–Larry Morey: *Biancaneve e i sette nani*
Medley of songs from Frank Churchill's music to Walt Disney's *Snow White and the Seven Dwarfs* 1937 animated musical

April 25, 1962 (10)

Singers:
Jula De Palma
Nini Rosso
Miranda Martino
Gloria Christian
The Swingers

Pino Spotti–Machel Montano: *Le tue mani* [Jula De Palma]
A successful 1954 song written for Jula De Palma

Ennio Morricone: *Concerto per radio e orchestra*
An original composition by Morricone

Franco Pisano: *La ballata della tromba* [Nino Rosso, trumpet]
A 1961 successful instrumental piece attributed, at times, to Berto Pisano, Franco's younger brother

Anonymous: *Cotton Reel*
A Virginian square dance with calls

Teo Usuelli–Virgilio Sabel: *Meravigliose labbra* [Miranda Martino]
A song launched in 1959 by Johnny Dorelli

Anonymous: *Biondina in gondoleta* [Fernando Zodini, bassoon]
A traditional Venetian song arranged for bassoon and orchestra

Nacio Herb Brown: *Sento di impazzire* [Gloria Christian]
From the 1936 musical film *Broadway Melody*

Ary Barroso: *Bahia* [The Swingers]
Famous Brazilian song written by Ary Barroso in 1938. Used to great acclaim in Walt Disney's 1944 film *The Three Caballeros*

May 2, 1962 (11)

Singers:
Fausto Cigliano
Gino Paoli
Renato Carosone
Renato Rascel
Helen Merrill
Jenny Luna
Chet Baker
The Swingers

Irving Berlin: *Let's Face the Music and Dance*
A song written in 1936 by Irving Berlin for the film *Follow the Fleet*, introduced by Fred Astaire

Angelo Montagna–Eduardo Nicolardi: *Sciuldezza bella* [Fausto Cigliano]
Neapolitan song that has held its popularity since it was written in 1905

Muzio Clementi: *Sonatina* [Roberto Pregadio, piano and harpsichord]
A spirited arrangement of the first movement of Clementi's *Sonatina* op. 36, no. 1

Gino Paoli: *Me in tutto il mondo*
A 1961 recording success for the intellectual, later turned politician, author/singer

Grigoras Dinicu: *Hora staccato*
Grigoras Dinicu, a Roma violinist and composer, achieved international fame in 1932 when Jascha Heifetz recorded and published his own transcription of *Hora staccato*, a Romanian hora-style piece written in 1906

Renato Carosone: *Gondolì, gondola* [Renato Carosone]
Presented first at the 1962 Sanremo Festival, this captivating song quickly reached international success

Ennio Morricone: *La naja*
La naja was a fantasy on military calls inspired by the Italian compulsory service identified in slang as naja, a Venetian contraction of the word tenaglia (pliers)

Renato Rascel–Pietro Garinei and Sandro Giovannini: *Arrivederci . . . e non addio* [Aura D'Angelo]
A 1961 Rascel success following his 1959 international hit *Arrivederci Roma*

Oscar Strauss: *La ronde*
Theme song from the 1950 film *La ronde*

Richard Rogers–Lorenz Hart: *Blue Moon* [Helen Merrill, Jenny Luna]
A 1934, yet timeless, beautiful ballad in the repertoire of a great number of artists

Gershwin: *It Ain't Necessarily So* [Berto Pisano, double bass]
From *Porgy and Bess* in an arrangement for double bass and orchestra

Chet Baker: *Il mio domani* [Chet Baker, trumpet and voice]
This jazz song, presented here for the first time, was recorded the following June and marketed as RCA Records 45-3080

Ennio Morricone: *Piccolo concerto*
The theme performed at the opening of each show was presented at the closing of the series featuring the orchestra leaving the stage one player at the time following the Haydn's "Farewell" Symphony model

Appendix 2

Canto Morricone

VOLUME 1—THE 1960S

1. Title: *Ho messo gli occhi su di te* (Lyrics: Sergio Bardotti)
Recording: RCA SP 8013 [Artist: Dino (Eugenio Zambelli)]
Film: *Menage all'italiana* (Menage Italian Style). Director: Franco Indovina, 1965.

2. Title: *Thrilling* (Lyrics: Sergio Bardotti and Gianni Musy)
Recording: RCA ARC AN 4068 [Artists: Rita Monico with I Cantori Moderni di Alessandroni]
Film: *La regola del gioco* (The Rules of the Game). Directors: Carlo Lizzani, Gian Luigi Polidori, Ettore Scola, 1965.

3. Title: *Se telefonando* (Lyrics: Ghico De Chiara and Maurizio Costanzo)
Recording: Rifi RFN NP 16152 [Artist: Mina (Mina Mazzini)]
Italian television show *Aria condizionata*, 1966.

4. Title: *Sapore di sale* (Lyrics and Music: Gino Paoli)
Recording: RCA PM45-3204 -1963 [Artist: Gino Paoli—Morricone, arranger and conductor]
Film: *Il successo*. Director: Mauro Morassi, 1964.

5. Title: *Quattro vestiti* (Lyrics: Franco Migliacci)
Recording: Fonit Cetra EPE 3164—1962 [Artist: Milva (Maria Ilva Biolcati)]

6. Title: *Fruscio di foglie verdi* (Lyrics: Audrey Stainton Nohra)
Recording: Ariete ARLP 2002 [Artist: Trio Junior]
Film: *Teorema* (Theorem). Director: Pier Paolo Pasolini, 1968.

7. Title: *Una stanza vuota* (Lyrics: Carlo Rossi)
Recording: RCA SP 8018 [Artists: Lisa Gastoni with I Cantori Moderni di Alessandroni]
Film: *Svegliati e uccidi* (Wake Up and Kill). Director: Carlo Lizzani, 1966.

8. Title: *In fondo ai miei occhi* (Lyrics: Sergio Bardotti)
Recording: RCA SP 8013 [Artist: Anna Moffo]
Film: *Menage all'italiana.* Director: Franco Indovina, 1965.

9. Title: *Nuddu* (Lyrics: Franco Pisano)
Recording: Parade PRC 5075/Jolly J 2054 [Artist: Fausto Cigliano]
Film: *Un bellissimo novembre* (Sweet November). Director: Mauro Bolognini, 1968.

10. Title: *Questi vent'anni miei* (Lyrics: Franco Torti and Guido Castaldo)
Recording: Ricordi ERL 210 [Artist: Catherine Spaak]
Film: *I Malamondo* or *Malamondo* (Funny World). Director: Paolo Cavara, 1964.

11. Title: *Tra tanta gente* (Lyrics: Luciano Salce)
Recording: Ricordi SRL 10-271 [Artist: Luigi Tenco]
Film: *La cuccagna* (The Land of Plenty). Director: Luciano Salce, 1962.

12. Title: *Deep Down* (Lyrics: Audrey Stainton Nohra)
Recording: Parade PRC 5052-1967 [Artist: Christy (Maria Cristina Brancucci)]
Film: *Diabolik* (Danger: Diabolik). Director: Mario Bava, 1968.

13. Title: *Je changerais d'avis* (*Se telefonando*). (Lyrics: Ghico De Chiara, Maurizio Constanzo, Jacques Lanzmann, and Françoise Hardy)
Recording: Vogue CLD 70230 [Artist: Françoise Hardy]. Arrangement by Johnny Hardy
Italian television show *Aria condizionata*, 1966.

14. Title: *Funny World* (Lyrics: Allan Brandt, Franco Torti, and Guido Castaldo)

Recording: Epic LN 24126 [Artist: Ken Colman]—from the original soundtrack
Film: *I Malamondo* or *Malamondo* (Funny World). Director: Paolo Cavara, 1964.

15. Title: *Il disco rotto* (Lyrics: Renato Rascel [Ranucci])
Recording: Italdisc MH-128 (1962) [Artist: Mina]

16. Title: *Hurry to Me* (Lyrics: Giuseppe Patroni Griffi and Jack Fishman)
Recording: CBS 70067-1970 [Artists: The Sandpipers]
Film: *Metti, una sera a cena* (Love Circle). Director: Giuseppe Patroni Griffi, 1969.

17. Title: *Penso a te* (Lyrics: Franco Migliacci)
Recording: Ricordi SRL 10-340 [Artist: Catherine Spaak]
Film: *I Malamondo* or *Malamondo* (Funny World). Director: Paolo Cavara, 1969.

18. Title: *Quello che conta* (Lyrics: Luciano Salce)
Recording: Ricordi SRL 10-271 [Artist: Luigi Tenco]
Film: *La cuccagna* (The Land of Plenty). Director: Luciano Salce, 1962.

19. Title: *Funny World* (Lyrics: Allan Brandt, Franco Torti, and Guido Castaldo)
Recording: Verve V6-8629 [Artist: Astrud Gilberto]
Film: *I Malamondo* or *Malamondo* (Funny World). Director: Paolo Cavara, 1964.

20. Title: *Cantata basilisca* (Lyrics: Lina Wertmüller)
Recording: RCA PM 45-3219 [Artist: Fausto Cigliano]
Film: *I basilischi* (Lizards). Director: Lina Wertmüller, 1963.

21. Title: *Scetate!* (Wake Up!) (Lyrics: Ferdinando Rossi)
Recording: RCA Italiana PML 10411, Napoli II, 1965 [Artist: Miranda Martino]
The music of this song is by Mario Costa arranged by Morricone.

VOLUME 2—WESTERN SONGS & BALLADS

1. Title: *Al Messico che vorrei* (Lyrics: Maria Travia)
Recording: RCA PM 45-3485 [Artist: Christy (Maria Cristina Brancucci)]
Film: *Tepepa* (Blood and Guns). Director: Giulio Petroni, 1969.

2. Title: *Death Rides a Horse* (Lyrics: Maurizio Attanasio)
Recording: RCA PM 45-3423 [Artist: Raoul (Ettore Raoul Lovecchio)]
Film: *Da uomo a uomo* (Death Rides a Horse). Director: Giulio Petroni, 1967.

3. Title: *Vamos a matar, compañeros* (Lyrics: Sergio Corbucci)
Recording: IT ZT 7009—1971 [Artists: Studio Choir]
Film: *Vamos a matar, compañeros* (Let's Go and Kill, Comrades). Director: Sergio Corbucci, 1970.

4. Title: *A Gringo Like Me* (Lyrics: Carol Danell)
Recording: RCA PML 10402—1965 [Artist: Peter Tevis]
Film: *Duello nel Texas* (Gunfight at Red Sands). Director: Ricardo Blasco, 1964.

5. Title: *Angel Face* (Lyrics: Maurizio Attanasio, alias for Grafman or Maurizio Graf)
Recording: ARC AN 4052 [Artists: Maurizio Graf with I Cantori Moderni di Alessandroni]
Film: *Una pistola per Ringo* (A Pistol for Ringo). Director: Duccio Tessari, 1965.

6. Title: *The Return of Ringo* (Lyrics: Maurizio Attanasio)
ARC AN 4069 [Artists: Maurizio Graf with I Cantori Moderni di Alessandroni]
Film: *Il ritorno di Ringo* (The Return of Ringo). Director: Duccio Tessari, 1965.

7. Title: *Lonesome Billy* (Lyrics: Peter Tevis)
Recording: RCA PM45-3352-1965 [Peter Tevis with I Cantori Moderni di Alessandroni]
Film: *Le pistole non discutono* (Guns Don't Argue). Director: Mario Calano, 1964.

8. Title: *Corri uomo çorri* (Lyrics: Audrey Stainton Nohra)
Recording: Eureka Parade EPC 1801 [Artist: Christy (Maria Cristina Brancucci)]
Film: *La resa dei conti* (The Big Gundown). Director: Sergio Sollima, 1967.

9. Title: *Eye for an Eye* (Lyrics: Maria Gioconda Gaspari and Audrey Stainton Nohra)
Recording: ARC AN 4083 [Artists: Maurizio Graf with I Cantori Moderni di Alessandroni]

Film: *Per qualche dollaro in più* (For a Few Dollars More). Director: Sergio Leone, 1966.

10. Title: *Per un pugno di dollari* (Lyrics: Peter Tevis)
Recording: RCA PM45 3352-1965 [Artists: Peter Tevis with I Cantori Moderni di Alessandroni]
Film: *Per un pugno di dollari* (A Fistful of Dollars). Director: Sergio Leone, 1964.

11. Title: *The Ballad of Hank McCain*, Part 1 (Lyrics: Audrey Stainton Nohra)
Recording: Jolly LPJ 5094 [Artist: Jackie Lynton]
Film: *Gli intoccabili* (Machine Gun McCain). Director: Giuliano Montaldo, 1969.

12. Title: *The Ballad of Hank McCain*, Part 2 (Lyrics: Audrey Stainton Nohra)
Recording: Jolly LPJ 5094 [Artist: Jackie Lynton]
Film: *Gli intoccabili* (Machine Gun McCain). Director: Giuliano Montaldo, 1969.

13. Title: *The Ballad of Hank McCain*, Part 3 (Lyrics: Audrey Stainton Nohra)
Recording: Jolly LPJ 5094 [Artist: Jackie Lynton]
Film: *Gli intoccabili* (Machine Gun McCain). Director: Giuliano Montaldo, 1969.

14. Title: *Faith—Upanisha* (Lyrics: Doug Fawlkes and Rocky Roberts)
Recording: GM GMS 0014 [Artist: Rocky Roberts]
Television series *L'uomo e la magia* (The Magic Man). Director: Sergio Giordani, 1971.

15. Title: *La canzone della libertà* (Lyrics: Luciano Lucignani)
Recording: Cetra LPB 35033 [Artist: Sergio Endrigo]
Film: *L'alibi* (The Alibi). Directors: Adolfo Celi, Vittorio Gassman, and Luciano Lucignani, 1968.

16. Title: *The Ballad of Sacco and Vanzetti*, Part 1 (Lyrics: Joan Baez)
Recording: RCA OLS 4 [Artist: Joan Baez]
Film: *Sacco e Vanzetti*. Director: Giuliano Montaldo, 1970.

17. Title: *The Ballad of Sacco and Vanzetti*, Part 2 (Lyrics: Joan Baez)
Recording: RCA OLS 4 [Artist: Joan Baez]
Film: *Sacco e Vanzetti*. Director: Giuliano Montaldo, 1970.

18. Title: *The Ballad of Sacco and Vanzetti*, Part 3 (Lyrics: Joan Baez)
Recording: RCA OLS 4 [Artist: Joan Baez]
Film: *Sacco e Vanzetti*. Director: Giuliano Montaldo, 1970.

19. Title: *Here's to You* (Lyrics: Joan Baez)
Recording: RCA OLS 4 [Artist: Joan Baez]
Film: *Sacco e Vanzetti*. Director: Giuliano Montaldo, 1970.

20. Title: *The Ballad of Sacco and Vanzetti* (Lyrics: Joan Baez)
Recording: Philips 6308 127-1971 [Artist: Scott Walker]
Film: *Sacco e Vanzetti*. Director: Giuliano Montaldo, 1970.

21. Title: *Marche de Sacco et Vanzetti—Here's to You* (Lyrics: Joan Baez, Georges Moustaki)
Recording: Polydor 205 610-1971 [Artist: Georges Moustaki]
Film: *Sacco e Vanzetti*. Director: Giuliano Montaldo, 1970.

VOLUME 3—THE 70S

1. Title: *We Are One* (Lyrics: Carol Connors)
Recording: Tam YX 7036 [Artist: Carol Connors]
Film: *Orca* (Orca: The Killer Whale). Director: Michael Anderson, 1977.

2. Title: *La califfa* (Lyrics: Alberto Bevilacqua)
Recording: Ricordi SMRL 6098-1972 [Artist: Milva]
Film: *La califfa* (Lady Caliph). Director: Alberto Bevilacqua, 1970.

3. Title: *Nata libera* (Lyrics: Sergio Bardotti and Gianfranco Baldazzi)
Recording: General Music GMS 0013 [Artist: Mireille Mathieu]
Italian television miniseries *I Nicotera* (1972). Music by Piero Piccioni, arranged by Morricone.

4. Title: *Viaggio senza bagagli* (Lyrics: Maria Travia)
Recording: Ricordi SMRL 6098 [Artist: Milva]
Film: *Il diavolo nel cervello* (Devil in the Brain). Director: Sergio Sollima, 1972.

5. Title: *Chi mai—Idiota* (Lyrics: Carlo Nistri)
Recording: IT ZT 7013 [Artist: Lisa Gastoni]
Film: *Maddalena*. Director: Jerzy Kawalerowicz, 1971.

6. Title: *J'oublie la pluie et le soleil* (Lyrics: Sergio Bardotti and Bernard Raduszinsky)
Recording: Philips 9101 702-1974 [Artist: Mireille Mathieu]
Film: *La califfa* (Lady Caliph). Director: Alberto Bevilacqua, 1970.

7. Title: *Metti, una sera a cena* (Lyrics: Giuseppe Patroni Griffi)
Recording: Ricordi SMRL 6098-1972 [Artist: Milva]
Film: *Metti, una sera a cena* (Love Circle). Director: Giuseppe Patroni Griffi, 1969.

8. Title: *L'eblouissante lumiére* (Lyrics: Michel Jourdan)
Recording: Philips 9101 702-1974 [Artist: Mireille Mathieu]
Film: *Giù la testa* (A Fistful of Dynamite). Director: Sergio Leone, 1971.

9. Title: *Io e te* (Lyrics: Daniele Pace)
Recording: LP CGD 132-1971 [Artist: Massimo Ranieri]
Film: *Metello*. Director: Mauro Bolognini, 1970.

10. Title: *Quando verranno i giorni* (Lyrics: Sergio Bardotti and Gianfranco Baldazzi)
Recording: General Music GMS 0013 [Artist: Mireille Mathieu]
Italian television miniseries *I Nicoter* (1972). Music by Piero Piccioni arranged by Morricone.

11. Title: *Una donna che ti ama* (Lyrics: Audrey Stainton Nohra)
Recording: CTI Italia 9702 [Artist: Astrud Gilberto]
Fim: *Gli scassinatori* (The Burglars). Director: Henri Verneuil, 1971.

12. Title: *Immagini del tempo* (Lyrics: Maria Travia)
Recording: Ricordi SMRL 6098-1972 [Artist: Milva]
Film: *Le foto proibite di una signora per bene* (Forbidden Photos of a Lady above Suspicion). Director: Luciano Ercoli, 1970.

13. Title: *Pas vu, pas prís* (Lyrics: Maurice Vidalin)
Recording: Barclay 71 471-1972 [Artist: Mireille Mathieu]
Film: *Gli scassinatori* (The Burglars). Director: Henri Verneuil, 1971.

14. Title: *Chi mai*—French version as *J'ai peur* (Lyrics: Carlo Nistri)
Recording: Previously unreleased [Artist: Lisa Gastoni]
Film: *Maddalena*. Director: Jerzy Kawalerowicz, 1971.

15. Title: *Questa specie d'amore* (Lyrics: Alberto Bevilacqua)
Recording: Ricordi SMRL 6098-1972 [Artist: Milva]
Film: *Questa specie d'amore* (This Kind of Love). Director: Alberto Bevilacqua, 1972.

16. Title: *Un amico*—French version (Lyrics: Daniel Beretta)
Recording: GM ZSLGE 55496 [Artist: Daniel Beretta]
Film: *Revolver* (Blood in the Streets). Director: Sergio Sollima, 1973.

17. Title: *Mon ami de toujours* (Lyrics: Mireille Mathieu)
Recording: Barclay 71 471-1972 [Artist: Mireille Mathieu]
Film: *Gli scassinatori* (The Burglars). Director: Henri Verneuil, 1971.

18. Title: *Argomenti* (Lyrics: Franca Evangelisti)
Recording: CTI Italia 9702 [Artist: Astrud Gilberto]
Film: *Gli scassinatori* (The Burglars). Director: Henri Verneuil, 1971.

19. Title: *Ridevi* (Lyrics: Maria Travia)
Recording: Ricordi SMRL 6098-1972 [Artist: Milva]
Film: *L'alibi* (The Alibi). Directors: Adolfo Celi, Vittorio Gassman, and Luciano Lucignani, 1968.

20. Title: *La donna madre* (Lyrics: Alberto Bevilacqua)
Recording: Philips 9101 702-1974 [Artist: Mireille Mathieu]

21. Title: *Un amico* (Lyrics: Daniel Beretta)
Recording: GM ZSLGE 55496 [Artist: Daniel Beretta—12-string guitar version]
Film: *Revolver* (Blood in the Streets). Director: Sergio Sollima, 1973.

VOLUME 4—THE 80S & 90S

1. Title: *It's Wrong for Me to Love You* (Lyrics: Carol Connors)
Recording: Applause APLP 1017-1982 [Artist: Pia Zadora]
Film: *Butterfly*. Director: Matt Cimber, 1981.

2. Title: *A brisa do coracao*, Part 1 (Lyrics: Francesco De Melis and Emma Scoles)
Recording: Epic EPC 480383 [Artist: Dulce Pontes with guitar soloist Filippo Rizzuto]
Film: *Sostiene Pereira* (Explain Pereira). Director: Roberto Faenza, 1995.

3. Title: *Sean Sean* (Lyrics: Leonie Gane and Amii Stewart)
Recording: BMG BL 74808-1990 [Artist: Amii Stewart]
Film: *Giù la testa* (A Fistful of Dynamite). Director: Sergio Leone, 1971.

4. Title: *Love Affair* (Lyrics: Alan and Marilyn Bergman)
Recording: Warner Bros. 9362-46254-2-1996 [Artist: K. D. Lang (Kathryn Dawn Lang)]
Film: *Love Affair*. Director: Glenn Gordon Caron, 1994 [song was not used]
Film: *Twister*. Director: Jan De Bont, 1996 [song used]

5. Title: *My Heart and I* (Lyrics: Leonie Gane and Amii Stewart)
Recording: BMG BL 74808 [Artist: Amii Stewart]
Italian television series *La piovra*. Director: Luigi Perelli, 1990.

6. Title: *The Loving Game* (Lyrics: Cesare De Natale)
Recording: Epic EPC 478475-2 [Artist: Simona Patitucci]
Film: *La notte e il momento* (The Night and the Moment). Director: Anna Maria Tatò, 1995.

7. Title: *Ho fatto un sogno (e l'ho chiamato Roma)* (Lyrics: Antonello Venditti and Sergio Bardotti)
Recording: Heinz 74321-1997 [Artist: Antonello Venditti] from the album *Antonello nel paese delle meraviglie* (1997)

8. Title: *C'era una volta la terra mia* (Lyrics: Maria Travia)
Recording: RCA PB 6807-1985 [Artist: Katia Ricciarelli]
Film: *C'era una volta il West* (Once Upon a Time in the West). Director: Sergio Leone, 1968.

9. Title: *Ricordare* (Lyrics: Giuseppe Tornatore and Pascal Quignard)
Recording: Sony Classical SK 52504 [Artist: Gerard Depardieu]
Film: *Una pura formalità* (A Pure Formality). Director: Giuseppe Tornatore, 1994). [Soundtrack by Ennio and Andrea Morricone]

10. Title: *Le secrét du Sahara* (Lyrics: Leonie Gane and Lang)
Recording: RCA BL 71947 [Artist: Debbie Davis]

Italian television miniseries *Il segreto del Sahara* (The Secret of the Sahara). Director: Alberto Negrin, 1987.

11. Title: *Sahara* (Lyrics: Jack Fishman)
Recording: Varese Sarabande STV 81211 [Artist: Cathy Cole]
Film: *Sahara*. Director: Andrew V. McLaglen, 1983.

12. Title: *Hurry to Me* (Lyrics: Jack Fishman)
Recording: BMG BL 74808-1990 [Artist: Amii Stewart]
Film: *Metti, una sera a cena* (Love Circle). Director: Giuseppe Patroni Griffi, 1969.

13. Title: *Di più* (Lyrics: Lucio Dalla)
Recording: MBG 461192 (1997) [Artist: Tosca (Tiziana Tosca Donati)]

14. Title: *Desire—Chi mai* (Lyrics: Leonie Gane and Amii Stewart)
Recording: BMG BL 74808-1990 [Artist: Amii Stewart]
Film: *Maddalena*. Director: Jerzy Kawalerowicz, 1971.
Note: The film original instrumental version was used as title theme for the nine-episode BBC television series *The Life and Times of David Lloyd George* (1981).

15. Title: *A brisa do coracao*, Part 2 (Lyrics: Francesco De Melis and Emma Scoles)
Recording: Epic EPC 480383 [Artist: Dulce Pontes with guitar soloist Filippo Rizzuto]
Film: *Sostiene Pereira* (Explain Pereira). Director: Roberto Faenza, 1995.

16. Title: *Could Heaven B*e (Lyrics: Leonie Gane)
Recording: BMG BL 74808 [Artist: Amii Stewart]
Film: *Voyage of Terror: The Achille Lauro Affair*. Director: Roberto Faenza, 1990.

17. Title: *Effacer le passe* (Lyrics: Giuseppe Tornatore and Pascal Quignard)
Recording: Sony Classical SK 52504 [Artist: Gerard Depardieu]
Film: *Una pura formalità* (A Pure Formality). Director: Giuseppe Tornatore, 1994. [Soundtrack by Ennio and Andrea Morricone] same base as *Ricordare* (see #9).

18. Title: *Libera l'amore* (Lyrics and music: Zucchero [Adelmo Fornaciari])
Recording: Polydor 841 125-1989. Song arranged by Morricone for the album *Oro, Incenso & Birra*

Bibliography

Agostini, Roberto. "Sanremo Effects: The Festival and the Italian Canzone (1950s–1960s)." In Franco Fabbri and Goffredo Plastino (Eds.), *Made in Italy: Studies in Popular Music*. New York: Routledge, 2014, 28–40.

Barbarani, Francesco (a cura). *Il sacro esperimento del Paraguay: Dagli scritti del gesuita Antonio Sepp*. Verona: Cassa di Risparmio di Verona, Vicenza, Belluno e Ancona, 1990.

Brizio-Skov, Flavia (Ed.). *Popular Italian Cinema: Culture and Politics in a Postwar Society*. London: I. B. Tauris, 2011, 107–52.

Calabretto, Roberto. *Pasolini e la musica*. Pordenone: Cinemazero, 1999.

Caprara, Valerio (a cura). *Spettabile pubblico: Carosello Napoletano di Ettore Giannini*. Napoli: Alfredo Guida Editore, 1998.

Caraman, Philip. *The Lost Paradise: The Jesuit Republic in South America*. New York: Seabury Press, 1976.

Collombin, Jean-Blaise. *Ennio Morricone: Perspective d'une œuvre*. Paris: L'Harmattan, 2016.

Conti, Francesca Romana and Mila De Santis (a cura). *Catalogo Critico del Fondo Alfredo Casella*. I. Carteggi; II. Scritti, Musiche, Concerti. Firenze: Leo S. Olschki Editore, 1992.

Cooper, David. *Bartók: Concerto for Orchestra*. Cambridge: Cambridge University Press, 1996; 2nd edition, 2004.

Cropsey, Eugene H. "*Sacco and Vanzetti:* An American World Premiere." *The Opera Quarterly*, vol. 19, no. 4 (Autumn 2003): 754–80.

Cucci, Stefano. *Lontane presenze . . . L'universo poetico di Ennio Morricone*. Lucca: Libreria Musicale Italiana, 2018.

Danese, Silvio. *Anni fuggenti: Il romanzo del cinema italiano*. Milano: Bompiani, 2003.

De Benedictis, Angela Ida and Veniero Rizzardi (Eds.). *Nostalgia for the Future: Luigi Nono's Selected Writings and Interviews*. Foreword by Nuria Schoenberg Nono. Berkeley: University of California Press, 2018.

De Fusco, Renato. *Made in Italy: Storia del design italiano*. Roma-Bari: Edizioni Laterza, 2007; 2nd edition, 2010.
Fabbri, Franco and Goffredo Plastino (Eds.). *Made in Italy: Studies in Popular Music*. New York: Routledge, 2014.
Fallaci, Oriana. *Un uomo: Romanzo*. Milano: Rizzoli, 1982. Published in English as *A Man*. London: Arrow, 1993.
Feisst, Sabine M. "Arnold Schoenberg and the Cinematic Art." *The Musical Quarterly*, vol. 83, no. 1 (Spring 1999): 93–113.
———. *Schoenberg's New World: The American Years*. New York: Oxford University Press, 2011.
Frayling, Christopher. *Spaghetti Westerners: Cowboys and Europeans from Karl May to Sergio Leone*. London: I. B. Tauris, 1981; 2nd edition, 1998; 3rd edition, 2006.
Frías, Pedro, Jose. *Memorias del músico Zipoli*. Córdoba: Ediciones Olocco, 1975.
Garinei, Lello and Marco Giovannini. *Garinei e Giovannini presentano: Quarant'anni di teatro musicale all'italiana*. Milano: Rizzoli, 1985.
Harrison, Nicholas. "Comprehensive Bibliography on *The Battle of Algiers*." *Oxford Bibliographies*, http://www.oxfordbibliographies.com/view/document/obo-9780199791286/obo-9780199791286-0140.xml.
Heldt, Guido, Tarek Krohn, Peter Moormann, and Willem Strank (Eds.). *Ennio Morricone*. München: edition text + kritik, 2014.
Iddon, Martin. *New Music at Darmstadt: Nono, Stockhausen, Cage, and Boulez*. Cambridge: Cambridge University Press, 2013.
Leinberger, Charles. *Ennio Morricone's* The Good, the Bad and the Ugly. Lanham, MD: Scarecrow Press, 2004.
———. "*Degüello*, 'No Mercy for the Losers': The Enduring Role of the Solo Trumpet in the Soundtrack of the Old West." *International Trumpet Guild Journal* (March 2015): 18–33.
Lucci, Gabriele (a cura). *Morricone: Cinema e oltre*. Milano: Electa, 2007.
Malvano, Andrea. *L'arte di arrangiar (si)*. Lucca: Libreria Musicale Italiana, 2015.
McNaspy, C. J. and J. M. Blanch. *Lost Cities of Paraguay*. Chicago: Loyola University Press, 1982.
Melis, Ennio. *Storia della RCA: La Grande Pentola*, a cura di Anna Maria Angiolini Melis e Elisa De Bartoli con una nota di Franco Migliacci. Lavagna, Genoa: Editrice ZONA, 2016.
Miceli, Sergio. *Morricone, la musica, il cinema*. Milano: Ricordi/Mucchi, 1994.
———. (a cura). *Norme con ironie: Scritti per i settant'anni di Ennio Morricone*. Milano: Edizioni Suvini Zerboni, 1998.
———. "Leone, Morricone and the Italian Way to Revisionist Westerns." In *The Cambridge Companion to Film Music*, edited by Mervyn Cooke and Fiona Ford. Cambridge: Cambridge University Press, 2016, 265–93.
Mininni, Francesco. *Sergio Leone*. Milano: Editrice Il Castoro, 1989; 2nd edition, 1994.
Montariello, Carlo. *La "Napoli milionaria!" di Eduardo De Filippo: Dalla realtà all'arte senza soluzione di continuità*. Napoli: Liguori Editore, 2006.

Monteleone, Franco. *Storia della radio e della television italiana*. Venezia: Marsilio, 1992.
Morricone, Ennio. *Lontano dai sogni: Conversazioni con Antonio Monda*. Milano: Mondadori, 2010.
———. *Inseguendo quel suono: La mia musica, la mia vita. Conversazioni con Alessandro De Rosa*. Milano: Mondadori, 2016.
———. *Ennio Morricone in His Own Words: Morricone in Conversations with Alessandro De Rosa*. Translated by Maurizio Corbella. New York: Oxford University Press, 2019.
Morricone, Ennio e Sergio Miceli. *Comporre per il cinema: Teoria e prassi della musica per film*. Venezia: Marsilio, 2001.
———. *Composing for the Cinema: The Theory and Praxis of Music in Film*. Translated by Gillian B. Anderson. Lanham, MD: Scarecrow Press, 2013.
O'Leary, Alan. The Battle of Algiers *at Fifty: End of Empire Cinema and the First Banlieue*. Available at https://filmquarterly.org/2017/01/10/the-battle-of-algiers-at-fifty-end-of-empire-cinema-and-the-first-banlieue-film/.
Panagoulis, Alexandros. *Altri seguiranno: Poesie e documenti dal carcere di Boyati*. Palermo: S. F. Flaccovio, 1972.
———. *Vi scrivo da un carcere in Grecia*. Milano: Rizzoli, 1974.
———. *Collected Poems*. Athens: Papazissis, 2002.
Plastino, Goffredo and Joseph Sciorra (Eds.). *Neapolitan Postcards: The Canzone Napoletana as Transnational Subject*. Lanham, MD: Rowman & Littlefield, 2016.
Restagno, Enzo (a cura). *Petrassi*. Torino: EDT (Edizioni di Torino), 1992.
Sciannameo, Franco. "Ennio Morricone at 85: A Conversation about His 'Mission.'" *The Musical Times*, vol. 154, no. 1924 in *The Musical Time* (Autumn 2013): 37–46.
Temkin, Moshik. *The Sacco-Vanzetti Affair: America on Trial*. New Haven, CT: Yale University Press, 2009.
Tortora, Daniela. *Nuova Consonanza: Trent'anni di musica contemporanea in Italia (1959–1988)*. Lucca: Libreria Musicale Italiana, 1990.
———. *Nuova Consonanza: 1989–1994*. Lucca: Libreria Musicale Italiana, 1994.
Trudu, Antonio. "La distruzione del tempio: John Cage a Darmstadt nel 1958 (e prima, e dopo)." In Sergio Miceli (a cura), *Norme con ironie: Scritti per i settant'anni di Ennio Morricone*. Milano: Edizioni Suvini Zerboni, 1998, 313–46.
Weissmann, John S. *Goffredo Petrassi* [in English]. Milano: Edizioni Suvini Zerboni, 1980.
Yule, Andrew. *Fast Fade: David Puttnam, Columbia Pictures, and the Battle for Hollywood*. New York: Delta Publishing, 1989.

Index

absolute music. *See* "musica assoluta"
Academy Awards, 98, 118
Adagio per oboe, violoncello, archi ed organo (Zipoli), 109
Adriana (sister), 12
aesthetic, 118
The Alamo (film), 48
Alessandroni, Alessandro, 43, 47, 65
Alfano, Franco, 117
Ali's Theme (Morricone, E.), 5, 99, *104*, 104–5
Almost a Man and a Half a Man. See Un uomo a metà
Altri seguiranno (Others will Follow) (Panagoulis), 95
Amapola, 70, 75n29
America, 69
American Academy in Rome, 78
An American in Paris, 40
Americanization, 10, 13
American literature, 68
American style, 34
"Animal Trilogy," 3, 67, 84–85
Anka, Paul, 2, 33
Anno Santo celebrations, 11–12, 28n10
anti-Fascism, 95
anti-Semitism, 97
applied music. *See* "musica applicata"
Argento, Dario, 3, 5, 67

arrangements, 6, 37–38, 44, 45n20; of commercial music, 2, 13, 27, 52–53; ghost, 13; of Neapolitan songs, 41; principles of, 33; at Teatro Sistina, 11
Arrangements (Morricone, E.), 44
Art Nouveau, 42
"Art of Arranging," 39
Asciolla, Dino, 80–81, 92n9, 140n8
atonality, 15
Aus Italien (Strauss), 39
Austin, Larry, 77
avant-garde techniques, 15, 22
Ave Maria Guarani (film), 110, 112
Aznavour, Charles, 36

Bach, Johann Sebastian, 5, 27, 53, 66, 86, 101–2, 114n14
Baez, Joan, 4, 96, 97, 122
The Ballad of Hank McCain, 122
Barabbas (film), 47, 51, 72n1
Barbetti, Maurizio, 93n10
Barboni, Enzo, 64
Bartók, Bela, 15, 16, 28n19
Barzizza, Pippo, 28n11
La battaglia di Algeri (The Battle of Algiers) (film), 4–5, 61, 95–102, 105, 114n16, 115n18, 126
La bataille d'Alger, un film dans l'histoire (film), 5, 99

Beethoven, Ludwig Van, 137
Begleitungsmusik zu einer Lichtspielscene, op. 34 (Schoenberg), 82
Bellugi, Piero, 141n27
Bensmail, Malek, 5, 99, 101
Berg, Alban, 124
Berio, Luciano, 23, 81, 117, 128, 134, 139n2
Berlioz, Hector, 81, 85
Bernstein, Leonard, 74n10, 107
betrayal, 69
The Betrothed. See *I promessi sposi*
Betti, Laura, 90
The Bible (film), 61, 75n25, 140n12
Biondo, Antonio Giuseppe, 32
The Birdcage (film), 87
The Bird with the Crystal Plumage. See *L'uccello dalle piume di cristallo*
birth, 9
Bixio, Cesare Andrea, 42–43
Black Panthers, 100
Blasco, Ricardo, 48
Blitzstein, Marc, 98
Blood and Guns. See *Tepepa*
Bolero, 47, 51
Bolt, Robert, 107
Brahms, 22
Britten, Benjamin, 73n4
Buck, Pearl S., 93n13
Bugsy (film), 120, 122, 123
Le buone notizie (Good News) (film), 92n5
Il buono, il brutto e il cattivo (The Good, the Bad, and the Ugly) (film), 2, 54–55, 64–65, 119
The Burglars. See *Gli scassinatori*
Burn!. See *Queimada!*

cabaret, 4, 90–91
Cadenza per flauto e nastro magnetico (Morricone, E.), 128
Caffarelli, Reginaldo, 9
Cage, John, 22, 23, 24, 29n22, 78
La Cage aux folles (film), 4, 86–87
La Cage aux folles II (film), 4
La Cage aux folles III (film), 4
Caggiano, Roberto, 9
Calvino, Italo, 85
Canone Inverso (film), 124
Cantico del Giubileo (Morricone, E.), 28n10
Canti per la libertà (Songs of Freedom) (film), 96
Canto Morricone, 6; Vol. 1-The 1960s, 159–61; Vol. 2-Western songs & ballads, 161–64; Vol. 3-The 70s, 164–66; Vol. 4-The 80s & 90s, 166–68
Canto sospeso (Nono), 24
capitalism, 61
Caput Coctu Show, 91
Carosello Napoletano (film), 40, 45n16
Carpitella, Diego, 12, 28n9
cartoons, 50
Carunchio, Carlo, 86
Casablanca (film), 103
Casals, Pablo, 133
The Case is Closed, Forget It. See *L'istruttoria è chiusa*
Casella, Alfredo, 15, 39, 132–33
Casorati, Felice, 133
Castelnuovo-Tedesco, Mario, 131–32
Casualties of War (film), 124
Catania, Francesco, 51
Catholicism, 11–12, 106, 110
The Cat O'Nine Tails. See *Il gatto a nove code*
C'era una volta il West (Once Upon a Time in the West) (film), 3, 56–60, 58–59, 64, 119
C'era una volta in America (Once Upon a Time in America) (film), 3, 54, 56–57, 67–70, 75n29, 118
C'era una volta la Rivoluzione (Once Upon a Time a Revolution) (film), 3, 56, 67–68
Les Chakachas, 105
chamber music, 22
Changes, Indeterminacy, and Communication (Cage), 24

Chaplin, Charlie, 49–50, 54
Chemins III (Berio), 81, 134
chess playing, 25, 124
children, 9
Christianity, 87, 102, 106, 135
civil rights, 96
classical musicians, collaborations with, 80–81
A Clockwork Orange (film), 50
Cockeye's Song, 70–71, *71*, 126
Cold Eyes of Fear. See Gli occhi freddi della paura
Colonne sonore (periodical), 29nn24–25
color, 81–82
Come, Sail Away (song), 6, 119, 120
comedy, 54
Comencini, Luigi, 82
commedia dell'arte, 49
commedie all'italiana (Comedies Italian Style) (film genre), 121, 140nn8–9
commercial music, 7, 118, 122; access to world of, 22; arrangements of, 2, 13, 27, 52–53; influence on, 2; success with, 79
communism, 97
Communist Party, Partito Comunista Italiano (PCI), 10
Compañeros. See Vamos a matar compañeros
Comporre per il cinema (Miceli & Morricone, E.), 1, 29n23, 92n9
composer/conductor, 6, 35
composition studies, 9
concert music, 35
Concerto for Orchestra (Bartok), 28n19
Concerto per flauto e orchestra (Petrassi), 128
Concerto per orchestra (Morricone, E.), 14–15, 17–22, *18–21*, 26, 28n20, 127
Concerto per violino e orchestra (Garofalo), 27n2
Concerto per violino in sol minore (Ferdinandi), 27n2

Concerto romano per organo, 3 trombe, 3 tromboni, archi e timpani, op. 43 (Casella), 133–34, 141nn27–28
concert works, 5–6, 7, 126–39
Conservatorio di Santa Cecilia, 9, 11–13, 141n24
Consolini, Giorgio, 74n16
Conspectus Tuus (Morricone, E.), *109*, 109–11
consumerism, 45n16
Continuo (Maderna), 23
Coppola, Anton, 98
Corbucci, Sergio, 60
Cori di Didone (Nono), 24
Coro di morti (Petrassi), 15, 16, 28n14
Costa, Mario Pasquale, 41
counterpoint, 16, 27, 53
Courboin, Charles-Marie, 133
Cucci, Stefano, 135
Curson, Ted, 88

D'amore si muore (One Can Die of Love) (film), 86
Dan Savio (pseudonym), 48
Darmstadt, 22–24, 29n22
death, 50
The Death of Klinghoffer, 139n4
Deborah's Theme, 70, *70*, 71, 118
De Filippo, Eduardo, 40
degree, 11
El Degüello (film), 48, 50, 53, 56, 71
Dell'Orso, Edda, 29n28, 55
De Ninno, Alfredo, 9, 27n2
De Niro, Robert, 69, 106
Denza, Luigi, 39
Deonna, Emmanuel, 101
De Palma, Brian, 122, 126
depth, 90
De Seta, Vittorio, 79
detective/crime stories, 93n10
Dimensioni sonore (Sonic Dimensions) (Morricone, E.), 3, 4
Dimensioni sonore, musiche per l'immagine e l'immaginazione, 83–84, 89

discipline of, 2
Disney, Walt, 58
Distacco I (Morricone, E.), 13
Distacco II (Morricone, E.), 13
Distanze (Morricone, E.), 22, 25, 29n27, 92n5
Divertimento (Bartok), 16
Divina creatura (*The Divine Nymph*) (film), 43
Donquishoot, Rabah, 99
Dreyfus, Alfred, 113n3
Duck You, Sucker!. *See C'era una volta la Rivoluzione*
Duello nel Texas (*Gunfight at Red Sands* or *Gringo*) (film), 48, 73n9

early life, 2, 9, 11
Eastwood, Clint, 2–3, 49–50, 74n13
easy listening, 34
economy, 40
education: at Conservatorio di Santa Cecilia, 9–11–13, 141n24; degree, 11, 12; graduation, 13
electro-engineering, 75n27
electronic music, 84
Elevator for the Scaffold, 88
emotions, 89
The End of a Mystery. *See La luz prodigiosa*
The Ennio Morricone Songbook, 121
Ennio Morricone un film una musica, 89
Un esercito di 5 uomini (*The Five Man Army*) (film), 60
Esposizione Universale Roma (EUR), 74n24
European Recovery Act. *See* Marshall Plan
Evangelisti, Franco, 23, 77–78
experimental works, 3, 78, 83, 84

Faith, Percy, 34
Fallaci, Oriana, 95
family, 12–14, 22, 92n6
fans, 6
fascism, 10, 74n24, 95

The Fascist. *See Il federale*
fatalism, 81
Il federale (*The Fascist*) (film), 86
The Feed-back, 78
Fellini, Federico, 2, 85
Ferdinandi, Antonio, 9, 27n2
Ferienkurse, 22, 23–24
Ferrara, Franco, 47
Ferri, Constantino, 9
Festival della canzone napoletana (*Festival of Neapolitan Song*), 41
fifths, 41–42
film, illusion in, 90
film music, 12, 82, 118; Cage and, 24; defining, 89; ghost arranging, 13; history of, 1, 123; horizontal application of, 90; income from, 7; Leone and, 24; recording studios and, 83; reputation in, 3; seminars in, 29n23; silence in, 24; from '64-'68, 61–63; theory of, 1; vertical application of, 90
film noir, 81–82
The Firebird (Stravinsky), 134
First Symphony (Brahms), 22
A Fistful of Dollars (film). *See Per un pugno di dollari*
The Five Man Army. *See Un esercito di 5 uomini*
Flamini, Alberto, 10
flashbacks, 69
Fleisher, Richard, 47
Fleming, Renée, 6, 119, 120
Folsom, Frank M., 31
Fonosynth, 83–84
For a Few Dollars More. *See Per qualche dollaro in più*
For a Fistful of Dynamite (film), 63
Four Flies on Grey Velvet. *See Quattro mosche di velluto grigio*
Francis, Connie, 37
"Frank's Allusive Theme," *59*
free jazz, 83
Frescobaldi, Girolamo, 5, 7, 102–3, *103*, 114n16, 136–37, *137–39*

friendships, 61
Fünf Sätze für Streichquartett, op. 5 (Webern), 25
funiculi funiculà, 39

Gabriel's Oboe, 108, 108–10, 119
Galeazzi, Enrico Pietro, 32
Gangi, Mario, 132
Garinei, Piero, 11
Garofalo, Carlo Giorgio, 9, 27n2
Il gatto a nove code (The Cat O'Nine Tails) (film), 3, 84
Gebrauchsmusik, 90–91
Germani, Fernando, 132, 133, 141n24
Gervasio, Raffaele, 39–40
Gestazione (Morricone, E.), 6, 126–27
Gesto-Azione (Morricone, E.), 126–27
Ghia, Fernando, 106–8, 110, 115n23
ghost arranging, 13
ghost composing/supervising, 13
Giacca, Dino, 41, 42
Giallo, 81–84
Gillo Pontecorvo's Return to Algiers (film), 99
GINC. See *Gruppo di improvvisazione Nuova Consonanza*
Giovanni, Francesco, 109
Giovanni, Sandro, 11
The Girl of Ipanema, 122
Giù la testa (film). See *C'era una volta la Rivoluzione*
Gli intoccabili (film), 122
Gli occhi freddi della paura (Cold Eyes of Fear) (film), 92n5
Gli scassinatori (The Burglars) (film), 122
Gli uomini che mascalzoni (What Scoundrels Men Are!) (film), 42–43
The Good, the Bad, and the Ugly. See *Il buono, il brutto e il cattivo*
The Good Earth (Buck), 93n13
Good News. See *Le buone notizie*
The Gospel According to St. Matthew. See *Il Vangelo secondo Matteo*
GRA (*grande raccordo anulare*), 31

Greek tragedy, 49
Griffes, Charles, 133
A Gringo Like Me, 48, 73n9
Gruppo di improvvisazione Nuova Consonanza (GINC), 3, 77–79
Gunfight at Red Sands or *Gringo*. See *Duello nel Texas*

Haazen, Guido, 101
Hammar, Ali, 115n17
Hancock, Herbie, 118–19
"Harmonica's Theme," 58
harmony studies, 9
Harold en Italie (Berlioz), 81, 92n9
The Hateful Eight (film), 122
The Hawks and the Sparrows. See *Uccellacci e uccellini*
Das heilige Experiment (Hochwälder), 115n23
Henrici, Christian Friedrich, 114n14
Herrmann, Bernard, 2, 12–13
Hill, Terence, 64
L'histoire du soldat (Stravinsky), 78–79
Hitchcock, Alfred, 2
Hochwälder, Fritz, 115n23
Holy Year, 11–12
horizontal application, of film music, 90
Huston, John, 75n25, 140n12

If You Meet Sartana Pray for Your Death. See *Se incontri Sartana digli che è un uomo morto*
illusion, in film, 90
improvisational music, 3
Improvvisazioni a formazioni variate dei compositori-esecutori, 78
Improvvisazioni melodiche (Melodic Improvisations), 96
income, 7, 22, 61, 92n6
Incontri di fasce sonore (Evangelisti), 23
infanticide, 54
Internationale Ferienkurse für Neuu Musik, 22–23
intrapreneurs, 2

invenzione (invention), 65
Invenzione per John, 65–66, 65–67
I promessi sposi (The Betrothed) (film), 120
Iraq invasion, 100
L'istruttoria è chiusa (The Case is Closed, Forget It) (film), 92n5
Italia, rapsodia per orchestra, op. 11 (Casella), 39
I Tempi della Fine (Time of the World's End) (film), 102
Ives, Charles, 127
I Wonder as I Wander, 73n4
I write from a prison in Greece. See *Vi scrivo da un carcere in Grecia*

Jamaica, 74n16
jazz, 28n11
Jeu de cartes (Stravinsky), 18
"Jill's Theme," 59
Joffé, Roland, 106–7, 113
Jones, Quincy, 118

Kammerkonzert (Berg), 124
Kapò (film), 100
Karamanlis, Konstantinos, 95
Ketoff, Paolo, 81, 83, 93n10, 93n15
Klinghoffer, Leon, 119, 139n4
Koussevitzky Foundation, 16
Kramer, Gorny, 13
Kraus, Peter, 37
Kubrick, Stanley, 50
Kurosawa, Akira, 73n6

Lacerenza, Michele, 46n22, 73n8
Lady and the Tramp (film), 58
Leftism, 61
legacy, 5–6
La leggenda del pianista sull'oceano (The Legend of 1900) (film), 120
Lehrman, Leonard, 98
Leibowitz, Renè, 100
Leone, Sergio, 118, 121; collaboration with, 2, 3, 48–50, 72, 73n8, 100; death of, 63; film music and, 24; Kurosawa and, 73n6; Mininni and, 49–50, 53–54, 57–58, 63–65, 68–70, 74n12
Leopardi, Giacomo, 15
Liberamente mosso (Morricone, E.), 128–29
"Library Music," 82–83
libri gialli, 82
The Life and Times of David Lloyd George, 125
Lo chiamavano Trinità (They Call Me Trinity) (film), 64, 75n26
Lonesome Billy, 48
Love Affair (film), 119–20
Lussu, Emilio, 54
Luttazzi, Lelio, 13
La luz prodigiosa (The End of a Mystery) (film), 119
Lynton, Jackie, 122

Ma, Yo-Yo, 125–26
Macchi, Egisto, 79
Madama Butterfly (Puccini), 22
Maddalena (film), 124
Maderna, Bruno, 23
madrigale drammatico. See *Coro di morti*
The Man Who Shot Liberty Valance (film), 54
"Man with a Harmonica," 58
Marcello, Alessandro, 86
Marchetti, Gianni, 72n1
Marcia degli accattoni (March of the Beggars), 66–67, 67
Marco (son), 14
Marco Polo (film), 92n9, 126
Marshall Plan, 27n5, 31
Martino, Miranda, 20, 42
Marxism, 87, 97, 102
Masonic Funeral Music K 477 (Mozart), 16
Meditazione orale, 91
Melis, Ennoi, 32
Melodic Improvisations. See *Improvvisazioni melodiche*

Menáge all'italiana (Menage Italian Style) (film), 121, 140n8
Merrill, Helen, 36, 45n21
Messico e Irlanda or *Mesa Verde*, 67
Metro-Goldwin-Mayer, 93n13
MEV. *See Musica Elettronica Viva*
Mexican Revolution, 64
Miceli, Sergio, 1, 29n23, 67, 92n9, 112
Mike Perkins (pseudonym), 48
military service, 13
Mininni, Francesco, 2df, 74n12; Leone and, 49–50, 53–54, 57–58, 63–65, 68–70, 74n12
Minnelli, Vincent, 40
Il mio nome è Nessuno (My Name is Nobody) (film), 64, 72
Miranda Martino—Napoli (Morricone, E.), 41
Miranda Martino—Napoli Volume II (Morricone, E.), 41
Missa Luba, 101
Missa Papae Francisci (Morricone, E.), 6, 135–36
The Mission (film), 5, 28n10, 100–101, 106–12, *108*, *111*, 113, 126, 135
Modugno, Domenico, 87
Mondadori, Arnoldo, 93n10
Montaldo, Giuliano, 4, 92n9
The Moon of the Caribbean (film), 48
Morricone, Andrea, 28n20
Morricone, Ennio. *See specific entries*
Morricone, la musica, il cinema (Miceli), 112
Morricone, Maria (wife), 14
Morricone, Mario (father), 9, 129
Morricone, Valentina (granddaughter), 7, 136, 138
Morricone—La musica nel cinema di Pasolini, 89
Moses (film), 126
Mozart, Wolfgang Amadeus, 16, 88
"musica applicata" (applied music), 79, 118, 123
"musica assoluta" (absolute music), 79, 118, 123, 125

Musica Elettronica Viva (MEV), 78
musical comedy, 4
musical theater, 86
Musica per 11 violini (Morricone, E.), 22, 25–27, 29n28, 55, 67, 92n5
Musica sul velluto (Morricone, E.), 42, 45n21
"Musica sul velluto," 43
Music for String Instruments, Percussion and Celesta (Bartok), 15, 16
Mussolini, Benito, 15, 74n24
My Name is Nobody. See Il mio nome è Nessuno

Naples, 40
Napoli milionaria (film), 40
Napoli milionaria (opera), 40
Nascimbene, Mario, 47
Nataletti, Giorgio, 12, 28n9
Nati per la musica (radio show), 13
Nazis, 15
Neapolitan songs, 40, 41, 45n20
Neri, Ennio, 42–43
New Music Ensemble (NME), 77
Nicolai, Bruno, 3, 13, 83, 84
Niles, John Jacob, 73n4
NME. *See* New Music Ensemble
Noche oscura (Patrassi), 15, 28n17
Nono, Luigi, 23, 24
Nuova Consonanza, 77, 78, 91n1
Nuovo Cinema Paradiso (film), 86, 120

object trouvés, 55
Obmra di lontana presenza (Morricone, E.), 6
Oboe sommerso (Quasimodo), 5, 105
Oboe sommerso (Sunken Oboe) (Morricone, E.), 13, 105–6
Ogni volta (Every Time), 2, 33
Ogro (Operation Ogro) (film), 100–101
Oh Danny Boy, 58
Olympics, 74n24
Ombra di lontana presenza per viola, orchestra d'archi e nastro magnetico (Morricone, E.), 81, 134

Once Upon a Time a Revolution. See C'era una volta la Rivoluzione
Once Upon a Time in America. See C'era una volta in America
Once Upon a Time in the West. See C'era una volta il West
On Earth as It Is In Heaven, 110, 135
One Can Die of Love. See D'amore si muore
O'Neil, Eugene, 48
On the Waterfront, 74n10
Opera XII (Frescobaldi), 136–37
Orchestra del Teatro La Fenice (Morricone, E.), 28n20
L'orchestrazione moderna nella musica leggera (Barzizza), 28n11
Oscar/Academy Award, 5, 118
Others will Follow. See Altri seguiranno

Panagoulis, Alexander, 5, 95–96, 113
Papadopoulos, Georgios, 95
Parlami d'amore Mariù, 42–43
Parri, Ferruccio, 95
Pasolini, Pier Paolo, 5, 64n24, 66–67, 87–89, 94nn26–27, 101; assassination of, 113; network of, 95; relationship with, 4
Pastures of Plenty, 47–48, 51, 73n5, 74n14
Pauli, Hansjörg, 79
PCI. *See* Communist Party, Partito Comunista Italiano
Pearls, 119, 120
Perspectives (Berio), 23
Per un pugno di dollari (*A Fistful of Dollars*) (film), 68, 71, 73n8; awards of, 77; Eastwood in, 2–3; Greek tragedy and, 49; Kurosawa and, 73n6; origin of sound of, 47–48; success of, 33, 48, 49, 51–52; themes in, 48; violence in, 50
Peters, Edith, 73n7
Petrassi, Goffredo, 11, 13, 74n25, 128; birth of, 14; as boy soprano, 14; death of, 28n16; emancipation from, 25; as heir to, 17; students of, 14
Petri, Elio, 79, 92n5, 96
Petroni, Guilio, 60
Philharmonie im Gasteig, 123–24
Piacentini, Marcello, 15, 74n24
Piaf, Edith, 122
Piccolo concerto (television show), 2, 33–39, 44n10, 45n21; April 4, 1962 (7), 153–54; April 11, 1962 (8), 154–55; April 18, 1962 (9), 155–56; April 25, 1962 (10), 156–57; December 13, 1961 (6), 146; February 7, 1962 (1), 146–47; February 14, 1962 (2), 148–49; February 21, 1962 (3), 149–50; February 28, 1962 (4), 150–51; March 7, 1962 (5), 151–52; March 14, 1962 (6), 152–53; May 2, 1962 (11), 157–58; November 8, 1961 (1), 143–44; November 22, 1961 (3), 144–45; November 29, 1961 (4), 145
Le pistole non discutono (*Pistols Don't Argue*) (film), 48, 74n10
Pistols Don't Argue. See Le pistole non discutono
Pius XII (Pope), 31–32
Per pochi dollari in più (film), 2
Pointe, Ali La, 5
pointillism, 22, 25, 85
Poiret, Jean, 4, 86
polyphony, 26–27
Pontecorvo, Gillo, 4–5, 98, 101–4
Porrino, Ennio, 132
Poverty Theme, 71, *71*
Primo Concerto (Patrassi), 16, 20
The Private Sea of Dreams, 78
professional emancipation, 22
professionalism, 57
public appearances, 6
Puccini, Giacomo, 22, 117, 139n1
Puttnam, David, 107
Per qualche dollaro in più (*For a Few Dollars More*) (film), 51–53, 59, 64, 74n17

Quarto Concerto (Morricone, E.), 6, 132–34, 141nn28–29
Quarto Concerto (Petrassi), 16
Quarto Concerto per Organo, 2 Trombe, 2 Tromboni e Orchestra "Hoc erat in votis" (Morricone, E.), 132
Quasimodo, Salvatore, 5, 13, 105–6
Quattro mosche di velluto grigio (Four Flies on Grey Velvet) (film), 3, 84
Quattro pezzi per chitarra (Morricone, E.), 131–32
Queimada! (Burn!) (film), 100–101
Quinto Concerto (Petrassi), 16–17, 19, 22, 28n19

Racial Laws, 132
radio, 10, 12, 13
Radiocorriere, 34–37, 44n9
Rai-TV national network, 22, 33, 92n9
Rawhide, 50, 74n13
Razionalismo, 15, 74n24
Razzi, Giulio, 12, 27n8
RCA Italiana, 2, 31–33, 39, 44, 83
RCA Italiana Symphony Orchestra, 33
realism, 50
Rebecca (song), 5, 105
recording studios, film music and, 83
repertoire, 38
Requiem (Mozart), 88
"Requiem Glorioso," 110
Requiem per un destino (Morricone, E.), 79, 91, 127
La resa dei conti (Sixty Seconds to What?), 52–53, 74n17
Respighi, Ottorino, 133, 135
Restuccia, Vincenzo, 29n28
Ricercare cromatico post il Credo (Frescobaldi), 102–3, *103*, 114n16, 136–37, *137–39*
Ridolfi, Libera (mother), 9
Rigel, Maria Tonini, 42
Rio Bravo (film), 48
Rodrigo, Joachím, 131–32

Roma (Morricone, E.), 6, 136–37, *137–39*
Roma (Thinking about Frescobaldi's Ricercar Cromatico) (Morricone, E.), 6–7
Roma Capomunni, 94n28
Roma città aperta (Rome Open City) (film), 10
Rome, 31
Rondinella, Giacomo, 40
Rossellini, Roberto, 10
Rota, Nino, 1, 2, 12–13, 40, 94n28, 120–21
Russo, Ferdinando, 41
Rustichelli, Carlo, 92n6, 100

Sacco, Nicola, 96–98, 113
Sacco e Vanzetti (film), 4, 96, 98, 122
Sacco-Vanzetti case, 96
Salce, Luciano, 86
Salinas, Franco, 99
Salò o le 120 giornate di Sodoma (Salò, or the 120 Days of Sodom) (film), 88–89
sampling, 83
Sanremo Song Festival, 13–14, 32, 40–41, 44n3
Savina, Carlo, 34–35, 36, 37
Scelsi, Giacinto, 78
Scètate!, 41–42
Schoenberg, Arnold, 23–34, 82, 93n13
Secondo Concerto (Morricone, E.), 127–28, *129*, *130*
Secondo Concerto (Patrassi), 15–16, 18, 20
Segovia, Andrés, 131–32
Se incontri Sartana digli che è un uomo morto (If You Meet Sartana Pray for Your Death) (film), 64–65
Semproni, Umberto, 9
Sequenza I (Berio), 128
Sequenza VI (Berio), 81, 134
serialism, 15, 25, 28n18
Serrault, Michel, 4

Sesto Concerto (Petrassi), 28n18
sex, 68, 82
sexuality, 82
Shakespeare, William, 49
siblings, 9
silence, in film music, 24
silent movies, 82
Sindoni, Vittorio, 79
Sinfonia romantica (Garofalo), 27n2
Sixty Seconds to What?. See *La resa dei conti*
social justice, 98–99
Sonata per ottoni, timpani e pianoforte (Morricone, E.), 13
Songs of Freedom. See *Canti per la libertà*
Sonic Dimensions. See *Dimensioni sonore*
Sorice, Stefano, 29n24
soundtracks, 6, 43, 55, 72n1, 85, 100–101, 122
Spielberg, Steven, 2
State of Grace (film), 122, 123
status, 38
St. Matthew Passion (Bach), 101, *101*, 102, 114n14
Stoppa, Paolo, 40
Strauss, Richard, 39
Stravinsky, Igor, 16, 18, 78–79, 134
Le Streghe (The Witches) (film), 94n21
subjectivity, 25
Sunken Oboe. See *Oboe sommerso*
Suoni per Dino (Morricone, E.), 3, 80–81, 134
symphony orchestras, 123–24
Syn-ket, 75n27, 84

Tears for Dolphy, 88, 94n22
"Teatro di rivista," 11
Teatro Eliseo, 11
Teatro Sistina, 11
television, 12, 34
Teorema (film), 88
Tepepa (Blood and Guns) (film), 60
terrorism, 100, 104

Terzo Concerto (Morricone, E.), 6, 132
Terzo Concerto (Petrassi), 16, 18
Terzo Concerto per chitarra classica amplificata, marimba e orchestra d'archi (Morricone, E.), 131
Tessari, Duccio, 52
Tevis, Peter, 36–37, 47–48, 73n5, 73n9, 74n15
They Call Me Trinity. See *Lo chiamavano Trinità*
3 Studi (Morricone, E.), 22, 25, 29n26
time, 69
Time of the World's End. See *I Tempi della Fine*
Tiomkin, Dimitri, 48
Toccata and Fugue in D Minor (Bach), 53
Toccate per l'Elevazione (Zipoli), 109
Tognazzi, Ugo, 4
Tommaso, Giovanni, 13
Tornatore, Giuseppe, 86, 94n24, 120
Un tranquillo posto di campagna (film), 67
Trapani, Enzo, 35, 36
Trastevere neighborhood, 1, 27n1
trumpet playing, 2, 9, 11
Tudor, David, 23, 24
Turandot (Puccini), 117, 139nn1–2
Turco, Peppino, 39

Uccellacci e uccellini (The Hawks and the Sparrows) (film), 87, 91
L'uccello dalle piume di cristallo (The Bird with the Crystal Plumage) (film), 3, 84
The Unanswered Question (Ives), 131
The Untouchables (film), 122, 126
Un uomo a metà (Almost a Man and a Half a Man) (film), 79
UT per tromba in Do, timpani—grancassa e orchestra d'archi (Morricone, E.), 129–30

Vamos a matar compañeros (Compañeros) (film), 60

Il Vangelo secondo Matteo (The Gospel According to St. Matthew) (film), 101
Vanzetti, Bartolomeo, 96–97, 113
Variazioni su un tema di Frescobaldi (Morricone, E.), 114n16, 137
Verrà la morte (Morricone, E.), 13
vertical application, of film music, 90
Via Tiburtina, 31–32, 44n1
viola, 81, 92nn9–10
violence, 50
Violin Concerto (Berg), 17
Vi scrivo da un carcere in Grecia (I write from a prison in Greece) (Panagoulis), 95
Volontè, Gian Maria, 54
Voyage of Terror (television film), 6, 120, 139n4
"Voyage of Terror," 119

Walk of Fame star, 7, 86, 138
Wallach, Eli, 54
We All Love Ennio Morricone, 6, 118, 119
Webern, Anton von, 25
Western all'Italiana (film), 121

Westerns, 72, 100; American, 47–48; archetypes in, 49; comic, 64; culture of, 63–65; international popularity of, 49; origin of sound of Italian, 47; scores for, 56–57, 60; sound devices in, 53; success of Italian, 2–3; traditions in, 50–51, 110. *See also specific films*
What Scoundrels Men Are!. *See Gli uomini che mascalzoni*
Willaert, Adriano, 26–27
Williams, John, 2
The Witches. *See Le Streghe*
World War II, 15, 31

Yacef, Saadi, 99
Yojimbo (film), 73n6
Yo-Yo Ma Plays Morricone (album), 6, 119, 125–26

Zammerini, Giovanni, 13
Zeitgenössische Musik II, 78
Ziad, Karim, 99
Zingarelli, Italo, 60
Zipoli, Domenico, 109
Zivelli, Vittorio, 34

About the Author

Franco Sciannameo is College of Fine Arts Distinguished Teaching Professor of Music in the School of Music at Carnegie Mellon University in Pittsburgh, Pennsylvania. Born in Apulia, Italy, violinist, musicologist, and cultural historian Sciannameo studied in Rome at the Conservatorio di Musica Santa Cecilia and later at the Accademia Chigiana in Siena, Accademia di Santa Cecilia in Rome, the University of Hartford, and the University of Pittsburgh.

Always concerned with the role of the artist in society, Sciannameo writes and lectures extensively on contemporary music and its relation to politics, cinema, and the arts. He has worked with a number of celebrated composers, including Giacinto Scelsi, Nino Rota, Ennio Morricone, and Paul Chihara, with whom he collaborated on performances and recordings. Sciannameo's articles and essays are featured in *The Musical Times* (London), and his books include *Nino Rota's The Godfather Trilogy* (2010); *Phil Trajetta (1777–1854): Patriot, Musician, Immigrant* (2010); *Music as Dream: Essays on Giacinto Scelsi* (2013); *Experiencing the Violin Concerto: A Listener's Companion* (2016); and *Musicians' Migratory Patterns: The Adriatic Coasts* (2018). Franco Sciannameo is currently working on the reconstruction of *The Venetian Maskers*, a comic opera by Philip Trajetta that premiered in New York on December 22, 1810.

www.ingramcontent.com/pod-product-compliance
Lightning Source LLC
Chambersburg PA
CBHW050906300426
44111CB00010B/1407